MISSION

Foundations of Mission Theology

Foundations of
Mission Theology

Edited by SEDOS

Translated by John Drury

MARYKNOLL DOCUMENTATION SERIES
ORBIS BOOKS ● MARYKNOLL, NEW YORK 10545

Second printing, November 1972

This translation has been made from the official French
version of the Symposium papers, originally published in
Spiritus No. 39 (1969) 321-521.

Manufactured in the United States of America

CONTENTS

Participating Theologians

D.S. AMALORPAVADASS, Bangalore, India
C. G. AREVALO, S.J., Manila, Phillipines
ATHANASE BOUCHARD, C.S.S.P., editor of *Spiritus,* Paris
ARNULF CAMPS, O.F.M., Alverna Gld, Holland
JEAN DANIÉLOU, S.J., Paris
G. DELCUVE, S.J., editor of *Lumen Vitae,* Brussels
A. M. FIOLET, Bilthoven, Holland
JEAN FRISQUE, Paris
JOSÉ-MARIA GONZALEZ-RUIZ, Madrid
DOMENICO GRASSO, S.J., Rome

A. M. HENRY, O.P., editor of *Parole et Mission,* Paris
HENRI de LUBAC, S.J., Lyon
STANISLAS LYONNET, S.J., Rome
JOSEPH MASSON, S.J., Rome
KARL MÜLLER, S.V.D., Rome
IGNACE de la POTTERIE, S.J., Rome
A. SANTOS, S.J., Madrid
JOHANNES SCHÜTTE, S.V.D., Rome
OTTO SEMMELROTH, S.J., Frankfurt
J. M. SETIEN, Santander, Spain
ANDRÉ SEUMOIS, O.M.I., Rome
T. TSHIBANGU, Kinshasa
A. VANNESTE, Kinshasa

Moderators of the Sessions

HENRI MONDÉ, S.M.A., superior general, president of SEDOS, Rome
JOSEPH LÉCUYER, C.S.S.P., superior general, Rome
THÉO van ASTEN, P.B., superior general, Rome
CHARLES HENRI BUTTIMER, F.S.C., superior general, Rome

Members of the Organization Committee

V. FECHER, S.V.D., Rome
C. A. DAILY, S.J., Rome
V. MERTENS, S.J., Rome
F. SACHETT, O.M.I., Rome

B. TONNA, secretary general of SEDOS
J. OVERBOSS, directress of the Secretariat
V. KARIC, secretary

ABBREVIATIONS

DOCUMENT SOURCES

AG   *Ad gentes.* Vatican II. Decree on the Missionary Activity of the Church. December 7, 1965.

Denz.   Denzinger-Schönmetzer, 1929. *Enchiridion symbolorum.*

DV   *Dei Verbum.* Vatican II. Dogmatic Constitution on Divine Revelation. November 18, 1965.

GS   *Gaudium et spes.* Vatican II. Pastoral Constitution on the Church in the Modern World. December 7, 1965.

IM   *Inter mirifica.* Vatican II. Decree on the Instruments of Social Communication. December 4, 1963.

LG   *Lumen gentium.* Vatican II. Dogmatic Constitution on the Church. November 21, 1964.

N.AE   *Nostra Aetate.* Vatican II. Declaration on the Relationship of the Church to Non-Christian Religions. October 28, 1965.

OE   *Orientalium ecclesiarum.* Vatican II. Decree on Eastern Catholic Churches. November 21, 1964.

PG   *Patres Graeci,* Migne.

PL   *Patres Latini,* Migne.

PO   *Presbyterorum ordinis.* Vatican II. Decree on the Ministry and Life of Priests. December 7, 1965.

PP   *Populorum progressio.* Encyclical of Paul VI. March 26, 1967.

SC   *Sacrum Concilium.* Vatican II. Constitution on the Sacred Liturgy. December 4, 1963.

UR   *Unitatis redintegratio.* Vatican II. Decree on Ecumenism. November 21, 1964.

Biblical passages are taken from the Jerusalem Bible translation, unless otherwise indicated.

Wherever possible, papal documents are cited in the translation provided by *The Pope Speaks Magazine* (Washington, D.C.); conciliar documents are cited from *The Documents of Vatican II,* ed. Walter M. Abbot, S. J. (New York: America Press, 1966).

Foreword

It was the initiative of various missionary institutes, which are members of SEDOS, that led to the organization of this conference.

It must be admitted at once that these missionary institutes are distressed, preoccupied, and concerned over the future of mission work, but that does not mean they are pessimistic. In a world of total transition, where new problems are posed every day, it is only natural that the missionary world should wonder about its own role in this rapid and often radical evolution. It was not so very long ago, for example, that in missionary territories the notion of nascent or local churches was practically unknown and certainly ill defined. Defined in terms of a vicariate apostolic, the local missionary church seemed to be more or less a prolongation or extension of the Western churches. It is not surprising that these missionary churches depended greatly, if not exclusively, on institutes which "benefited" from the "facilities" inherent in the existing colonial regime. But now profound changes have taken place in the field of missionary activity, as we all know.

We have been present at the end of the colonial era. We have seen the awakening of national consciousness, the thrust of young nations toward independence in their political affairs, their struggle to safeguard their own cultures and personalities in every domain, including the religious domain.

We were glad to see the establishment of a hierarchy in most of the mission countries. It has represented a great step forward. The newly established churches began to take cognizance of their own proper personality and responsibilities. They also began to show less dependence on Western churches. The latter, in turn, have had to change their missionary outlook and to promote further the full maturity of these nascent churches. But it has called for a new spirit of service and collaboration, devoid of paternalism and nostalgia for the past.

Then came Vatican II. The very presence of numerous bishops from mission countries and their influence on the discussions concerning the missionary theology of the universal Church helped the time-honored churches of East and West to see clearly the importance, the vitality, and the aspirations of the nascent churches. We all know the history of the Decree on Missionary Activity. After the Dogmatic Constitution on the Church (*Lumen gentium*) had proclaimed that the whole Church was missionary of its very nature, what need was there for a special document on missionary activity? Well, the vast majority of Council Fathers clamored for a charter document on the missions, and so *Ad gentes* was produced. Let me reiterate here the message of all these admirable documents: "The duty of the Church is to assemble all the people of earth into the People of God ... The Church is summoned to save and renew every creature, so that everything may be recreated in Christ and that all men may form a single People of God in him ... The work of evangelization, then, is a fundamental duty of God's People."

What do we see of this ideal, proclaimed by the Council, in the deeds and actual life of the Church? After the impulse for renewal was sent out, have we not felt a state of crisis and some regression? Have the Bishops' Conferences in our Western countries really begun to implement the universal dimensions of the doctrine of collegiality, which certainly obliges them to establish concrete and effective communion with the younger and poorer churches? On every side we hear talk of crisis: a crisis of priestly and religious vocations in the older churches, and a crisis of identical nature in the younger churches. How are we to remedy it? What is a community without priests or a Eucharistic life, such as we often find in the younger churches? What is a church without a well-formed and responsible laity? And who will train and sustain this laity if there are no living communities nor spiritual animators?

We are all aware of a further fact here: Geographically and sociologically, the missionary apostolate is framed within the countries of the underdeveloped world. The development problems of these people is one of the key problems of our epoch, so much so that the Holy Father has not hesitated to say that development is the new name for international peace.

Missionaries have confronted this problem since the early days of their apostolate. But theological reflection has trailed behind. The encyclicals *Mater et magistra* and *Populorum progressio*, the visits of Pope Paul VI to the United Nations, India, South America, and Africa, the creation of the Commission for Justice and Peace (with its subcommission for human betterment) represent important stages in the domain of doctrine. They are concrete signs and effective steps toward action in the new conditions of our present day.

This effervescence of ideas and initiatives has challenged missionary institutes, and they have begun to ask questions of themselves in turn. How can we frame the work of evangelization within the work for development? Granting the important contribution of the missionary Church to the betterment of peoples, how can we make this work more effective today and integrate it into the pastoral ministry? How can we make it a visible sign of Christ's charity, who wishes to save all men? Thousands of missionaries are prepared to dedicate themselves to this task, but there is still too much hesitation and uncertainty, too little in the way of directives and coordinated effort.

So you see, there are many questions. We are submitting them to the consideration of theologians. As missionaries, we do not expect ready-made formulas. But as Saint Paul did at the start of the Church's missionary activity, we should like to link reflection and action in a new synthesis suited to our day. Finally we expect this convention to provide us with a fresh awareness of the missionary responsibilities that are incumbent on the whole People of God.

A BRIEF NOTE ON THE HISTORY OF THE SYMPOSIUM

The idea of a meeting of theologians to study mission questions was first proposed by Father V. Fecher, S.V.D. on February 17, 1967, during the thirteenth meeting of superiors general who are members of SEDOS. As first envisioned, it was to be a joint effort undertaken in cooperation with the Gregorian University in Rome. When hopes for such a joint venture faded, Father J. van Kerchoven, superior general of the Missionaries of the Sacred Heart, urged SEDOS to take further steps on its own at the next meeting of superiors general (April 11, 1967). An organization committee was formed, and its report was approved at the fifteenth meeting of superiors general (July 20, 1967). This committee met several times, under the direction of Father J. Schütte, who was then president of SEDOS. The symposium, the term applied to the committee's project, would be distinct from the missiology study weeks held at Burgos, Louvain, and Milan. It would be directly concerned with a truly high-level discussion of missionary theology, involving eminent theologians. Besides the theologians who participated in it, others were invited who could not be present: Bouvy, S.J.; R. D. Chenu, O.P.; Y. Congar, O.P.; A. Dulles, S.J.; C. Giblet; J. Glasik, M.S.C.; J. Kaspar; H. Küng; J. Loew, O.P.; R. Mackenzie, S.J.; G. Moran, F.S.C.; I. Pycke, C.I.C.M.; K. Rahner, S.J.; J. Ratzinger; E. Shillebeeckx; R. Schnakenburg; G. Thils; G. Van Akeren, S.J.

The organizing committee prepared a long list of possible subjects and asked for comments from the theologians invited. Eventually the list was reduced to two fundamental questions, both related to the basic concern of the missionary institutes as to why there should be mission work at all: (1) Salvation through Non-Christian Religions; and (2) Mission Work and Development.

The committee, presided over by Father V. Fecher, proposed to involve the house of superiors general in the theological discussion, requesting them to participate in two open sessions and preparing them for these sessions by distributing to them the documents of the theologians.

The symposium was first scheduled for September 1968 at Nemi, near

Rome. Since this date was not convenient for many of the theologians, the symposium was held March 27-31, 1969 at Rome.

SEDOS (*Servizio documentazione e studi*, via dei Verbiti 1, cp. 5080, 00100 Rome) was founded at the end of Vatican II by a group of missionary institutes. It was designed to be an organism of interinstitutional cooperation charged with providing its members information, documentation, studies, and plans that would help them to carry out their missionary task and to bolster their collaboration in this domain. While this organism has since opened its doors to institutes that are not specifically missionary (there are now twenty-nine congregations or societies in it), its aim remains exclusively missionary. Its work is presently shared by some ten offices or commissions, involved with: documentation; personnel statistics; inquiries to missionaries about their problems and difficulties; formation; the social communications media; development in general; health and sanitation work; educational projects; mission theology.

Henri Mondé
President of SEDOS

CARDINAL AGAGIANIAN

Theology and Missionary Formation

CHAPTER ONE

It is a particular pleasure for me to bring the greetings of the Sacred Congregation concerned with evangelization to this audience. You are directly engaged in missionary activity and interested in the study of the doctrinal questions that are posed to it today. These questions may have varying degrees of legitimacy and relevance, but they share a note of uncommon urgency.

My presence here is meant to be, first of all, an encouragement to the superiors general of the diverse institutes engaged in missionary work, under whose auspices you are holding these few days of missionary study that I have the honor to inaugurate. They bear living witness to your desire for mutual understanding and your spirit of collaboration.

As the recent Council reminds us, it is the duty of the Sacred Congregation for the Evangelization of Peoples "to direct and coordinate missionary work throughout the world" (AG 29). So it has an obligation to encourage useful forms of collaboration between missionary institutes at various levels. *Ad gentes* itself recommended that on the territorial level there should be conferences of male religious and unions of women religious working in close collaboration with the Bishops' Conference of a given mission area; they could then undertake joint initiatives that are judged necessary or useful: "Communities engaged in missionary activity in the same territory should find ways and means of coodinating their work" (AG 33). Such national federations of religious men and women are already in operation in some localities.

The same conciliar decree also recommends collaboration between missionary institutes in the various home countries. They could thus collaborate in joint missionary initiatives, particularly with respect to the formation of future missionaries, refresher courses for young missionaries, and relations with civil and international organisms: "With equal reason, all these recommendations can be appropriately extended to include the cooperation of missionary communities in the home lands. Thus common problems and projects can be handled more easily and with less expense: for instance, the doctrinal formation of future missionaries, courses for the present missionaries, relations with public authorities and with international and supranational organizations" (AG 33). Here it is a question of setting up various confederations of institutes with a missionary aim in mind. Such confederations could obviously function in widely different ways and under widely different norms.

On the international level, the Union of Male Superiors General has existed in Rome with official status since 1957, and it has a missionary commission. The international Union of Female Superiors General has been in existence since 1965. Support for these official organisms was urged by the conciliar decree *Perfectae caritatis* (no. 23). But there is no reason why private associations of major superiors cannot be set up on a more restricted scale to pursue specific missionary objectives. They could offer some guarantee of effectiveness, provided they obtained a direct and determined commitment from the major superiors themselves.

My presence here is also meant to encourage all those who are whole-heartedly concerned with the study of doctrinal questions relating to the missionary apostolate. The general theme of the symposium we begin today is: "A Mission Theology for Our Times." My encouragement goes out to the participants in the study groups, to the reporters, and to all those who will follow the public sessions.

The Sacred Congregation for the Evangelization of Peoples is ever anxious to ground its missionary administration on clear-cut theological doctrine. At its founding in 1622, it placed great value on the best work in this domain, the *De procuranda salute omnium gentium* of Thomas de Jésus, which had appeared in 1613. And it has continued to surround itself with experts, including some in the area of missionary theology, whom it has engaged in the role of consultors. Here and there during its history, it may well have been the victim of specific currents of thought that were circulating in the Christian world or among missionary personnel, especially when preoccupation with mission theology was almost nonexistent. But its own efforts have always been oriented around a serious study of the problems; and it has not been afraid to run counter to strong currents of opinion; e.g., those concerning the native clergy at the turn of this century, when its doctrinal study clearly indicated the road to take. In modern times one cannot ignore the considerable role exercised by the major papal encyclicals on mission-related doctrine, or the role assumed by the mission dicastery in promoting missiology and rendering it effective in the formation of future missionaries.

The Sacred Congregation concerned with evangelization is a missionary center that is administrative in character, to be sure. But its administration is based strictly on direct information, on missionary experience and research, and on missiology studies. So it is both an administrative center and a source of impetus.

In 1777, in an era when, unfortunately, little attention was paid to the expert training of future missionaries and when missionary activity was going through a grave crisis, an instruction issued by this Sacred Congregation took up this question: "Are missionaries bound *sub gravi* to devote themselves earnestly to studies that will prepare them properly for their apostolic functions?" Here is the answer given:

> There can be no doubt about this matter. It is certain that a person is normally bound to make himself fit for the task he envisages. This obligation is all the more serious insofar as the task is more important. It would be a truly grave fault for any minister if he, because of his negligence (God forbid!), were to occasion the loss of the least of those for whom Christ shed his blood. That is why sacred ministers must devote themselves, first and foremost, to learning the doctrine that is necessary for them to carry out their functions properly. And they must look for this doctrine in the work of sound authors, particularly in the work of those who have dealt with missionary questions (April 17, 1777; *Collectanea I, 522, p. 323).*

Basic apostolic and missionary formation is necessary for all those who intend to dedicate themselves to missionary work. This is particularly true in our day, when the problems facing missionary activity are delicate; and when the attraction to purely humanitarian or secularized objectives can entice people who are consecrated specifically to the missionary effort of the Church, so that they are distracted from the specific ends of missionary work. These ends, as everyone knows, are: the implantation of new, autocthonous local churches that have their own proper means of life and development; through proclamation of the gospel, the formation of a native clergy and of a lay elite; the progressive setting up of Christian cells as living communities of faith, practicing liturgical worship, fraternal charity, apostolic zeal, and service to society in forms of life style and expression that are Christian and autochthonous.

Thus the conciliar decree demands that all future missionaries be initiated into the various branches of missiology: "It is above all necessary for the future missionary to devote himself to missiological studies: that is, to know the teaching and norms of the Church concerning missionary activity, the roads which the heralds of the gospel have traversed in the course of the centuries, the present condition of the missions, and the methods now considered especially effective" (AG 26). It also calls for some initiation into the religion and culture of the people he is to evangelize, and into "those branches of knowledge which it would be useful for them to master. They will thereby gain a general knowledge of peoples, cultures, and religions, a knowledge that looks not only to the past but to the present as well. For anyone who is going to encounter another people should have a great esteem for their patrimony and their language and their customs" (AG 26).

One point is worth noting here. Study of the major religious and moral systems of a non-Christian nature and broader study of the varied cultures in missionary territories is most useful in teaching the missionary to adapt to various cultures and to accept their values with respect. But such study should not take place without a corresponding exploration of the theological doctrine and personal commitment that is proper to Christian living. Inadequate knowledge of, and appreciation for, the Catholic religion could nullify all the efforts made to deepen one's knowledge of native religions, philosophies, and cultural systems, when it comes to the practical work of evangelization. Cultural study of the people who are to be evangelized should especially be accompanied by adequate formation in missiology. For if the missionary undertakes the study of religions and cultures, he does so as a missionary. It is and should be undertaken in the light of the missionary work to be carried out in these religious and cultural milieux. His viewpoint, then, is not that of the ethnologist or the historian of religion. His work in these areas is to be viewed from the standpoint of missionary activity. And this calls for corresponding in-depth study of missiology.

What is more, the study of missiology should not be regarded as mere intellectual enrichment or the acquisition of new information and knowledge. Missiology is a scholarly discipline that is wholly ordered toward action, toward the missionary apostolate; and it is studied by people with a vocation consecrated to mission work. So it should always be undertaken with a view to exercising more zealously and ably the practical apostolate in those countries where the Church is making an effort to implant itself as the grass-roots sacrament of Christ's redemptive work.

We certainly cannot demand that every future missionary become a specialist in one or another branch of missiology, or in some other discipline that is useful to the missions. The important thing for every missionary is a proper human, ecclesiastical, and spiritual formation that will put him on the right track in his missionary enterprises. And here I should like to stress the importance of giving a proper spiritual formation to all those who devote themselves to the missionary apostolate. This formation is truly the foundation for an authentic and fruitful apostolic life. We must offer them a Christian spirituality that is solid and apostolically oriented. A work such as that of André Seumois (*L'anima dell'apostolato missionario,* Editrice Missionaria Italiana, 2nd edition, 1961) could serve as a sound guide for a worthwhile apostolic and missionary spirituality. It would do much to inculcate a sound theological formation in future heralds of the good news of salvation in Jesus Christ. Deeper specialization in missiological or other disciplines will be the task of some carefully selected people, both among foreign missionaries and the native clergy. As *Ad gentes* points out: "Some should receive an especially thorough preparation in missiological institutes or in other faculties or universities. As a result they will be able to discharge special duties more effectively and to be a help, by their learning, to other missionaries in carrying on missionary work. In our time especially, this work presents very many difficulties and opportunities" (AG 26).

It is highly desirable that the various missionary districts, at least at the level of Bishops' Conferences, should have available to them a sufficient number of specialists in missionary questions. These would be capable of serving as expert advisors to the responsible organs, of competently organizing the formation of young foreign missionaries and the native clergy, and of directing specialized centers in a specific pastoral or apostolic field. Today our nascent missionary churches feel a keen need to prepare good theologians among the native clergy. Imbued with a solid formation, they would be able to tackle the weighty problems involved in the encounter between Christianity and native cultures and religions. Thus they would help to bring about solid missionary adaptation in various areas: e.g., presenting the Christian message to outsiders, catechesis, liturgy, the Catholic press, religious literature, and so forth.

The formation of such specialists should insure that they are not tempted to view their future involvement in an isolated way, that they are not dominated by a desire to introduce new fads or startlingly novel thoughts. The dominant motifs should be a spirit of humble service and total dedication to the missionary function of the Church. This calls for a spirit of frank and loyal collaboration with the Holy See. It requires wholehearted adhesion to the guidelines and directives of Vatican II: not only those contained in *Ad gentes* but also those of the other conciliar decrees, particularly those contained in *Lumen gentium*. Finally it must be firmly based on the teachings of the Church relating to all the sectors of ecclesial thought and activity; these teachings should guide their initiatives and orient their attitudes around service to Christ, the People of God, and the nations that are to be sanctified in the normal and fully rounded path to salvation.

Now the formation of specialists depends in large measure on the scholarly progress and development that takes place in missiology and other disciplines that are useful for the missions. That is why it is important to promote scholarly research and publications in these domains, and to improve the quality of the courses offered in missiological institutes. That is why we must encourage missiology congresses and meetings of specialists on missionary questions, such as the one that we are inaugurating today under the auspices of SEDOS.

The whole problem of missionary formation will be given due consideration at the next plenary session of the Sacred Congregation for the Evangelization of Peoples, which will be held April 22-25. This problem is at the head of the agenda for that plenary session, and we hope that it will achieve some practical and useful results.

Effective work in this domain also depends to an important degree on the involvement of superiors general and the available experts.

Our closing wish is that they too will be able to do good work in this domain, with the result that the crisis of confidence that now surrounds the Church's missionary vocation and task will fade away. Hopefully it will soon be replaced by a revitalized missionary enthusiasm, based on solid conviction and open to the bright prospects envisioned in the Lord's mandate: "Go out to the whole world; proclaim the good news to every creature" (Mark 16:15). Hopefully we will follow in the footsteps of the Apostle to the Nations: "I should be punished if I did not preach it!" (1 Cor. 9:16).

STANISLAS LYONNET

The Novel Aspect of the Gospel

CHAPTER TWO

One of the problems that may well be uppermost in the minds of missionaries, who are charged with the responsibility of preaching the gospel, is that of determining the specific content of the message they are supposed to transmit to the world. Put another way: to spell out clearly the novel element in the gospel. Now in defining the mission of the priest, Vatican II (PO 2) explicitly referred to Saint Paul and his description of his own missions in Romans 15:16: "He has appointed me as a priest of Jesus Christ, and I am to carry out my priestly duty by bringing the Goods News from God to the pagans, and so make them acceptable as an offering, made holy by the Holy Spirit."

We might well ask Saint Paul how he saw the new element of the Christian message in priestly service. We might try to find out what constituted in his eyes the distinctive and specific character of Christian revelation.

In general, a closer reading of his epistles reveals that he made every effort to define this message both with reference to the Old Testament and to the Judaism that he had known and lived before his conversion. In relation to the Old Testament, Christian revelation did not constitute a rupture in his eyes; rather than being opposed to Old Testament revelation, it brought it to fulfillment. To be sure, there is an element of "surpassing" as we move from the Old Testament to the New Testament, but that is not surprising. Prophecy, by definition, is surpassed by the event it foretells, as the type is by the antitype. The paschal lamb is surpassed by the immolated and risen Christ, the manna by the Eucharist, the covenant sacrifice of Moses on Sinai by the New Covenant sacrifice of the Eucharist. Such surpassing, however, may prevent someone who sticks close to the letter from seeing that the latter truly continues and fulfills the former. But the passage from one to the other does not involve any rejection, and hence does not constitute a conversion in the strict sense.

7

The case is different when we come to Judaism. By Judaism we mean the religion of the Old Testament as it gradually came to be understood by at least one part of the Israelites, that part to which Paul himself belonged. Here we cannot talk about surpassing, here we have a real breakaway. In passing from one to the other, as Paul himself tells us forthrightly, he had to renounce all the benefits that he once thought ensured salvation to himself: circumcision, the Israelite race, irreproachable observance of the Law (he being more zealous in its observance than most, as he tells us in Galatians). All these advantages he would now regard as disadvantages:

> But because of Christ, I have come to consider all these advantages that I had as disadvantages. Not only that, but I believe that nothing can happen that will outweigh the supreme advantage of knowing Christ Jesus my Lord. For him I have accepted the loss of everyting, and I look on everything as so much rubbish if only I can have Christ and be given a place in him. I am no longer trying for perfection by my own efforts, the perfection that comes from the Law [i.e., which he expected to get from observance of the law], but I want only the perfection that comes through faith in Christ, and is from God and is based on faith (Phil. 3:7-9).

In other words, conversion does not come from activity that is exclusively my own, but from the activity of Christ in me. It presupposes that Another has died and risen for me, that he communicates his own risen life to me, and that he asks me to accept this life in a free act which is the act of faith in the Pauline sense of the term.

Such a conversion is no less radical or difficult than that from paganism to Christianity, for it demands that he turn his back on all the notions he had held previously. Indeed it is more difficult in one sense, as Paul himself found out. For he saw pagans accept the gospel while the Jews as a body persisted in their refusal of it.

The text from Philippians brings us directly to that which Paul certainly saw as the essential new element of Christianity. But before we spell it out, we would do well to recall several other aspects. They are not so radically new, to be sure. But they are more external and hence easy to grasp, and their delineation will furnish a good part of Saint Paul's preaching. We shall then be in a better position to appreciate the "essential new aspect" that we have alluded to.

The Whole Law Is Summed Up in One Precept: Love of Neighbor

There is no doubt that the fundamental principles of Old Testament and Jewish morality remains absolutely unchanged. The Christian, like the Israelite and the Jew, is by definition a man who knows what pleases God and does it. His conduct (*peripatein*) is in conformity with the will of God, for "pleasing God" essentially means doing his will; or, as the other biblical formulas put it, "doing the truth," "knowing God."

The new religion, like the old, is viewed as a "way" (*hodos*). Indeed this term will be used to designate it without elaboration: "I persecuted this Way" (Acts 22:4); "What I do admit to you is this: it is according to the Way which they [i.e., the Jews] describe as a sect that I worship the God of my ancestors" (Acts 24:14). This "way" is also called "the way of God" (Matt. 22:16; Acts 18:25), "the way of salvation" (Acts 16:17), "the way of justice" (Matt. 21:32), and "the way of truth" (2 Peter 2:2).

Whether he writes to the Thessalonians, the Romans, or the Corinthians, the only thing that concerns Paul is that his readers know and carry out the will of God: "What God wants of you all is to be holy" (1 Thess. 4:3); "Let your behavior change, modelled by your new mind. This is the only way to discover the will of God and know what is good, what it is that God wants, what is the perfect thing to do" (Romans 12:2); "What we ask God is that through perfect wisdom and spiritual understanding, you should reach the fullest knowledge of his will" (Col. 1:9). And if it seems that Paul is here stressing the "intellectual" aspect, asking the Colossians to have "wisdom" and "understanding," he is in fact only picking up the two terms (*sophia* and *synesis*) that Deuteronomy used to describe the conduct of the Israelite who observes the Law perfectly: "I teach you the laws and customs that you are to observe . . . Keep them, observe them, and they will demonstrate to them your wisdom (*hokmah*) and intelligence (*binah*). When they come to know of all these laws they will exclaim, 'No other people is as wise and intelligent as this great nation.' And indeed what great nation is there that has its gods so close as Yahweh our God is to us whenever we call to him? And what great nation has laws and customs (*mishpat*) to match this whole Law that I put before you today?" (Deut. 4:5-8).

The first novel aspect of Christianity enters with the work of specifying this will of God. For the Jew, it is entirely determined by the ensemble of commandments in the Law as they are inscribed in the Mosaic code. To these commandments tradition has added a series of precepts, in order to ensure their complete carrying out. For Christianity, the ensemble of commandments is reduced to a single precept that embraces all the others: "You will love your neighbor as yourself." This cast is only relatively novel, insofar as the Old Testament was already moving toward such a simplification, notably in the teaching of the prophets; and insofar as several Jewish doctors had already glimpsed and taught this. But it is truly novel nevertheless, particularly with regard to Judaism, for it certainly had not been the common teaching.

A RELATIVELY NOVEL FEATURE

We can cite the statement which the Talmud attributes to Hillel the elder, the grandfather of Gamaliel, who was Saint Paul's teacher. For him the Law could as well be summed up in the "golden rule," which he formulated in terms of Tobias 4:16: "Do to no one what you would not want done to you"; "that is the whole Law, the rest is merely explanation" (Bonsirven, *textes rabbiniques*, n.633). And we know that the same formula is found in the Targum where it comments on the two passages in Leviticus (19:18,34) that promulgate the precept: "Love your neighbor as yourself."

Now this sentence quite faithfully reflects the "summary of the moral code" which is presented in various parts of the Bible. As examples we may cite Psalm 15 (14) and Psalm 24 (23). They in turn, as the Jerusalem Bible reminds us, evoke many passages from the message of the prophets: Isaiah 1:16-17; 26:2-3; 33:15; Micah 6:6-8; Zacharia 8:16-17; Ezechiel 18:7-9. Here too, the teaching of Deuteronomy is even more clear, if that is possible. In Chapter 6 it sums up the whole Law in the one commandment urging love of God (Deut. 6:4-5), and Christ will call it the "first of the commandments." In the context of that day, love of God means essentially fidelity to God and obedience to his law, as Moran has shown.[1] Then, in Chapter 10, the formula is picked up and spelled out in a series of expressions that are practically equivalent: "fear Yahweh your God . . . follow all his ways . . . love him, serve Yahweh your God with all your heart and all your soul . . . keep the commandments and laws of Yahweh" (Deut. 10:12-13).

This series of expressions is in turn condensed into one precept: "Circumcise your hearts, therefore, and be obstinate no longer" (10:16). Paul will take up this notion to explain how the pagans can actually practice the law without knowing it (Romans 2:29). Finally verse 19 spells out what "circumcise your heart" means concretely. After explaining that God is a great God who "is never partial, never to be bribed . . . sees justice done for the orphan and the widow . . . loves the stranger and gives him food and clothing" (10:17-18), it concludes: "Love the stranger then, for you were strangers in the land of Egypt" (v.19). This is exactly what is said in Leviticus 19:34, where the precept of loving the alien as oneself is also related to Israel's alien status in Egypt. In short, Deuteronomy teaches that the whole Law is summed up in love for God, which involves carrying out the will of God, which in turn involves imitating Yahweh's disinterested love. There we already have the injunction of the Sermon on the Mount: "You must be merciful (or perfect) just as your heavenly Father is merciful (or perfect)." There we already have in germ the injunction laid down by Christ at the institution of the New Covenant: "Love one another as I have loved you."

BUT TRULY NOVEL ALSO

There are three differences, however, which make the Christian message novel even in terms of the content of the law of Christian love. (The nature of this law involves an even more radical difference.)

The first difference is that Judaism, going against even the import of the Deuteronomic formula, often limited "neighbor" (Heb. *ger*, translated "proselyte" in Greek) to Israelites alone. It restricted it to members of the People of God alone, excluding the "enemies of God" who are also, by definition, the enemies of his People. This limitation led to invectives that are familiar to us from the Psalms: "Yahweh, do I not hate those who hate you, and loath those who defy you? I hate them with a total hatred, I regard them as my own enemies" (Ps. 139:21-22; *cf*. Ps. 16:4; 125:5; 137:8-9). This sentiment is found at Qumrân: "Love all the sons of light, each according to his rank in the congregation of God; and hate all the sons of darkness, each according to his culpability, in accordance with God's vindictive will" (*Manual of Discipline* 1:9-11). It clearly justifies Christ's words: "You have learnt how it was said, 'You must love your neighbor and hate your enemy.' But I say this to you: love your enemies . . . in this way you will be sons of your Father in heaven, for he causes his sun to rise on bad men as well as good and his rain to fall on honest and dishonest men alike" (Math. 5:43-45).

Christ seems merely to be going back to the teaching of Deuteronomy that we have just seen. In any case, this explains why Saint Luke was able to present the parable of the Good Samaritan as a commentary on the two precepts. As in Deuteronomy, the second commandment becomes the means of practicing the first. And the only remaining question is: "Who is my neighbor?" (Luke 10:25-37).

The second difference is that although the Old Testament knew that we were supposed to love all men as God loves us, no one then could have imagined the lengths to which God's love for man would go. He would become man so that he could go so far as to die for them out of love. He would not only become the Shepherd of Israel in search of the stray sheep (Ezek. 34:11-16); he would go so far as to give his life for his flock (John 10:11-16). It is not simply a matter of not doing to others what you would not have done to you, or of doing to them what you would have done to you. We would never expect that another would die in our place. But Christ himself died for us, and he formulates his precept: "I give you a new commandment: love one another; just as I have loved you, you also must love one another" (John 13:34). And even as the practice of the Mosaic Law was to distinguish the Jew from the pagan, so the practice of fraternal charity is to be the singular sign marking the authentic disciple of Christ (John 13:35).

The third difference, particularly vis-à-vis Judaism, is the insistence with which the precept of love of neighbor is promulgated as the embodiment of the whole Law. In Judaism, the statement of Hillel the elder is cited repeatedly because it is practically unique. In the New Testament, by contrast, it is the common teaching reiterated by all the books that comprise it.

As early as the Sermon on the Mount, Christ proclaims it as clearly as one could, and in terms that come very close to those of Hillel: "So always treat others as you would like them to treat you; that is the meaning of the Law and the Prophets" (Matt. 7:12). This golden rule is tied to another statement of Christ: "Do not imagine that I have come to abolish the Law or the Prophets. I have come not to abolish but to complete them" (Matt. 5:17). This suggests at the very least that Christ "fulfilled all the precepts of the law down to the last iota." Because all the precepts are summed up in the precept of love of neighbor as expressed by the golden rule, and because he himself loved as no one else ever had, he prescribed a single commandment for his disciples: that they love their brothers. What is more, as we shall see, he gives them the power to love them by communicating his own love.

Under these circumstances we are not astonished to see how Matthew concludes the whole teaching of Christ, just before beginning his passion narrative. He describes the day of judgment, in which people are categorized solely on their practice of love of neighbor: "Come, you whom my Father has blessed. . . . For I was hungry and you gave me food. . . . Go away from me, with your curse upon you. . . . For I was hungry and you never gave me food. . . . in so far as you neglected to do this to one of the least of these, you neglected to do it to me" (Matt. 25:34-46).

The fourth Gospel gives even greater stress to this teaching, if that is possible. The precept of love of neighbor becomes the very Law of the New Covenant, promulgated at the most solemn moment of his life when he performs and fulfills the new passover (John 13:34-35; *cf.* 15:12).

Saint Paul, in turn, proclaims this teaching without equivocation: "The whole of the Law is summarized in a single command: Love your neighbor as yourself (Gal. 5:13). This one precept contains all the others, so much so that love of neighbor is "the answer to every one of the commandments" (Romans 13:8-10). All the other precepts, which he has occasion to bring up in his letters, are related to this one precept. If the Christian must divest himself of vainglory and pretention, it is because he must imitate Christ and serve his brothers (Phil. 2:3; *cf.* Romans 12:3 ff.). If he must work, it is so that he will not be a burden to others (1 Thess. 2:9; 2 Thess. 3:8); or, even more, so as to "be able to do some good by helping others that are in need" (Eph. 4:28). And Paul himself set this example so as to get across the lesson, which he deemed of capital importance (Acts 20:34-35). When he chastises the greedy and the covetous, who seek more than they need and usually at the expense of others, he does so because they are thereby treating their neighbor as an instrument of pleasure or profit instead of serving him (1 Cor. 5:10-11; 6:9-10; Col. 3:1; Eph. 5:3-5; *cf.* 1 Thess. 4:6). If Timothy is charged to maintain sound doctrine, it is to promote charity (1 Tim. 1:5). This alone "edifies," i.e., builds up the community; knowledge merely "gives self-importance" (1 Cor. 8:1). Prayer, which holds such a great place in his teaching and his life, is usually conceived as an essentially "apostolic" prayer. This is a typically biblical depiction (Abraham, Moses, Aaron, etc.), representing prayer as a struggle which the Christian engages in with God for the welfare of those entrusted to his care.

What is true for Saint Paul holds true for the other apostles. For Saint James: "pure, unspoilt religion in the eyes of God our Father is this: coming to the help of orphans and widows when they need it, and keeping oneself uncontaminated by the world" (James 1:27). This is what he will call "the supreme law of scripture" in the next chapter. And it is always formulated in the same terms: "You must love your neighbor as yourself" (2:8). Or, using another category that is typically Jewish but also Johannine and Pauline, he will call it "the law of freedom" (2:12). It is the law of the new covenant that sets the Christian free as the first covenant, in the opinion of the Jews, set Israel free.

As for Saint John, one need only read his first Epistle; the anecdote related by Saint Jerome about it is an eloquent commentary. He makes a point of saying that we respond to God's love for us by loving our brothers: "Since God has loved us so much, we too should love one another" (1 John 4:11). He does not say what we might have probably said: that we shoud love him in return (*cf.* C. Spicq, *Agapè*, III, p. 284). But this should not astonish us, for it is by doing this that we do his will, and please him, and imitate him. Saint Catherine of Siena saw this clearly when she wrote these words to Peter Benuccio: "I want you to realize that a person can love God . . . only through his neighbor" (Letter 77).

Here we certainly have the correct interpretation of the *logion* which, unlike the passages studied so far, sums up the whole Law in two precepts rather than one: "The greatest and the first commandment" and "the second resembles it" (Matt. 22:38-39), upon which "hang the whole Law and the Prophets" (Matt. 22:40). The first formula, that of the Sermon on the Mount, Saint Paul, Saint James, and Saint John, sums up the whole Law in love of neighbor; and it is true that it could furnish a pretext for "secularism" if interpreted too strictly, as if "love of God was only a way of symbolizing love of neighbor" (Van Buren).[2] But the second formula, which offers two precepts, also involves a certain danger. Some might be led to believe that there are some things commanded only by love of God and not by love of neighbor; that, despite the assertions of Saint Paul and Christ himself, love of neighbor does not contain the whole Law in it!

The Church Fathers were not led astray on this point. For Saint Augustine, "the ten commandments come down to these two: love of God and love of neighbor. And those two come down to the one commandment: Do not do to others what you would not have done to yourself. In it are contained the ten commandments and the two great precepts" (Sermon 9,14, or Sermon 96; PL 38,86). Saint Thomas feels no differently, when he comments on John 15:12: "This is my commandment: love one another." He asks how it is that Christ could mention only the single precept of love of neighbor, when Scripture specifies many others. He answers this question by citing Romans 13:8-10 and Saint Gregory the Great's explanation of the same passage in Saint John's Gospel. "Charity is the root and end of all the precepts," the source from which it comes and the end to which it tends (Homily 27:1 on the Gospels; PL 76:1205). And he does not hesitate to draw his conclusion: "Thus all the precepts are ordered to this end, that man do good to his neighbor instead of doing him wrong"(*Super Joannem 15*, lect. 2, Ed. Marietti, n. 2006).

And now, in its Dogmatic Constitution on the Church, Vatican II proclaims: "The People of God has as its law (*habet pro lege*, in the singular) the precept of loving as the Lord loved us." And the reference to John 13:34 shows clearly what kind of love it is talking about.

This insistent stress certainly constitutes one of the characteristics of Christianity which, by virtue of its external and more clearly visible aspect, most struck the people around them: "See how they love one another!" It follows, then, that anything added to this precept from without, which does not bear a connection to this precept and which does not bring out the subordination of every other precept to this one, runs the risk of concealing and disfiguring, to a greater or lesser extent, the authentic teaching of Christ. That is why, for example, the new penitential discipline (*Paenitemini*, February 17, 1966)—the first postconciliar Constitution—takes pains to remind us that if fast or abstinence is to be in accord with the law of the Church, it must be a witness of asceticism and charity for the poor. This is in line with the most traditional doctrine, that of Saint Leo the Great and Saint Gregory the Great. For the former, "the abstinence of the faithful should be the nourishment of the poor" (PL 54:172,190, etc.). And in his *Regula pastoris*, the latter bids the Lenten preachers to remind the faithful that "their abstinence will be pleasing to God only insofar as they give to the poor the nourishment that they are giving up." And he calls this: "sanctifying the fast" (*Regula pastoris* 3:19; PL 77:83).

Love of Neighbor: Participation in the Love with Which God and Christ Love Us in the Spirit

For Saint Paul, however, the real novelty of Christianity lies elsewhere. It is radically new in comparison with Judaism. But instead of contradicting the teaching of the Old Testament, it actually fulfills what the latter proclaimed in abstract terms.

"CIRCUMCISION OF THE HEART"

Deuteronomy is not content to sum up the precepts of the Law in one single precept ("Circumcise your heart . . . and be obstinate no longer"; Deut. 10:16), and to explain that this comes down to befriending the alien in the concrete (Deut. 10:18-19). In Chapter 30, circumcision of the heart is presented not only as a precept imposed on man but the work of Yahweh himself. He alone is able to "circumcise your heart and the heart of your descendants, until you love Yahweh your God with all your heart and soul, and so have life" (Deut. 30:6). Thus, for the writer of Deuteronomy, it was not within man's power to circumcise his heart on his own. He had to have the personal intervention of Yahweh, an interior renewal that only God could bring about.

This is the only such passage in Deuteronomy. But it is the same interior renewal which Jeremiah, almost certainly relying on Deuteronomy to some extent, proclaimed in his talk about a "new covenant." God would engrave this new covenant on men's hearts rather than on stone tablets: "Deep within them I will plant my law, writing it on their hearts" (Jer. 31:33). About twenty years later, Ezekiel would pick up the same notion in Jeremiah's terms, but substituting the term "spirit" for "law": "I will put my spirit in you" (Ezek. 36:27). The gift of God's law engraved on the heart is identical with the gift of the very Spirit of Yahweh.

The consequences seem inescapably clear. If the law of God is interiorized to this extent, if the Spirit of God becomes the very principle of our actions, then it is clear that to the extent that this interiorization takes place (to be completed only in heaven), our conduct will necessarily be conformed to the will of God. Is this not the aim that Jeremiah ascribes to the gift of this interior law: "There will be no further need for neighbor to try to teach neighbor . . . No, they will all know me, the least no less than the greatest" (Jer. 31:34). For "knowing God," as the Bible understands it, is identical with the carrying out of his will. And one is quite right to remark on this text: "To know Yahweh is to possess in the depths of one's being the law of Yahweh as the supreme principle of one's actions" (P. E. Langerin, *Sciences ecclesiastiques* 19, 1967, p. 398). In even clearer terms Ezekiel ascribes the same aim to the gift of Yahweh's Spirit: "I shall put my spirit in you and make you keep my laws and sincerely respect my observances (Ezek. 36:27).

This doctrine is not peculiar to the passages of Deuteronomy, Jeremiah, and Ezekiel cited above. It is the sense in which we must interpret a theme that is familiar throughout the Bible: In eschatological times, God himself will teach his People (e.g., Isaiah 48:17; 54:13 which will later be cited in John 6:45, *Erunt omnes docibiles Dei, didaktoi Theou*; 55:1-3; Song of Songs 8:2, "There you would teach me," an allusion to the covenant). It is closely allied to the theme of Wisdom inviting men to its table, all the more so because we know that Paul's Jewish contemporaries identified Wisdom with the Law: "Wisdom . . . has laid her table . . . 'Come and eat my bread and drink the wine I have prepared! Leave your folly and you will live, walk in the ways of perception' " (Prov. 9:2-6). "Whoever fears the Lord will act like this, and whoever grasps the Law will obtain wisdom. She will come to meet him . . . give him the bread of understanding to eat and the water of wisdom to drink" (Sir. 15:1-3). "Approach me, you who desire me . . . They who eat me will hunger for more, they who drink me will thirst for more" (Sir. 24:19-21).

A variation on this theme is that of the messianic banquet which was foreshadowed by the gift of manna in the desert (Ps. 22:27; 23:15; Isaiah 26:6; 65:13), and which found fulfillment in the Eucharistic repast where Christ communicates his own love to us. All these themes find echoes in the fourth Gospel. Right from the prologue on it takes pains to set up a contrast between

Moses, through whom was transmitted "the Law" of Sinai, and Jesus Christ, through whom have come "grace and truth" (John 1:17).

So here we have the essential new element of the Gospel that Paul is commissioned to proclaim to the pagans: namely, the very person of Jesus Christ. He is the mediator of a covenant that no longer involves the gift of a law engraved on stone which could be transmitted by a mere human being like Moses. His covenant involves the gift of God's own Spirit, of the mutual love between Father and Son. Christ communicates this to men through his death and resurrection; to be more exact, through a death which, insofar as it is the supreme act of love by a God-man, is quite the opposite of death and forms a single mystery of life with the resurrection.

LOSING ALL TO GAIN CHRIST

We often overlook the extent to which Paul's teaching is dominated and clarified by the two oracles of Jeremiah and Ezechiel. People do cite the classic passage in Second Corinthians where Paul contrasts the letter that kills with the Spirit that gives life. The former, engraved on tablets of stone, is explicitly tied up with the old covenant promulgated by Moses; the latter, engraved on fleshly tablets of the hearts, is explicitly tied up with the new covenant (2 Cor. 3:3-7). Less often do we note that the Epistle to the Romans picks up this same opposition between the "outworn letter" and the "new spirit." It is already present in 2:29, where Paul talks about pagans who observe the commandments of the Law without knowing them—a passage of obvious missionary interest. It is to be found especially in 7:6, where Paul ushers in the thoughts he will develop in Chapter 8: about Christian existence being a life in the Spirit.

But even long before he wrote the great theological epistles, right from his First Epistle to the Thessalonians, we see him setting forth Christian morality in terms of these two oracles; and they provide the key. He reminds the Thessalonians "of the life God wants, as you learnt from us, and as you are already living it" (1 Thess. 4:1). "What God wants is for you all to be holy" (1 Thess. 4:3), he explains. As the Jerusalem Bible notes, this does not simply mean that God enjoins them to be holy; it also means that God's will is what brings about their holiness. And Paul will say this in his second epistle to them: "God chose you from the beginning to be saved by the sanctifying Spirit ..." (2 Thess. 2:13). Now the person who refuses to let himself be sanctified, "is not objecting to a human authority, but to God, who gives you his Holy Spirit" (1 Thess. 4:8). Thus he does not simply oppose a precept promulgated by man, or even one promulgated by God; he sets himself up in opposition to an "activity of God" operating at the very core of the Christian through God's gift of his Spirit. And the use of a present participle (*didonta*), now preferred in critical editions to the aorist participle (*donta*), underlines the continuity of this activity of God in the very core of our being through his Spirit: "Who *gives* his Holy Spirit." Saint Thomas describes it as "working out love in us."

It is clearly an allusion to the gift of the Spirit of Yahweh which, according to Ezekiel, was to typify messianic times. As we have seen, it is a gift that is essentially ordained to permit men to lead a life pleasing to God.

The next verse of First Thessalonians refers no less clearly to the prophecy of Jeremiah. For him, the gift of a law engraved on men's hearts would have this effect; people would no longer need to teach each other because they all will be directly taught by God to know Yahweh, i.e., to act in accordance with his will. It is in the light of Jeremiah's prophecy that we must understand verse 9 of First Thessalonians 4: "As for loving your brothers, there is no need for anyone to write to you about that, since you have learned from God yourselves to love one another." In other words, God has not simply taught the Thessalonians about the existence of a precept obliging Christians to love one another. Nor has he simply taught them the exact content of this precept: i.e., that they must love each other as Christ loved them. He has taught them to love each other by engraving on their hearts the precept of love (Jeremiah), by "circumcising" their hearts (Deuteronomy), and by giving them his own Spirit (Ezekiel). Or, to put it in other words, he has done it by communicating to them his own love which, in the person of the incarnate Jesus Christ, has become an authentically human love.

Paul will never weary of reiterating this same message, fully aware of its radical novelty in comparison to any notion that made the law observed by man a real mediator of salvation. The formulas vary, but the doctrine remains the same and the backdrop does too.

Epistle to the Galatians   "I live now not with my own life, but with the life of Christ who lives in me. . . . I cannot bring myself to give up God's gift; if the Law can justify us, there is no point in the death of Christ" (Gal. 2:20-21).

Epistle to the Philippians   "Life for me, of course, is Christ" (1:21). "For him I have accepted the loss of everything, and I look on everything as so much rubbish if only I can have Christ and be given a place in him. I am no longer trying for perfection by my own efforts, the perfection that comes from the Law, but I want only the perfection that comes through faith in Christ, and is from God and based on faith. All I want is to know Christ and the power of his resurrection" (Phil. 3:8-10). And as Huby explains quite well, knowing the power of his resurrection does not mean knowing directly the power that resurrected Christ, but knowing "the power of the risen Christ, all that the resurrection bestows and realizes; in particular, the inauguration in us of a new life with Christ in the Spirit, which is essentially identical with the life of the glorified Christ while not yet fully developed in eternal radiance as his is" (*Epîtres de la captivité*, p. 348).

Epistle to the Romans   "The law of the spirit of life in Christ Jesus has set you free from the law of sin and death." Through Christ, God has accomplished what was impossible for the Law. "In that body [Christ's] God condemned sin. He did this in order that the Law's just demands [i.e., what the Law as the expression of God's will demands of man, which is summed up in love of neighbor] might be satisfied in us [in the passive voice, because it is the work of Christ and his Spirit more than ours], who behave not as our unspiritual nature but as the spirit dictates" (8:2-4).

Epistle to the Colossians   The Colossians were in danger of being enslaved to a brand of gnosticism that took its inspiration from Judaism. In it religion would involve a series of carefully kept observances. Under the protection of angels, people were to watch what they ate and drank, and to observe particular festivals (*cf*. 2:16-23). Paul reminds them of the essential element in his message, that which makes it novel: "the mystery hidden for generations and centuries and [now] revealed to his saints" (1:26). Paul defines it in three words: "Christ among you" (1:27).

This does not simply mean that the salvation message, formerly reserved for Israel alone, has now been preached to them too. It means that Christ, who is the sole source of salvation for both Jews and pagans, has now become their life. He has communicated his spirit to the Colossians, the very Spirit of God. Thus they can now please God and carry out his will: i.e., love one another as God loves and as Christ has shown us by his example. This is what Paul, in verse 25, described as "making the world of God fully known" (Gr. *eis hymas plerôsai ton logon toû Theoû*); and I do not think one could find a better definition of "evangelization." It is not simply announcing Christ or preaching him. It is implanting the gospel economy; seeing to it that men love one another as Christ loves us, that they realize that this love has been given to them by an Other, an Other who loved them so much that he chose to communicate his very own love to them by dying and rising for them and by making himself their food in the Eucharist.

In Paul's thinking, this is the fuller sense of the profession of faith recalled in Romans 10:9: "If your lips confess that Jesus is the Lord and if you believe in your heart that God raised him from the dead, then you will be saved." To be sure, this does affirm the divinity of Christ and his Resurrection. But to proclaim that Christ is resurrected from the dead is not simply to affirm the historical reality of a past event that was localized in time and space. It is also and primarily to affirm, as Paul did to Festus (Acts 25:19), that "This Jesus, who had died, is alive today." And he is not only alive "in heaven," where he sits at the Father's right hand and intercedes for us (Romans 8:34); he is also alive in his Church and in the heart of every one of his disciples. He is the Christ who, in the Spirit, lives, prays, and loves in me.

One can readily see how far we are from any moralism wherein man would simply expect religion to teach him what he is to do without giving him the capability of doing it. Paul does lay great stress on man's incapacity to perform what he sees as good. But he does so because the Judaism which he was opposing readily conceived the gift of the Law as an education in what man had to do to please God, it being understood that, in creating him free, God had given man's nature all he needed to carry out his duty. For Saint Paul, on the contrary, man in his present real-life condition is a slave of sin and incapable of doing good: "Though the will to do what is good is in me, the performance is not" (Romans 7:18).

Man's nature, to be sure, is not totally corrupt. He can still wish good. (The Greek verb *thelein* suggests a desire and a tendency rather than a decision of the will: "desire" or "yearn for" good.) For Saint Augustine and the whole patristic tradition, this good is most often present to man's conscience as a law "which truth has inscribed on the heart of every man, even the pagan, through the hand of the Creator: 'Do not do to others what you would not have done to yourself'" (St. Augustine, *On Psalm 57,1;* PL 36,373). Augustine therefore calls it a "natural law." It is the same law that sums up "the whole Law and the Prophets," according to Hillel, Christ, and Saint Paul. But even if I can "yearn for" this good, and even if all men in all ages and places do yearn for it—unless they are "de-natured"—we cannot love with a truly disinterested and universal love unless Christ himself, in the Spirit, loves in us.

Under these conditions we can readily understand why the concrete exercise of such charity is presented as the criterion of God's indwelling in us. It is so presented by the Church Fathers, Saint Augustine and Saint Leo, who follow the lead of Saint John the Evangelist in this matter.

> If a person wants to know experimentally [*experiri*] whether God dwells in him . . . then let him scrutinize the depths of his heart. Let him examine whether he fights pride with humility, and envy with a proper interior goodwill. Let him ask to what extent he avoids falling prey to flattering words, and rejoices over the success of others. Let him ask whether he refuses to return evil for evil and prefers to forget wrongs done to him . . . In short, let him see whether he finds charity, the mother of all virtues, in the most intimate recesses of his heart . . . to such an extent that he wishes for his enemies the same good he wishes for himself. If a person finds these dispositions in himself, then he need not doubt that God guides him and dwells in him. And his response to God will be all the greater if he boasts in the Lord rather than in himself (Saint Leo, *Sermon 38, 3;* PL 54,262).

Saint Paul defined Christianity in relationship to the Old Testament and to Judaism. He showed how it fulfilled the former and was opposed to the latter. He detected one novel aspect of Christian revelation right away in the very content of the new law: i.e., that it is fully embodied in the single precept of loving our brothers as Christ loved us. But he detected an even more radical novelty in the nature of this law, which made it truly "new." It is a law no longer engraved on stone and imposed on man from without, but inscribed on man's heart as an interior dictate. It is not just a "spiritual law": i.e., a law "given by the Holy Spirit." It is a "law of the Spirit": i.e., a law "which the Holy Spirit accomplishes in us" (Saint Thomas, *On Rom. 8,2*). Only Christ, the mediator of the new covenant, is capable of communicating this Spirit to us; and he does so in fact by his death and resurrection. We in turn accept the Spirit by submission to God. And this submission to God is faith (Romans 1:5), a faith "that makes its power felt through love" (Gal. 5:6) and whose sacrament is baptism.

Now such a message seems as relevant today as anything could be. To preach a message of brotherly love is to heed the aspirations of men in every age, but perhaps even more so the aspirations of men today. That is why "missionary activity is closely bound up too with human nature and its aspirations" (AG 8). By the same token Paul's message, which opposed the Judaic notion that the law was the true mediator of justification and salvation, is no less radically opposed to modern atheism. It is opposed to "systematic" atheism, which "gives man freedom to be an end unto himself, the sole artisan and creator of his own history" (GS 20). And it is opposed to that more insidious and widespread form of atheism whereby "some never get to the point of raising questions about God, since they seem to experience no religious stirrings nor do they see why they should trouble themselves about religion" (GS 19).

Surely evangelization will mean preaching to all men, whatever religion they may already profess, that they must love one another; that this is the only thing which God demands of them because it "is the basic law of human perfection and hence of the world's transformation" (GS 38). The decree on Ecumenism aptly reminds us that "an ecumenical dialogue could start with discussions concerning the application of the gospel to moral conduct" (UR 23).

But that would only be the beginning, if we remember what "evangelize" meant for Saint Paul. His definition of it in the Epistle to the Romans (5:19) is practically untranslatable: To evangelize is "to effect the carrying out of Christ's gospel." Or, as Benoit translates a similar formula in the Epistle to the Colossians (1:25): "To effect in your midst the coming of God's word." Put in other words: To evangelize is to implant in a specific community the very activity of Christ—since the gospel is, for Paul, "the power of God saving all who have faith" (Romans 1:16).

The missionary will not be content to preach the law of love and its obligations. He will work to see it carried out in practice. As *Ad gentes* puts it: "Closely united with men in their life and work, Christ's disciples hope to render to others true witness of Christ, and to work for their salvation, even where they are not able to proclaim Christ fully" (AG 12). With this aim in view, the task of the missionary will also be to reveal to men the authentic source of their aspirations for dignity and fraternal union, and of the achievements they have won so far. God did not wait for the moment of the Incarnation to communicate his love to our humanity, as Paul knew and Vatican II has reminded us (LG 16; DV 3). But the fact is that he has done it exclusively through the death and resurrection of Christ, so that without them this love would never have been communicated to any human being and no salvation would have been possible.

But even that message will not satisfy the task of "implanting the gospel." The essential task of the missionary is that of every priest: to educate people in the Christian way of life. It is a life of love lived in a community where the Christian, like the child in his family, learns to love his brothers around the Eucharist: the expression and source of this love. As *Presbyterorum ordinis* says so well, he must educate them to "a sincere and active charity, and to that freedom with which Christ has made us free ... the attainment of Christian maturity" (PO 6).

NOTES

1. William M. Moran, S.J., "The Ancient Near Eastern Background of the Love of God in Deuteronomy," *Catholic Biblical Quarterly* 25 (1963) 77-87.
2. Quoted in Richardson, *Le Proces de la Religion* (Paris: Casterman, 1967), p. 41.

OTTO SEMMELROTH

Revelation and Salvation Outside the Visible Church

CHAPTER THREE

The conviction that there is no salvation outside the visible Church has always been the driving force behind the Church's missionary activity. Moreover, this missionary elan has felt itself free from the confusion that people had between the necessity of faith in God and his salvific action in Christ for salvation, and membership in the Church which carries this message and bears witness to this faith. Today we see that it, too, is prone to this confusion. People are prepared to recognize faith as an existential attitude that determines the decisions of conscience, while the Church readily falls prey to the same suspicions we have about *the establishment* and any organized power. A formula from the Council of Trent shows us that it is quite proper to make a distinction between the two, even with respect to what is necessary for salvation. Among the causes of justification, it specifies as an instrumental cause baptism, and hence membership in the visible Church. Thus it does not directly tie up what is necessary for salvation with membership in the Church but with faith, of which baptism is the sacrament.[1]

So the question may be asked: Is there revelation and salvation—which are in fact received in faith—outside the Church established and made real by baptism? Even though baptism and faith are truly made for each other, as sign and thing signified, can they be found disjoined from one another; in other words, can salvation in faith be received without its sacramental sign? Or, to put it in a way that makes it of pointed interest to missionaries: Can one propagate the faith without bringing entrance into the Church into the picture?

This is the issue we are going to examine in what follows. First we shall consider the tension that exists between God's universal salvific will and its finite materialization in the sacrament. Then we shall examine the relationships between revelation, salvation, and the Church. From there we shall move on to establish that there is more than one way for the Church to carry out its salvific function.

God's Universal Salvific Will and Its Finite Materialization

In exploring the relationship of revelation and salvation to the visible Church, we come upon a point of tension that cannot be treated lightly.

THE "SACRAMENTS OF FAITH"

The point of tension occurs between two truths of faith, both of them attested to by the Bible and promulgated by the magisterium. One is the truth proposed in First Timothy as the basis for offering prayers for all men: "To do this is right and will please God our Savior, who wants everyone to be saved" (1 Tim. 2:4). But the New Testament just as clearly attests that outside the Church, which is finite, there is no salvation.[2] This tension is embodied in the very person of Jesus Christ himself. His words proclaim the Father's universal salvific will, but this salvation is bound up with his finite God-man form (Matt. 11:27; 1 Cor. 3:11).

So here on the one hand we confront a gospel proclaiming God's universal salvific will. In the confrontation with Jansenism, the universality of God's salvific will and Christ's redemptive will became pointed objects of the magisterium's pronouncements.[3] Missionary activity has always been understood as service to this universal salvific will. In his missionary activity, Paul considered himself God's co-worker in the salvation of men (1 Cor. 3:9; 2 Cor. 1:24). In Third John 8, missionaries are called fellow-workers for the truth. Assuming responsibility for this universal salvific will, missionaries of every age have felt compelled to go to the ends of the earth. Yet, at the same time, they were the emissaries of the Church: not only in the sense that the Church sent them out as stakes in the fulfillment of this salvific plan; but also in the sense that they were to bring men into the Church's own sphere of life, because in it the salvation willed by God possesses a sacramental, incarnate form.

It is truly astonishing that the incontestability of the Church's mission has not suffered shipwreck on this tension which is immanent to it. On the one hand she feels she has inherited this mission from God, who "wills that all men without exception be saved even if all are not saved in fact."[4] On the other hand she experiences in herself and her missionary activity that the ecclesial materialization of this salvific will hardly seems to attest to its universality.

What is more, no less real than the universality of God's salvific will is the relation of man's salvation to factors that mark out its limits. First of all, salvation is linked to faith, and this in turn to a revelation that comes from God: "Now it is impossible to please God without faith, since anyone who comes to him must believe that he exists and rewards those who try to find him" (Heb. 11:6; see also Rom. 10:9-13). And the revelation, to which this saving faith is to open up, does not appear in the New Testament as a purely personal and interior communication of God; it appears as something fleshed out (i.e., materialized) in the proclamation of messengers sent by the Church. "But they will not ask his help unless they believe in him, and they will not believe in him unless they have heard of him, and they will not hear of him unless they get a preacher, and they will never have a preacher unless one is sent" (Rom. 10:14). Then reception of the message about God's revelation and the response of the receiver are to be materialized in signs that represent a concrete encounter between God and man. These signs have been called the "sacraments of faith" by Trent[5] and Vatican II (SC 59). So it is not enough for man to take interior cognizance of God's revelation and accept it with an interior faith. The saving encounter between God and man must go by way of the materialized form that Christ has chosen to give it in the word and sacrament of the Church.

The Church is this sacrament established upon man's community and history. It is the sacrament wherein God's salvific will for humanity and man's willing subjection to God find expression in the way God himself has willed it. The Church itself is not salvation, of course, but the latter is materialized in the Church sacramentally. And if a person wants to obtain salvation, he is supposed to express this salvation requirement concretely through his life in the Church.

It is there that we come upon the tension that we have just alluded to. If it were simply a matter of God's salvific will in itself, it would not be too difficult to believe confidently in its universality. But if salvation is tied up with acceptance of God's revelation in faith, and this in turn with the proclamation of the Church, and our response to this proclamation with the sacraments, then God's salvific will either seems to be something not universal or else appears to lack the energy required for its carrying out.

Right up into the nineteenth century, the magisterial pronouncements of the Church have reiterated the principle of Cyprian: "Outside the Church there is no salvation";[6] or, "If one is to have God as his Father, he must have the Church as his mother."[7] The straightforwardness and literalism of these pronouncements appear to transform the tension into outright opposition.[8] Even in 1832, in his encyclical *Mirari vos*, Gregory XVI put the label of indifferentism on any interpretation which held that "salvation could be obtained in just any profession of faith, so long as its moral principles are guided by the norms of goodness and uprightness."[9] And he rejected such an interpretation without any reservations.

Twenty years after this rigid proclamation, his successor Pius IX reiterated the necessity of belonging to the visible Church to be saved; but he toned down its absolute character. "We must hold *de fide* that no one can be saved outside the Roman Church, that it is the one and only ark of salvation and that all those who do not enter it are destined to perish in the deluge. But we must also hold with just as much certainty that those who are in ignorance of the true religion, when this ignorance is invincible, do not bear any fault for this in the eyes of the Lord."[10] In his encyclical *Quanto conficiamur,* the same pope says: "Both We and you know that if people are in invincible ignorance of our sacred religion, and if they nevertheless zealously observe the natural law and its precepts inscribed by God on the hearts of all men—leading an honorable and upright life in obedience to God, then they can obtain eternal salvation through the power of God's light and grace."[11] Here, for the first time, the necessity of belonging to the visible Church in order to be saved is no longer proclaimed in the purely objective way it had been previously. Now a personal factor enters into consideration, and this represents an important new element for us in our attempt to answer the question posed in this paper. A response of the Holy Office during the reign of Pius XII, sent to the archbishop of Boston in 1949, strongly rejected the excessively rigorous and literal interpretation of the American Jesuit Feeney with regard to "outside the Church, no salvation."[12] One cannot help but note how forcefully the tension is present once again in the last two documents cited.

SALVATION AND GRACE GO BEYOND THE LIMITS OF THE VISIBLE CHURCH

This same tension between God's salvific will and its material embodiment in the Church is evident in the declarations of Vatican II. Even more forcefully than in the documents of earlier days, stress is placed on God's universal salvific will; even though the necessity of belonging to the visible Church is not passed over in silence. The possibility of obtaining salvation is recognized, not only for people who do not live in the community of the visible Church, but also for those who do not live in the Christian community of faith. The possibility of salvation is not ruled out even for those who, through no fault of their own, have not arrived at a knowledge of a personal god (LG 15-16). It is not surprising that the missionary impetus should feel that it has been set back, or at least called into question, by the statements of Vatican II. If one feels that salvation is guaranteed only within the bounds of the visible Church, then it is easy to inspire a zealous missionary commitment. But if the Church says that men can obtain God's salvation, even if they know nothing of the Church or even a personal God, then the missionary dynamism must become somewhat ill at ease.

In the declarations of Vatican II we find express mention of the two poles that confront each other in the tension mentioned previously. The Council tells us that people, who have never been visited by a missionary, can also arrive at the salvation which the missionary is not only supposed to proclaim but also bring about among them through the intermediary of the Church. But the same Council also holds firmly to the evangelizing mission of the Church and to the necessity of belonging to her. When discussions began on the schema concerning the missionary activity of the Church, the pope was present in person to confirm his personal approval of it, exposing himself to the risk of seeing it rejected as inadequate. This indicates the great importance which the Church, today as yesterday, attaches to her evangelizing mission. The necessity of belonging to the visible Church in order to obtain salvation was confirmed (LG 14). And it did not accept the treatment of its doctrine on freedom of conscience in matters of religion until it had impressed on people's minds that a religion and a church founded by Christ and based on faith in him was a necessity for salvation. There was more than one debate on this question, but the Council did not want this affirmation to be left out.

Thus, in the same breath, the Council tells us that salvation and grace go beyond the limits of the visible (hence finite) Church, because they are provided by God's universal salvific will; and, at the same time, that the attainment of salvation is tied up with the People of God, who finds its realization in the Church (DH 1).

Revelation—Salvation—Church

In order to give a response to the whole problem outlined in the preceding section, we must first examine the relationships of revelation, salvation, and Church. The meaning of these three notions may seem fairly evident to any Christian who has had some formation. But he often finds that he must make a further effort to understand them properly when he is asked to explain their mutual relationship. He then perceives that his understanding of them is frequently correct but far from complete, and that partial knowledge has been mistaken for complete understanding.

THE NOTION OF SALVATION

Let us start with a rough outline of the three notions: revelation, salvation, and Church. We shall start with the notion of salvation as it is often conceived, then see how people depict the revelation of God and its relationship to salvation, and finally examine the role that is attributed to the Church.

As regards the nature of salvation, one is quite right in saying that it is a reality effected by God himself in man, whose communication to us has been earned by Christ and his work. Through this grace, which the New Testament calls justification or eternal life, man is transformed into the new creation of which Paul speaks (2 Cor. 5:17; Gal. 6:15).

This response certainly cannot be labelled false. But we should note that there is a danger: over and above our consideration of salvation as a gift from on high, the role which has been given to man in the salvation economy may be overlooked. The fact that God comes toward man through grace and communicates himself to him does not transform man into a mere object manipulated by God, so that he simply ends up with grace as the effect of God's action. In reality, through the grace of God's self-revelation, man is stimulated and rendered capable of personal vitality in relation to God. He can live an encounter with God which is a participation in the encounter of the Son with the Father in the unity of the Holy Spirit, and which can therefore be characterized by the cry of "Abba, Father" (Rom. 8:15; Gal. 4:6). Thus salvation is achieved in a union that inaugurates a dialogic process of personal encounter between God and man, one that participates in the encounter that is intrinsic to the Trinity of Father, Son, and Holy Spirit.

Related to the incomplete conception of salvation, which depicts man simply as the object of God's action, is an inadequate interpretation of the nature and import of revelation. If salvation is presented simply as a state which will be completed in direct contemplation of God in heaven, even though it has its beginnings here on earth in the grace of union with God, then God's revelation seems to have no internal tieup with salvation. Its only purpose seems to be to communicate knowledge of the supernatural gifts without which man could not take a personal stand for or against it. There can only be a personal decision where man knows that on which he must take a stand. But his natural intelligence and experience cannot inform him of the gifts and ends to which he is ordered in God's salvific plan. So if he is to arrive at them with a personal decision, he must be given knowledge of them by God himself. Thus he needs God's revelation to know what has been fixed for him and what is to be the object of a personal decision on his part.

This definition is almost wholly epistemological and theological in nature. And even Vatican I interpreted divine revelation primarily in terms of this very definition. It defined supernatural revelation as necessary, "because God in his infinite goodness has destined man for a supernatural end, i.e., a participation in divine realities, which wholly surpasses the understanding of his mind."[13] To be sure, Vatican I also said that it pleased God "to reveal himself and his eternal salvation plans."[14] But its justification of the necessity for revelation does not seem to make the latter a part of the carrying out of salvation itself. Instead, salvation seems to be simply the object and content of God's revelatory communication.

As a result, the role of the Church, too, cannot help but seem relativized and somehow estranged. The Church readily seems to be an auditorium in which people gather if they want to hear or learn God's revelation, or an assemblage of those who are destined to be touched by salvation. There is a twofold source of imperfection in such an interpretation of salvation, revelation, and the Church. First of all, the Church and its sacraments are interpreted too strongly as instruments of action that are in the hands of God; man stands passively before them as one in whom grace is brought about with the aid of these instruments. But then it becomes difficult to explain how any man can experience the effect of God's action even when this instrument is not used. Secondly, it is difficult to understand how a person who has not managed to hear the word of God's revelation from the mouth of the Church, and who therefore has not attained knowledge of these supernatural gifts of salvation, could nevertheless participate in these gifts.

CHURCH AND GRACE

We must deepen and round off our understanding of these three notions: salvation, revelation, Church. And this involves getting a proper understanding of a twofold duality: on the one hand, salvation-and-revelation and revelation-and-salvation; on the other hand, the Church and its visible salvific action.

Vatican II contributed an essential complement to the declarations of Vatican I in that it carried the meaning of revelation beyond a purely epistemological-theological function and interpreted it as a part of the very carrying out of salvation. Salvation is not the unilateral process of God's action on man. In his salvific action God reveals himself to men in such a way that they are "divinized" and rendered capable of a real communal life with God. They can encounter God in such a way that their human and personal process is a real participation in the encounter that takes place and unfolds within the Trinity. In revealing himself to men, God gives them the capacity to reveal themselves to him in turn, in a real association. Introduced into a united life with the Son of God, whose Incarnation is the most intense form of divine revelation, human beings touched by salvation take part in the encounter of the Father and the Son in the Holy Spirit.

This process is not simply brought to our awareness by what we are accustomed to call revelation. Rather, this revelation is an essential part of it. Vatican II describes revelation this way: "In His goodness and wisdom, God chose to reveal Himself and to make known to us the hidden purpose of His will, by which through Christ, the Word made flesh, man has access to the Father in the Holy Spirit and comes to share in the divine nature. Through this revelation, therefore, the invisible God out of the abundance of His love speaks to men as friends and lives among them, so that He may invite and take them into fellowship with Himself" (DV 2). Revelation, then, is not simply a teaching about salvation, which is something separate and apart from the former; revelation is a part of the whole working out of salvation. That is why equal stress is placed on the fact that revelation is not only God's word but also God's activity: "This plan of revelation is realized by deeds and words having an inner unity; the deeds wrought by God in the history of salvation manifest and confirm the teaching and realities signified by the words, while the words proclaim the deeds and clarify the mystery contained in them" (DV 2). When God reveals himself as salvation, he summons man personally. And this summons is not situated outside the salvation effected by God: God reveals himself with the activity of his grace and man, in heeding this summons, abandons himself to God so that he becomes one with him in the grace of a communal life.

Now what is the place of the Church and its salvific action within this process of revelation and salvation? Vatican II labels the Church as the "universal sacrament of salvation" (LG 1 and 9; AG 1). It is "a sacrament or sign and an instrument of intimate union with God and of the unity of all mankind" (LG 1). So we would be justified in regarding the Church, in its visible worldly form and in its saving action through word and sacrament, as the expression of this personal encounter between God and man in which salvation is effected. Man is an incarnate being linked to the world and society; a personal encounter is possible for him only in some expression of his interior abandonment to the partner in this encounter. In this expression he voices his yes or no, not only to the partner but also to the world and the society in which he is rooted. If God wills the salvation of human beings as such, he must summon them as incarnate beings with ties to a given world and a given community. That is why Christ, who entered our human history as the original sacrament of God's universal salvific will, founded the Church as the sacramental sign of God's salvific will.

John the Evangelist depicted the sacramental nature of the Church in the opening of Christ's side on the cross; from his side flowed blood and water, symbolizing the foundation sacraments of the Church, baptism and the Eucharist (John 19:34). From the very beginning, tradition has interpreted this as the founding of the Church: the second Eve springing from the side of the second Adam. Thus we should consider the Church as a sacramental sign in which God, through Christ, manifests his operative salvific will for mankind. And since God's signs are true, the Church is a pledge of obtaining salvation for the person who, in turn, accepts this sign in faith and truly lives a life of faith in the visible Church.

To be sure, we consider the necessity of the Church for salvation as a "necessity of means" (*necessitas medii*).[15] But instead of regarding this *medium* as a means of action in an instrumental sense, we must regard it as a means of personal expression. If a person wants to obtain salvation in his encounter with God, he must express his desire to be saved through the sign in which God expresses his will to save: i.e., in the Church established by God. In the Church, the person who is entrusted with the priestly function by virtue of the sacrament of orders plays the role of Christ, as Vatican II noted more than once (LG 17); there is brought about the salvific encounter between God and man in Jesus Christ, who "is the head of his body, the Church" (Col. 1:18).

The Church and Salvation

But how does the Church carry out its salvific function? Or, to put the question another way: How are we to interpret the principle, "no salvation outside the Church." so that we may preserve its valid sense?

THE CHURCH: LOCUS OF MAN'S ENCOUNTER WITH GOD

Christ willed the visible Church as a human society, and he established its fundamental elements. No matter how the prepaschal Christ may have chosen to carry out its foundation in detail, the Catholic *Credo ecclesiam* cannot contest the primitive sense of the declaration. This means that the Church is to carry out its salvific work as a pledge and sign expressive of the saving encounter between

God and man; to be specific, it does so through the fact that the people gathered together in it unite to form the ecclesial structure established by Christ as an encounter with the Lord in word and sacrament. The Church as the People of God, Body of Christ, and Temple of the Holy Spirit, is not just a reality which is there at the start and which men must join up with to become participants in the grace of God's self-giving—of which the Church is the expression and pledge insofar as it is a society permeated by the Spirit of God. The Church and her life are also the expression of something else, the expression which was validated by Christ's institution: man declares before God that he chooses to receive his gratuitous gift, and he abandons himself to God in return. People can encounter each other only in some form of expression that is similar and common. So if God chooses to encounter human beings in a form that expresses the human, then there is nothing else for man to do but to seek out the expression of his abandonment to God that was established by God himself. And when this expression takes the form of life in a community with worldly features, then it can be effected only by belonging to this community and actively participating in its life.

Thus mission work, insofar as it brings about participation in God's salvation, must always be the mission of the Church. This holds true in more than one sense. It is not just that the Church appoints messengers who carry forward the message of Christ himself: the good news of a merciful God and Father. It also implies that the missionary effort strives to incorporate people into the Church itself, so that by living in it they can realize their encounter with God in faith, hope, and love. It is precisely this aspect that allows the Church's missionaries in every age to experience the limits of their possibilities. Once upon a time mission work met violent repression and bloody martyrdom; today it meets with indifference and rejection of the *Establishment*. There is no longer the *odium fidei* that formerly gave a special luster to the martyr on the level of a purely terrestrial experience. Considering such experiences, the Church's missionary asks himself just what salvation involves for people who remain outside the confines of the message that is announced by him and tied up with the earthly society of the Church. If salvation is not refused to them anyway, he naturally wonders what is the import and sense of his Church-associated missionary activity.

THE CHURCH: SIGN OF SALVATION

This brings us to a second way in which the Church can express its sacramental function.

Life in the Church is a personal sign of the encounter between God and man, a sign set up by Christ. This leads us to consider an analogous phenomenon that is present in people's relations with each other. These relations, too, involve preestablished signs through which people stimulate each other. One must use signs that the other person understands. The parties must use the same language, or one or more languages that will enable them to understand each other. But what happens when one only haltingly and imperfectly speaks the language of the other? They try to understand each other as best they can. If they are attuned to each other, then they will understand each other even if the signs, words, and phrases of one express his thought to the other only confusedly. A child who is still quite inarticulate cannot be understood by a stranger, but his mother knows what he is trying to say.

Now membership in the Church founded by Christ, and a way of life in accordance with the ecclesial forms instituted by him, may be the means of expression through which man is to concretize his desire for salvation. But that does not change the fact that many people do not know or recognize this means of expression willed by God. They are not aware of its significance as the receptacle of God's personal revelation, and they cannot give their will to believe the sacramental form of a profession of faith.

From God's viewpoint, however, the Church remains the sign of salvation in accordance with the purpose of its foundation. Some men, with no personal fault of their own involved, may set up signs other than that of life within the Church founded by the Lord in order to express their desire for salvation. Others, through their faults and negligence, may continually transform the image of the Church and their way of life into a distorted expression of God's revelation. But the fact remains that God has inserted the Church, founded by his Son, in the world and its history as a seal confirming and manifesting his salvific will to all men. There is indeed a Church; and in it the evidence of God's saving revelation is preserved, proclaimed in a living way, and sacramentally arranged. Even for those who have not managed to enter into formal contact with the Church, this fact is a pledge of God's salvific will and of man's desire for a salvation that will bring him to God's presence.

We could say of such people that they have obtained salvation "outside the Church," in the sense that they do not live within the bounds of the visible Church. But we could not say it in the sense that they do not live within the Church's sphere of influence, within the sphere of all that she manifests as a sacramental sign. Their desire to be saved could be embodied in expressive signs that only partially and incoherently point to the authentic sign that the Church is. But even for such people, the sign that expresses God's salvific will remains the same: it is the fact that there is a Church in the world, and that in it we find the proclamation of God's Word and the celebration of the sacramental signs of salvation.

It is certainly true that faith is necessary for salvation. But faith is a response that is correlative to God's revelation. Where God's revelation has not reached men in its complete form, there faith cannot be required in the same form of expression as it is where the Word of God has been proclaimed and understood. At one point Vatican II says: "Nor does divine Providence deny the help necessary for salvation to those who, without blame on their part, have not yet arrived at an explicit knowledge of God, but strive to live a good life, thanks to his grace" (LG 16). Now one may well ask, as was indeed asked at the Council, why there is no mention of the necessity for faith in God's revelation. The Council's reply to this question was that the words "thanks to His grace" sufficed. This indicates that an interior personal revelation of God, which is brought about through grace, is certainly not the objective, articulated revelation that comes to man in the word of Jesus Christ and the proclamation of the Church; but it also indicates that it does lead to salvation people who do not encounter this articulated revelation. Despite the difference, their salvation still remains salvation through the will of Christ and the Church; for Christ and his Church are the seal and pledge and sign expressive of God's salvific will for men.

Does this make the missionary activity of the Church meaningless? The answer seems to be "no" for two reasons. First of all, the fact remains that the Church is the seal that God has stamped on his salvific will for mankind. Because this salvation is a living encounter between God and man, the Church and life within the Church perdures for man, too, as the authentically willed expressive sign of his encounter with God. Hence the Church—that is, the people who come to know these relations as members of the Church—must see to it that people's salvific encounter with God finds the materialized shape and expressive form which God has established as the expression of his will.

Beyond that, the mission of the Church must realize that this effort and this introduction of man into the internal life of the Church are not the only aspects of its activity. Even for those people who do not know the Church and hence do not find their way to it, the Church remains the pledge and seal of God's salvific activity; so the people who make up this Church must see to it that Christ's features radiate from the visage that she presents to the human beings around her. Was this not the chief desire of the Council itself, as it states in its dogmatic Constitution on the Church: " . . . to shed on all men that radiance of His which brightens the countenance of the Church" (LG 1).

That is why we must add at once that missionary activity directed outwards must be supported by the life within the Church, by the quality of the communities already existing. The communities and members of the Church cannot rest content with the fact that Christ did in fact found the Church as the sign of God's salvific will for the human community, and that it therefore shares in the immortality of God's promise. That it is a sacrament of salvation, established by Christ, is a real part of the mystery of the Church; but it must live out this mystery in human decisions. This, too, is part of the missionary task of the Church: Through the efforts of all its members, it must present itself as an authentic sign of God's salvific will and radiate this fact around it.

THE CHURCH: PERPETUATING CHRIST'S WORK

There is a third way for the Church to exercise its salvific function. We must now consider this way and try to rediscover its significance, for it is rather alien to today's pragmatic outlook. It concerns the suppletory function of the

Church: filling up the deficiencies in the relations between men and God. If a person believes that in the Church Christ has his salvific activity carried on through the Holy Spirit, then he must also believe that the Church is commissioned to act as a deputy or substitute for Christ's activity and suffering on behalf of men. The duty of the Church is not just to distribute the fruits that Christ won by his saving work. Vatican I began its constitution on the Church with these words: "The eternal Shepherd and Overseer of our souls willed to give permanent duration to his work of redemption and salvation; for that reason, he decided to set up the Holy Church.[16] Thus the raison d'être of the Church is to keep the work of Christ himself perduringly present in her history.

Now the work of Christ is distinct from that of an earthly nature precisely insofar as it does not show up solely in material results and accomplishments. In the physical, material realm, one instrument can usually be replaced by another, of course; but in the authentic sense of the term, one instrument cannot be used as a substitute for another. The latter exchange is possible only between persons. And the Christian faith says that this has in fact happened in the activity of the God-Man on behalf of men: "For our sake God made the sinless one into sin, so that in him we might become the goodness of God" (2 Cor. 5:21). The nature of his redemptive activity is that of suppletory expiation; but this of course does not dispense us from the duty of entering into his expiation and doing penance ourselves. However, since our penance could never have presumed to reach God, the Son of God carried out our obligation in a way which gave new possibilities to our human penance. What we could not do, he did for us. He stands before God as our replacement.

Now the significance of the Church for salvation is also stamped with this particular activity. The necessity of the Church for salvation is not embodied solely in the fact that men enter it to lead their life in the presence of God therein. Nor is it embodied solely in the fact that the existence of the Church in this world is the seal that confirms that God has provided for the salvation of all men. It is also embodied in the fact that the Church can and should present itself before God as a substitute for those who do not live in her and even for those who work against her. In the Church we should see realized what Christ realized and uttered on the cross: "Father, forgive them; they do not know what they are doing" (Luke 23:34). The first martyr did the same thing as Christ: "Lord, do not hold this sin against them" (Acts 7:60). This the Church must continue to do over and over again, following in Christ's footsteps.

Certainly it is not easy to make this duty understood. More than one person could readily be tempted to wish that he had never heard of "substitution for others," that he could simply enjoy its benefits. Consider all those who do not concern themselves with the Church and its exigencies. The temptation is all the stronger in that one cannot see or evaluate the effect of this activity. Indeed, one cannot demonstrate it in any strict sense. We are simply forced to believe in it, keeping our eyes on Christ, who continues to live in his Church. Intent on following him, we must do our part in carrying out this salvific feature of the Church's activity.

NOTES

1. Council of Trent, Session 6, Chapter 7, Denz. 1529.
2. *Cf.* A. Friedrichsen, "Eglise et sacrement dans le Nouveau Testament," *Revue d'histoire et de philosophie religieuse* 17 (1937) 346.
3. Denz. 2005; 2304.
4. Council of Quiercy in 853; Denz. 623.
5. Denz. 1529.
6. Cyprian, Epistle 73, 21.
7. *Ibid.*, 74, 7.
8. *Cf.* Boniface VIII (Denz. 870); Council of Florence, Decree on the Jacobites, Denz. 1351.
9. Denz. 1730.
10. Pius IX, encyclical *Singulari quadam*, Denz. 2685 (preliminary remark).
11. Denz. 2866.
12. Denz. 3689.
13. Denz. 3005.
14. Denz. 3004.
15. Denz. 3868.
16. Denz. 3050.

DISCUSSION

The reader should remember that all the discussions were spontaneous, and that remarks were made extemporaneously. But the participants have had a chance to reexamine and correct their remarks, as they were taken down by several reporters: A. Sacchi, P.I.M.E.; Th. R. Laube, F.S.C.; R. Haramburu, O.M.I.; and J. Hardy, S.M.A.

—Editor

J. M. GONZALEZ-RUIZ   The question posed here is: What purpose does the Church serve for salvation? But it was not posed properly because it was only considered in the context of the individual, not in terms of its collective and historical aspect. I would prefer to start from the concept of salvation in the Bible, situated in a historical context. For the Bible, the history of salvation does not end. It will find an answer beyond the frontiers of history. It is the kingdom of God that is to come. The kingdom of God will be the result of the presence of the Church, of ecclesial communities, through the course of human history. If, *per impossibile*, this presence were eliminated, the kingdom of God would not come and then there would be no salvation for anyone. Let me give a simple, concrete example: Olympic games are going to take place in Rome. A person can reserve a seat, but first one must build a stadium and have games; otherwise, the reservation is of no use. In the same way, the kingdom of God must be built and set up. If the Church does not build this kingdom—that is to say, if there are no churches, no ecclesial communities—then there will be no salvation. The reservation would be of no use. Today the Church does not know what her frontiers are. She simply has the duty of expanding her visible presence everywhere, through every human community. So the Church must expand, otherwise there will be no kingdom; for the latter will be precisely the result of the Church's presence in human history. That is what justifies the missionary activity of the Church.

J. M. SETIEN   To determine the efficaciousness of the sacraments, we must start from the tension that exists between the gratuitousness of God's gift and the disposition or subjective approach of its recipient. In considering the Church as a "sacrament," with the aim of grasping the raison d'être of its mission works, one might well start from the same tension: between the gratuitousness of God's gift communicated through the Church, and the subjective disposition of peoples (their natural uprightness, their religious life). One cannot examine the gratuitousness of God's gift apart from human dispositions. But neither can one make an abstraction of the gratuitous character of God's gift, which is communicated through the sacraments and, consequently, through the Church considered as a sacrament. We cannot determine exactly what God does and what man does; that holds true both on the level of the individual and the level of a whole community. In my judgment, however, there is a special efficaciousness to the action of the Church as sacrament, which derives from the gratuitousness of God's gift, which *is rendered present in the Church*.

A. SANTOS   Two principles must be maintained. It is true that "outside the Church there is no salvation." But it is not true that outside the Church there is no revelation, and this second aspect can always be defended. Thus any pagan can arrive at the act of faith and at salvation, because he can arrive at a certain revelation of God by ways that only God knows.

A. SEUMOIS   It seems to me that Semmelroth's text considers the Church to be only a mission, to have no other nature than that of forming a magnetic field between God and humanity. One could see in this the theology of the Dutch Pentecostal-Calvinist, J. C. Hoekendijk, which denies any and all structural reality to the Church. But this is obviously an incomplete view because the Church, before being a mission sent into the world, is something objective; it possesses an existence of its own. It is the People of God, formed objectively as a special entity by the incorporation of its members into the very humanity of Christ and enlarged to worldwide dimensions. It is this total body of Christ which, on this earth, is commissioned to pursue Christ's universal redemptive mission in the world. Membership in the Church is normally open and visible, through the sacramental incorporation of baptism. But there is also a suppletive, invisible membership, sufficient in certain circumstances for man to attain his salvation in Christ, and deriving from a theological life (supernatural faith, hope, and charity) combined with the at least implicit desire for baptism. The central question here is to know how the "pagan" can arrive at the act of supernatural faith *propter auctoritatem Dei revelantis*. To explain this, we must take into account not only the revelations of the Old and New Testaments, but also the primitive, proto-evangelic revelation (i.e., the promise of a future redeemer) made at the origin of the human race. This primitive revelation, alas, is too often disregarded today by theologians.

A. M. HENRY   We have much talk of "the Church" here, but we must define this term. It has more then one meaning: organization of God, etc. It is important for us to know what definition of the Church one is starting from when he talks about the Church and salvation. Moreover, I think we would do well to recall the lecture of Lyonnet that we heard yesterday evening. The novel aspect of the gospel is simply this: "There is only one commandment." In carrying out this commandment, we fulfill man's desire. But then man comes to realize that he, all alone, cannot carry out this task of loving everyone as Christ loved us. Saint Paul himself pointed out this impossibility in terms of the law. Man must rely on the divine source: the Holy Spirit, given visibly in the Church. Would it not be worthwhile to start with this excellent lesson and then move on to discover the rest: revelation, salvation, Church, etc.?

G. DELCUVE   Semmelroth offers a nice complement to Lyonnet's lecture, notably in terms of a Trinitarian viewpoint: i.e., in terms of man's real participation in the life of the Trinity. That seems to be an important point to me.

J. FRISQUE   I should like to add a word of support for the remarks of Gonzalez. We must reach some agreement on the collective, historical, and cosmic dimension of the Church. Here I am thinking of the extent to which a certain conception of the adage, "no salvation outside the Church," can concretely influence a missionary pastoral effort. An individualistic conception tends to initiate a missionary strategy that is much too shortsighted. Only a more global vision of the Church will resolve many of the questions and certain sources of uneasiness.

J. MASSON   I should like to make two points. First, as Setien has remarked, we must bring more balance to the sacramental efficaciousness of the Church and of revelation, with respect to their value as signs and their value as instruments. The latter aspect was left very much in the dark by Semmelroth's treatment. But I realize that it is time to spotlight the free, responsible, personal, and interior character of each individual's act of faith. My second point concerns a question of vocabulary. We must link up with the text of *Lumen gentium* (no. 10) and comprehend the Church in its totality as being visible and invisible, as an interior communion and an exterior society. It would be clearer if we spoke of visible membership or invisible membership in the Church.

C. G. AREVALO   The Church, defined as a sociological reality, is a clear notion for everyone. We must define more clearly the meaning of the Church as a community, as a prophetic community in particular.

D. S. AMALORPAVADASS   I would offer two remarks. 1. It is necessary to situate the Church's mission and apostolate in a historical and cosmic context.

Salvation is proposed to peoples taken as whole groups and living their own religion, so it must be studied in this context. 2. Secondly, as presented up to now, salvation seems to me to be depicted too much as coming from the outside. Without denying this aspect, I should like to see it considered under another aspect: as a discovery coming from within, as something imbedded within peoples and nations.

G. GRASSO   The definition of the Church given by Semmelroth is too restricted. It is a sign which expresses but also gives the grace of salvation; this makes it easier to justify the missionary activity of the Church. Grace comes from the Church and orders human beings to the Church. Thus the latter's witness is necessary to bring human beings from the implicit to the explicit. And thus we can see more clearly why the Church must reform itself to be a better sign of God's countenance.

K. MÜLLER   How does revelation take place outside the Church? And another question: Do you think that God's direct influence on man, without the proclamation of the word, is sufficient for faith?

A. CAMPS   The adage, "no salvation outside the Church," has a whole history of its own that must be clarified if we are to have a more precise view. Moreover, Semmelroth says that in Christianity there is a summons from God, which is revelation, and a response from man. But do not these two things also exist in non-Christian religions: revelation from God in one way or another, and response from man as an individual or as a member of a community? And if so, then what is the relationship and the difference between these two responses, the one given inside Christianity and the other outside it?

A. BOVEHARD   Salvation is already given in Christ, so we must distinguish the questions involved here. On the one hand, how do individuals attain this salvation? On the other hand, what is the role of the Church as a collectivity vis-à-vis humanity as a collectivity? Apropos of Gonzalez's remarks, the role of the Church as a collectivity may not be simply the construction of God's kingdom. It may also be God's positive will that this salvation, given by Christ, be effectively signified to all humanity before the end of time. As Hillman has indicated in *The Church as Mission,* humanity exists not only as religious groups but also as ethnic and cultural units: this is the biblical sense of "nations." It is to these ethnic and cultural units, which represent all humanity, that salvation is to be signified. Likewise an idea of Comblin, expressed in his book *Le témoignage de l'Esprit,* seems interesting to me: the announcement of salvation to all humanity plays the role of bringing personalization to humanity. The role of the Church is not so much to bring salvation, for it it Christ who saves, as to help every man to come to the light by confronting him with the question of Christ. This question, then, must be posed to all humanity before the end of time.

I. DE LA POTTERIE   Semmelroth has underlined the tension that exists between implicit and explicit, between revelation and man's response. To better understand these two aspects of mission theology, we might better start from the clearer notion of the "word of God," i.e., revelation. This word of God must first be preached and proclaimed; all modern hermeneutics reminds us of this, following in the footsteps of Saint Paul (Romans 10 in particular). Then the word of God must be still further interiorized; this is the whole Johannine theology of the progressive interiorization of God's word. Finally, there is a corresponding third aspect: the Trinitarian aspect. The word of the Father has come among men. It has become incarnate in Christ, and it is personalized and interiorized through the Spirit. Here we find the third member of the triad: Revelation, Church, Salvation. Salvation is effected precisely by the acceptance and interiorization of the word, and this interiorization is man's response. Thus there is a collective and exterior aspect to mission work: i.e., the Church must continue the work of Christ by preaching the word. But there is also an interior aspect and a salvific aspect.

H. DE LUBAC   As Gonzalez stressed, if we are going to complete Semmelroth's treatment, then we must spotlight the historical and collective aspect of salvation, the aspect of waiting for God's kingdom, and the role of the Church in relationship to this salvation. But neither can we forget the intrinsic relationship that exists between this role of the Church (necessary to the collective salvation of humanity if history is to end up in the kingdom of God) and the personal, interior aspect of salvation. It is possible for there to be a collective revelation and for the kingdom to come, because this word in history has a personal efficaciousness for the one who receives it.

T. TSHIBANGU   From the pastoral viewpoint, it would be important for us to focus more precisely on the definition of salvation and the extension of the term "Church" that have been used here. At the very least, one would have to indicate the present state of theological study, so that these notions might be clarified.

A. VANNESTE   Semmelroth says that the Church is the means of explicitating God's salvific will and man's response. To stay within the lines of modern philosophy, we would have to say that something which is not explicitated does not exist. So if this offer of salvation is not made incarnate in human history, if it is not explicit, then it does not exist. What creates a problem here, it seems, is not salvation outside the Church but the role of the Church. I feel we must return to the traditional framing of the problem: How are men saved who do not arrive at an explicit knowledge of God? What can salvation signify for them? We must revise the notion of salvation, which is employed here in too heavy-handed a way.

JOHANNES SCHÜTTE

Why Engage in Mission Work?

CHAPTER FOUR

Mission work throughout the world has become a problematic issue today. It is not just the form of its existence that is being called into question but its very nature and existence. It finds itself in difficulty when it tries to define itself and to justify its existence. This paradoxical state of affairs affects not only the mission theologian but also the missionary in action. The latter is even more affected; he is deeply disturbed because the reason and purpose of his missionary activity is being challenged, along with his very existence as a missionary.

MISSION WORK AND "ANONYMOUS CHRISTIANS"

The salvation of souls, taken in an exclusivist sense as far as salvation was concerned, drove Saint Francis Xavier through wide expanses of the Far East. This motive is no longer convincing today. Indeed at Vatican II the Church defined, as an explicit doctrine, Saint Paul's affirmation (1 Tim. 2:4) about God's universal salvific will. God's will cannot remain vain and without effect. Therefore God offers his salvation in an effective manner, as an authentic and realizable possibility and as an personal summons, to all men of all nations and ages, even to the most primitive of them. The countless numbers of non-Christians, who comprise the overwhelming majority of the human race, can (and must) find their salvation outside the visible Church. The fact that we cannot comprehend the way this is carried out does not change the reality, for it forms an integral part of the unfathomable mystery of God.

Now if this is true, why should we compromise their chances for salvation by confronting them with the proclamation of Christ? For this proclamation can be for the world a cause of judgment as well as of salvation, of death as well as of life. It has a dramatic aspect because it obliges man to take a position for or against Christ and his gospel, once they have been proposed to him.

Why should mission work disturb men's consciences and lead them into a critical situation that they have neither wished for nor looked for? Would it not be better to leave them in the path determined by their history and situation, in the religion into which they were born, to which they are naturally tied, and toward whose founders they feel an obligation? Would it not be better to leave them in the religion in which, through God's design, they can find and achieve their salvation? In the last analysis, is not this salvation that of Christ and his Church? If all these people are already "anonymous Christians," related in some way or other to Christianity, could not the missionary effort be content to proclaim this hidden attachment? If people's own religion is the normal path of salvation for all men, provided for them by God, then why can it not be the right and legitimate path of salvation for them? If we seek by every means to take men away from their own religion and path of salvation, are we not exerting influence on consciences in an unjustifiable way, restricting and doing damage to the freedom of conscience that was solemnly proclaimed by Vatican II, and conditioning their personal decision in an arbitrary way?

How much more logical and in accord with reality it would be to teach these people to delve more deeply into their own religion and follow it more faithfully. We would help the good Hindu to become a better Hindu, and the good Moslem to become a better Moslem.

Eventually we could commit ourselves to being an active and effective minority in a general worldwide sharing of all these religions. By sharing human values with them in a disinterested way, we would illuminate and actualize the mystery of God in a new humanity. For this we would simply need the presence of the Church in a mission land in some discreet way, however hidden and reserved it might be. It would serve as a sign and a witness, in such a way that individuals would have a chance and an opportunity to encounter and find Christ if they were led to pose questions earnestly and on their own initiative. But missionary initiatives would not be forced on them otherwise.

Now obviously such an approach would represent a fundamental challenge to mission work as it is conceived today. It would no longer correspond to the present-day situation, and it would be stripped of any sense of urgency or priority. Why should missionaries and their institutes put up with so much hardship, and invest so much effort in the missionary process? Such questions obviously go to the very core of the mission effort, challenging both our way of understanding it and its very existence.

Now some people may not try to explain mission work as a necessity for the salvation of the individual. They may prefer to see the implantation of the Church (*plantatio ecclesiae*) as its aim and goal. But even then one runs into difficulties, if one tries to work out an authentic and convincing justification. And our hesitation would seem to be simply the byproduct of ecumenical theology and the spirit of Vatican II. Do they not regard non-Catholic Christian communities as ecclesial communities, in the theological sense of the term? Do they not accord them a real function in the salvation economy?

Moreover, there is the danger of an ecclesiocentrism running up against the incomprehension of people today, particularly if one sees the Church as an institution and not as a living organism (i.e., as the holy People of God). The Church is not there by its own volition. It does not find its meaning and purpose within itself; it cannot affirm and extend itself of its own will. The Church is a sign and a way; it finds its meaning in service.

What we have to do, then, is to express the reality of "mission work" in a new way, to rediscover its full meaning and urgency. In short, we must present it in the framework and dimensions of current theological thought. In my opinion, the commandment in Matthew's Gospel (28:18-20) still remains the surest and most convincing basis for mission work. But we must reinterpret it in the light of the new theology, and point out the force and salvific import of its terms.

The Epiphany of God's Sovereignty Among the Nations

"All authority in heaven and on earth has been given to me. Go therefore . . ." If Christ appeals to the power he has received over all things, then for the apostles this is not only the authorization for their mission but also its reason and goal. It derives from the fact that in him, the glorified Christ, the eschatological sovereignty of God, the *eschaton*, has been inaugurated. According to the will of Christ, the mission effort is in the service of the eschatological glorification of God, which has begun to shine and which is in some way anticipated in the risen and glorified Christ.[1]

THE FAITH OF PAGANS AND THE UNIVERSAL CHRIST

For Scripture, the *eschaton* is the end (and hence the beginning also), the universal omnipotence of God, the "Day of Yahweh" that predominates in the Old Testament promises. It is the revelation of God as the master of the whole earth and history, and hence of the whole future including its very last reaches. In the end, God will be "all in all." This future day has already begun in the glorified Christ. Through him and with him, the *eschaton* has already penetrated the present day; it is here as a ferment of salvific unrest, and as a point of departure for a living dynamism that expands the horizons of earth and history to encompass ever new goals and an ever greater future. Christ is the eschatological fulfillment of God's glorification, and hence the fulfillment of missionary hopes and expectations. Mission work is essentially a postpaschal event.

The Old Testament and the historical Jesus did not know "mission work" in its proper sense. Both were aware of the universality of salvation, which affects all nations, but without the consequent notion of missionary activity. The salvation of the nations, awaited at the end of time, is the work of God himself. With the epiphany of God's glory, all nations will be drawn toward him and will crowd into the house of God on Mount Zion. This is the idea of Isaiah above all (2:2-3), and of Micah (4:1-2). "Nations come to your light" (Isaiah 60:3). And there is also the notion of the eschatological banquet prepared by God on Mount Zion, which "Yahwah Sabaoth will provide for all peoples" (Isaiah 25:6).

During his ministry on earth, Jesus picks up these two ideas. "Men from east and from west, from north and from south will come to take their places at the feast in the kingdom of God" (Luke 13:29). "But the subjects of the kingdom will be turned out into the dark" (Matt. 8:11), because they do not believe in the one sent by God to carry the eschatological proclamation of grace and salvation.

The pagan nations, who journey from the ends of the earth, are assembled into the kingdom of God. We are given a glimpse of the eschatological future at the fullness of time when God's kingdom will have arrived in all its fullness. Even though the historical Jesus is aware that he has been sent exclusively to the "lost sheep of Israel," he at the same time realizes that he is the inauguration of these eschatological events. In the faith of pagans, a faith which his own people refuse to him (Matt. 8:5-10), and in the Greeks who approach him (John 12:20 ff), he sees the inauguration of the eschatological age. In him all pagans and all nations are called, once for all time, to share in the kingdom of God and the feast he is preparing. At the institution of the Eucharist during the Last Supper, the Lord somehow anticipates this eschatological event by saying the words: "This is the blood of my covenant, shed for many." They have a missionary dimension that is unlimited. The "many" are the nations, the pagan nations, the same people for whom the suffering servant gives his life as a ransom (Isaiah 53:12). Already in the Last Supper, then, Jesus sees the universal significance of this in a very direct way. A new economy has been inaugurated, a new covenant has been concluded: salvation is offered to all nations.

The institution of the Eucharist is an anticipation of Good Friday and of Easter, which will give birth to this completely new economy. The point of view is now different and the salvation economy has progressed. For between the earthly activity of Jesus and that of the risen Christ we have the most important happening in the history of salvation, and it has eschatological import at the same time: it is the passion and resurrection of Christ. The paschal Christ gives the irrefutable order to commence the universal mission that is to assemble the nations for the approaching eschatological hour. The foundation for the universality of the commission is the universality of Christ's sovereignty: his authority in heaven and on earth, his power over the whole cosmos. Mission work has the essential aim of making evident and fully effecting Christ's position as the universal sovereign, in whom the epiphany of God's glory has become a reality.

ESCHATOLOGICAL PERSPECTIVES ON THE MISSIONARY FUNCTION

Mission work as we conceive it, then, is founded on the risen Christ. It is a postpaschal phenomenon. The summons to mission work presupposes the glorification of Christ, his enthronement in heaven, the integration of the Son of

Man into the Son of God. The missionary effort derives from the mandate of the risen and glorified Lord, and from the power of the Holy Spirit. In effect, the order concerning missionary work is not, in the last analysis, a phrase spoken between the resurrection and the ascension. It must be interpreted within the framework and context of Christ's universal glorification and his sending of the Spirit.

The mission mandate, the specific summons to "go forth" and gather the nations, is an new element. Previously the pilgrimage of the nations was considered to be the inauguration of God's sovereignty and to be accomplished solely by him. Now the Lord calls for the collaboration of the apostles, of missionaries. They are to help carry on his work in time and bring it to completion. Thus all those to whom Christ addresses his appeal have a duty which must be framed within salvation history and which, in the last analysis, must be understood within the great eschatological context.

Is it not precisely within this eschatological perspective and this salvation-history framework that we could give our missionaries effective and solid motivation for their commitment and collaboration in the full-blown coming of Christ's eschatological sovereignty? It was in these perspectives that Paul understood his missionary function. They accounted for his sense of impatience and urgency regarding his mission work: "I should be punished if I do not preach the Gospel!" (1 Cor. 9:16). If we look at it in terms of the imminent manifestation of God's eschatological sovereignty in Christ, then the question as to whether individuals can find salvation by another road is secondary. That is God's affair. Our duty is to commit all our energy and resources to Christ's *eschaton*, to his "Day," to the coming and fulfillment of his reign, and to the epiphany of God that has come to light in him.

All Nations as Disciples of Christ

"Make disciples of all the nations!" In the mission mandate, it is not a question of converting individuals but of converting peoples and communities. More precisely, it is a question of making them disciples. Being a disciple does not signify "anonymous" membership of a vague or uncertain sort. It signifies that one professes, follows, and is taken into the light.

THE MISSION: BUILDING THE PLENITUDE OF CHRIST

The duty and the mission of inducing all nations to become disciples, which we have received from the Lord, also has a specifically eschatological dimension. Christ is the heart and center of all creation and, above all, of salvation history. He is the center of a saved world. The goal envisioned here is the great *anakephalaiosis* of all things in Christ (Eph. 1:10), so that in and under him, the Head, the whole earth may be reassembled into unity and reconstituted in salvation. In this way the eschatological plenitude of Christ will reach its fulfillment and its termination. The nations are to be oriented toward this plenitude; they are to accept it and be inserted into it.

This presupposes that we address ourselves to the nations, that we reach them as communities, i.e., as religious, cultural, and societal complexes. Today some make much of the fact that the figures and statistics render a verdict against missions and point to the more than two billion non-Christians in the world, whose numbers never cease to increase. All the more, they say, because the population explosion is strongest in the developing countries; i.e., in the non-Christian nations of the Third World—excepting Latin América. To judge by the demographic data, we find ourselves in a desperate situation. What good is it to fight against such odds? All our calculations and statistics show that mission work cannot even hope to make a worthwhile dent. Despite all our efforts, it will not be able to make any substantial change in the way things are developing; the course cannot be changed.

Faced with these arguments, we must first remind ourselves that the mission of salvation, and hence the missionary activity of the Church, cannot be restricted to figures and statistics. Weights and measures are not the determining factors for it. On the contrary, it is framed in the mystery of Christ; and only in faith can it be understood and affirmed. When confronted with this mystery and this faith, all figures and statistics lose their meaning and value. If a person is carrying out God's orders, he need not try to inquire after the external results.

Moreover, we should realize that in Christ's mission it is not a question of piling up figures for statistical charts. It is a question of inducing nations to become his disciples. Seen from this angle, the weight of figures is far less disconcerting than the fact that the Christian mission effort has certainly not yet penetrated to the level of cultures and religions on a world scale—not to mention any talk about *presence* at this level. For the number of individual conversions is not important by comparison with the fully efficacious presence of Christ and his Church within these cultural and social dimensions. Will we manage that task? Is it even possible? And if so, how?

We must face the reality: The Christian mission effort cannot keep pace with the galloping population rate. In future days Christians will find themselves in the minority; and the Church will find herself in a *diaspora* situation, scattered throughout the world. And this will be even more true in mission areas. But this fact does not give us the right to succumb to the temptation of seeing ourselves as a "little flock" or a holy remnant, in the sense of a sect. Christianity's ambition remains universal. We cannot renounce or scale down this ambition because it is directly rooted in the eschatological character of Christianity. What we must do is find new ways of turning it into a reality.

First of all, the hard facts cannot provide us with a pretext for doing nothing, or for shedding our corresponsibility and collaboration in the universal mission of the Church. The Church does not have the right to rest content with being present as a mission effort in some discreet, sheltered way: i.e., a hidden sign and witness. It must struggle, with all its being and energy, to render Christ, and itself in Christ, fully present in a total and vital way. It must try to place as many human beings as possible in the presence of Christ's gospel, and hence of Christ himself; and to foster, through this confrontation, their taking a stand for Christ and their own salvation. The Church is mandated by God to unsettle men, to keep them from being lulled into contentment or sleep. That is her prophetic role. She is a herald in the desert, the messenger of God's kingdom and of salvation in Jesus Christ. So long as human beings do not feel any intimations about this restless yearning for the Good News and Christ's truth, the Church must awaken them to this restless yearning. It must "give man the possibility of responding to Christ" (Uppsala). And the mission effort must awaken and stimulate this response by its proclamation. If man is to respond, he must first be approached, set questioning, and summoned.

THE MISSION: INCARNATION OF CHRIST

The fact is that we only reach and address a fraction of humanity, despite all our efforts. And the fact is that only a fraction of those reached react and respond positively to Christ and his message. But this does not invalidate Christ's order. Failure cannot be a reason for disavowing the will of God when it is clearly known.

Now Christ's commandment is not primarily aimed at the conversion of the individual, at challenging him and winning a response from him. Rather, it demands that we strive to make disciples of all nations. Peoples, as communities, are to become Christ's possession; and they must be helped to follow him. Christ is to be alive in them: i.e., he is to become a living presence in a new incarnation. Following in the footsteps of the God-made-man, the Christian mission effort must go out of itself and enter into the mission nation. It must be merged in that nation's own personality, so that Christ can live and be fashioned in it. It is not simply a matter of proclaiming Christ and his good news, but of incarnating Christ anew in the culture, thought, and mentality of another people. What it calls for is a missionary proclamation that is adapted to them, that can touch the innermost core of a community, tribe, or nation to flesh out Christ in them.

Like Christ, the missionary Church must be humble and forget herself. She must forget her occidental cast, many things relating to her history and tradition, and everything which is not essential in her but which she has acquired and assimilated in different ages and places; only then can she become the incarnation of Christ in a community. She must adopt the spirit and outlook proper to a given community or societal group, so that Christ can be at home there. It calls for the proclamation of Christ within the aura of this particular culture and its mentality, as evinced by sociological, cultural, and religious data.

In and because of this perspective, she must find a new way of presenting and teaching philosophical and theological truths. They must be in tune with the spirit and life of this particular community, which has grown up on the soil of its own culture and religion and which ponders and expresses revelation in the light and framework of this culture and religion.

Any group or people or community must discover Christ as *their* Lord and Savior. They must feel that Christ and the Church have come to visit them in the very core of their soul. They must feel at home with these realities, in accordance with their own nature and mode of living. Only then will it be possible for the missionary effort to take hold of a people and penetrate their community. This is a duty which the Lord himself entrusted to us when he bade us to make disciples of all nations. The degree to which the mission effort penetrates and suffuses the soul of a people or nation, inducing them to become Christ's disciples, has no relationship to figures or statistics. It cannot be weighed and measured, for it is a living process of penetration and transformation that molds and leavens. We cannot mark the start or the endpoint of this process. But it is a strict duty for us missionaries, and it deserves the full expenditure of our resources and personnel.

In this connection, Professor Kaspar feels that the idea of representativity is a theological category of central importance in "helping us to tie up the reality of a diaspora-minority status with the universal aims that the Church proposes for herself. The notion of representativity, which is so important in the Old and New Testament, corresponds with the social character of man . . . In terms of what he is of himself and before God, each individual is conditioned by what the others are." This is not only a moral but also an ontological structure. "The being of another touches my very being. Humanity is thus linked by a community destiny from which one cannot separate himself. The Christian profession and witnesses rendered to Christ is an event which, by way of representativity, touches all men. Mission work, then, is in the service not so much of individual salvation as of societal salvation: i.e., a salvation touching humanity as a whole."[2] This notion of representativity might also be important for clarifying the way in which people become disciples of Christ.

A World At Peace

"And baptize them!" First of all, baptism signifies the sacramental remission of sins: that is, reconciliation and peace with God. It creates a new salvific situation for man, a salvation order for things and the world that is embodied in the salutation: *shalom*—"peace." As it is used in the Bible, peace is a notion pregnant with meaning. It has a universal dimension that embraces all reality in all its forms. It indicates that everything is whole and in good shape, fully integrated and complete. According to the Bible, this peace comes from God alone. By himself, man cannot be at peace. That is why peace is an integral part of God's eschatological promises, his grace, and his salvation. The salvific function of mission work, too, is in the service of reconciliation (2 Cor. 5:18); and hence it bears witness to serving the cause of peace.

MISSION WORK: PEACE AND RECONCILIATION

The salvific function of mission work is not confined to a "pastoral commission." Instead, it involves taking custody of man in his totality and the world in its totality, for their well-being, their salvation and, in particular, their peace and unity. Like the Church in general, the missionary Church in particular is to be a *signum et sacramentum unitatis* (LG 1). Through baptism it reconciles men with God and introduces them into the saved world; by virtue of this fact, it reconciles individuals and whole peoples with each other, establishing peace among them. Peace and reconciliation with God are the basis for peace and reconciliation among men and nations.

Today there is a pervasive feeling that peace is threatened. If people feel that it is a value worth working for, then they will also realize that unity and harmony among different groups and nations is a burning problem and a critical duty. Is it not here that we must look for the new guiding and effective motif behind mission work and the efforts of the missionary? Must they not collaborate in the work of bringing peace among men and nations, of establishing God's universal and definitive peace in history and for the *eschaton*? This peace is ever threatened and ever new, and we are entrusted with the task of bringing it about in history.

Thus mission work and its salvific function are intimately tied up with the major preoccupations of our time: the yearning for peace and unity among human beings. It is in this connection that it can serve as the connecting link, redefining itself and presenting itself in a more comprehensible fashion. This new perspective, framed in a communal outlook, can contribute much to the problem of the relationship between mission work and aid to developing countries. Paul VI has told us that "development is the new name for peace." Development aid is in the service of a unified and saved world, of a united and pacified mankind. Development aid and mission work call out for each other, and render mutual assistance to one another. They are both necessary because of the representative function of Christians, upon which all men, especially the poor and the underdeveloped nations, have a claim. Both are necessary for a world that wishes to be united and saved.

The Growth of Christ's Body

Baptism does not just effect reconciliation with God. It also brings about sacramental incorporation into Christ and his Mystical Body, the Church. Here the Church is not conceived so much as an institution as it is a living organism: the living prolongation of Christ, the holy People of God. It is in this sense that the growth of the Church (i.e., the growth of Christ's Mystical Body) is the primary aim and end of mission work. This outlook does away with the charge of ecclesiocentrism, whereby the Church would see herself as the aim and end of her mission. Her true aim is Christ, the growth of his Body, the diffusion and expansion of his life.

This growth and diffusion relates to the most intimate core of the Church's being. For she derives her origin and nature from the activity whereby God gives a share of himself to creatures through the sending of the Son and the Holy Spirit (AG 2). The Church is aware of her resultant commitment, and she must act accordingly; for the law determining her nature is also the norm of her activity. She realizes that, in the last analysis, she is essentially dependent on God's plan. During her journey here, she is essentially missionary (AG 2). She must do as much as her strength and resources allow to carry out the Father's salvation mission; to establish Christ—and herself in Christ—as the universal sacrament of salvation. By God's design, she is the Mystical Body of Christ; and she deduces the laws governing her growth and activity from this fact. The proper activity of this Body is to grow and flourish. It must expand until it becomes the fullness (*pleroma*) of Christ, until it arrives at the plenitude of time in Christ and recapitulates all men and all things in the eschatological plenitude of Christ, thus giving glory to the Trinity.

We can find the identical motif in the Church insofar as she is the love of God that has become incarnate and visible in Christ. It is a love that has been poured out lavishly and rendered visible in all the members of the Body by the Holy Spirit. It is a love that essentially involves sharing and participating in God's own love and life. It is a love of overflowing measure that strives to communicate itself and spread; so it impels all the members of the Body to share with others, those who are still outside, the inexhaustible treasury of divine life and love that is placed at their disposal. This same love impels the members to offer themselves for mission work, so that it may become a sharing of love and a participation in the *koinonia*, in accordance with the most intimate nature of the Church.

Clearly mission work flows from the deepest nature of the Church (AG 6). For us missionaries, then, the motif of Christian love is the solid ground behind our missionary activity: It is the *agape* which God shares with us through his Spirit, and which impels us to share with all men the spiritual treasures of salvation and life in Christ. The *koinonia*, grounded in *agape*, is the communication and sharing of that which we ourselves have received: God, our inalienable treasure.

Why Mission Work in the Restricted Sense?

When we talk about "missions in the world" or "mission work" here, we are referring to the missionary activity of the Church as described in *Ad gentes*. It is the proclamation of Christ and the implantation of the Church among peoples and groups who do not yet know Christ, or among whom the Church has not yet been implanted. Perhaps it would be better to say: among whom the Church has not yet been solidly established for growth. This mission work is a special sector, a specific function, of the Church's mission: i.e., of the universal sacrament of salvation that embraces it. It is distinct from, but implied in, the general mission of the Church. The latter involves applying and accomplishing the salvific mission of Christ for the entire world through its ever-changing situation in history. Mission work is not essentially different from the Church's overall salvific mission; but it is different in terms of the specific situation in which it carries out this mission, in terms of the ways and forms in which it carries out its activities with its own proper means. But its existence and intrinsic justification are grounded on the Church's universal mission.

The question is: Does this distinction still have validity and meaning today? Are not France and Germany mission countries too? Do we not find, in every modern metropolis, countless people who do not know Christ, who have not encountered and confronted him so that they could make a personal decision about him? Is not "mission work" to be found everywhere? May we not justifiably reiterate the slogan of the World Council of Churches (New Delhi, 1961; Uppsala, 1968): "Mission work in six continents!" (Even though I have heard a Protestant missiologist speak about getting back to a more specific conception of mission work.) Why do we make a distinction between the "missionary situation" in our own native lands and "mission work" in foreign lands?

The situation in our homelands, to be sure, is a missionary one. But these countries do have an established, adult church with means and resources at its disposal. The home church should be able to handle its missionary needs with its own internal resources and spiritual treasury. Compared to this, the mission-land church is a mere infant without resources. It greatly needs help, either because the church has not yet taken firm root, or because it is just beginning to grow and is totally dependent on aid from outside. Is not the relationship between the mission-sending and the mission-receiving country best described as that of a mother to her child? France is a mission country, but it has twice as many priests as Africa and Asia put together. While the Church in France may be in a similar missionary situation, could one equate it with the situation of Africa? The latter is in danger of being choked by its own development. Her priests have had to contend sometimes with 5,000 new Christians or catechumens, not to mention the countless pagans. It is just not fair to speak about "missionary" activity, in the strict sense, with regard to our homelands.

Christ himself was aware that he had been sent first to the lost sheep of Israel; but he ordered his disciples to make disciples of all nations. And there is no doubt that the nations (*gentes*) in question were the pagans and non-Jews who were alienated or still in a state of nonbelief.

Why engage in mission work? We can sum up our answer this way. Mission work is necessary by virtue of the epiphany of God's eschatological sovereignty among the nations, which was inaugurated in Christ. It is necessary by virtue of Christ's commission to make disciples of all nations. It is necessary by virtue of the Church's salvific function on behalf of reconciliation and peace, on behalf of a world unified and saved in peace. It is necessary for the growth of Christ's Body. It is necessary by virtue of the love which makes all the members of this Body aware that they are commissioned, in the Holy Spirit, to communicate God's life and love to all men. Finally, mission work is necessary because it flows naturally from the most intimate nature and existence of the Church.

NOTES

1. See W. Kaspar, "Warum noch Mission?" *Ordenskorrespondenz* *9* (1968) 247-61.
2. *Ibid..*, pp. 259 ff.

DISCUSSION

J. M. GONZALEZ-RUIZ   Here we must pick up the terminology of Saint Paul, particularly that in his Epistle to the Romans. We must first distinguish cosmic revelation, which is the manifestation of God to all men, outside the prophets, the Church, etc. This is the *phanerosis.* Then there is positive ecclesial revelation, the revelation of a special message from God through the Church. This is the *apocalypsis.* We must also make a distinction between the "power-state" and the "nations." It is the latter who are addressed in the summons to "preach the gospel to all nations." Thus the gospel must reach all peoples. Above all, we must recall the element of challenge and debate involved in the Christian message. The Church has a mission to challenge people. Her message is inserted in the inner dynamism of nations, which involves conflict.

J. M. SETIEN   I should like to make four points. 1. If we find an epiphany of God's sovereignty in all peoples who live a life of charity under the influence of the Spirit, then what does the explicit presentation of Christ's message contribute? 2. Those who live lives based on charity are truly "sons of God"; to find out what living such a life means, we must explore the novel aspect of the gospel mentioned by Lyonnet. 3. The author talks about peace (*shalom*). But how are we to understand this notion? Is it an encounter in friendship with God or with men? The mission of the Church will have to be determined in terms of this two-edged human peace. 4. In my opinion, the novel aspect of Christianity is first and foremost the dialectic between life and death that is implied in charity. Charity leads us to death in self-giving. The novel aspect of Christianity lies in the fact that it gives meaning to this dying, and that meaning is the Resurrection. So if we are to escape the temptation to evasion, the question of bearing witness to charity must be framed in the perspective of structural transformations. I think that this social aspect of bearing witness to charity is essential, and that it was overlooked by Lyonnet.

A. SANTOS   The biblical text, *unum pastor et unum ovile* ("one flock and one shepherd"), is an important one; and it is directed toward pagans. It is the Johannine outlook on the Church, situated under Jesus Christ. It seems to me that it has more powerful force in providing motives and justification for mission work than does the text in Matthew.

A. SEUMOIS   Schütte's paper prompts me to make two observations. 1. Eschatology should not be situated outside ecclesiology. 2. It seems to me that his presentation of salvation is too collective. "Make disciples of all the nations," of course. But we must not neglect the individual aspect: "He who believes will be saved" (Mark 16:16).

A. M. HENRY   First of all, I do not share Schütte's unease about mission work. To begin with, we must appreciate the leavening power of the gospel in the world, even from a purely human viewpoint. Without the gospel, the world would be debased. Secondly, we must remember the eschatological character of mission work. The Church has an enormous fringe of influence, even outside her visible institutions. If the Church is faithful to herself, the gospel leaven will work everywhere, even among people who remain in their own religion. I am thinking here, for example, of the influence of Christianity in certain Islamic circles that coexist with Christian circles. The Church is already at work in non-Christian religions through such contact. The Church is the sacrament of the kingdom, but she is distinct from the latter; the kingdom is more widespread than the visible Church. Mission work fashions the kingdom everywhere, but the latter will be revealed only on the last day. Finally, I should like to point out that the problem of statistics mentioned by Schütte does not always have the significance which is accorded to it. The dialectic is no longer between mother-church (Europe) and daughter-church (mission lands), but between the Church and the world. Vatican II rediscovered and proclaimed the autonomy of the world. If she is faithful to her mission, the Church will be everywhere; and everywhere she will be "in mission" because the world is everywhere.

G. DELCUVE   I should like to make a few points and pose a few questions. 1. It seems to me that this paper minimizes the role of Israel as a missionary people among the nations, and the activity of the prophets sent by God. 2. It was said that mission work is a postpaschal event. Why and how? 3. It speaks about the epiphany of God's sovereignty among the nations, but it does not define the word "nations." And what is God's sovereignty? 4. Lyonnet gave a good description of the relations between God and men. But it seems to me that he has not satisfactorily pointed out that this participation in the Trinitarian love between Father and Son is revealed in the paschal mystery of

Christ first and foremost. And this latter point should be stressed in any missionary theology.

D. GRASSO　In reply to Henry, I should like to stress that there is a real missionary crisis. It is no myth, particularly where Asia is concerned. There is a lack of vocations, of course, but also a lack of motivation for the missionary apostolate. Quite a few people readily commit themselves to work for development, but few commit themselves to the service of the Church. We must remember that Christianity is not a humanism, for there is always the danger of pure horizontalism. As for Schütte's remark about Saint Francis Xavier: It is true that he denied there could be salvation outside the Church at the beginning of his missionary apostolate, but when he got to Japan he affirmed the possibility of salvation outside the visible frames of the Church.

O. SEMMELROTH　The kingdom of God is dialogue. It is not just revelation that comes down from God above; it is also man's response. Schütte says that men's salvation is their contact with the epiphany of God, which is effected through the Church. But then what about the salvation of men who are not in contact or relation with this revelation of God's epiphany in the Church.

A. CAMPS　Schütte says that the fact of men's salvation outside the ecclesial epiphany would become a secondary question. For me it is not a secondary question, particularly with respect to the motivation of missionary activity. This is especially true with regard to such activity in Asia.

A. BOUCHARD　It seems to me that we must carefully distinguish between the fruits of mission work, which have often been described, its motivations, and its aims. We must first clarify the primary aim of mission work. In other words, what is the Church supposed to accomplish in regard to humanity as a whole before Christ's return? When we have found out this primary aim, then we can discover the proper place and means of mission work.

I. DE LA POTTERIE　It seems to me that we must properly relate three aspects of mission theology that are often neglected: the eschatological aspect, the collective aspect, and the individual aspect. The eschatological aspect of the missionary task is to lead humanity to its total fulfillment in the kingdom. I think that the collective and individual aspects are balanced well in Schütte's treatment. "Make disciples of all the nations": "all nations" gives the collective dimension of salvation, in the sense of Daniel 7 and Apocalypse 7. "Disciples" gives the individual aspect. The word of God is to be interiorized in faith by Christ's disciples. On the other hand, the notion of peace is less clearly expressed. Finally, I should like to see Lyonnet's treatment of charity filled out in terms of Johannine theology. We must not separate charity and faith, charity and truth; if we do, we run the risk of falling into moralism on the one side, or intellectualism on the other.

H. DE LUBAC　Evangelical charity is really more complex than we seem to think, in terms of its relationship to faith. There is an essential, organic, and intrinsic tieup between faith and charity; and it is a theological tieup, not a philanthropic one.

T. TSHIBANGU　We must spell out the place of Christ, his central place in salvation and revelation, as an essential new aspect of Christianity. What motivates mission work is the presence of Christ everywhere. Christ's historical presence in creation leads it to its fulfillment. Everything else is a consequence of this.

A. VANNESTE   Schütte's question, "Why engage in mission work?" relates not only to missionaries but also to young priests in mission lands. When they see young people of their own age working for the development of their homeland, they are led to question the meaning of their own vocation. Moreover, we must see to it that all the theological categories employed here in the discussion have concrete meaning and import for missionary activity.

JEAN DANIÉLOU

Non-Christian Religions and Salvation

CHAPTER FIVE

Today we encounter contradictory judgments on non-Christian religions, sometimes uttered by the very same theologians. In the continuing development of Karl Barth's theology, for example, they are seen to be man's pretentious effort to lay hands on God; the feeling is that revelation should destroy them. Or they are regarded as an improper sacralization of nature and power, which is happily being blotted out by secularism. At the other extreme, some see them as means of salvation, in such a way that the boundary lines between them and Christianity are blurred; this tends to water down and debilitate the missionary élan of the Church. The two extreme attitudes are both inadmissible, because they involve some false judgments on the true nature of religions. So we must spell out this nature before we try to establish the relationship of these religions to salvation.

RELIGIONS, MYSTICISMS, RITES

The various non-Christian religions are essentially diverse and secondary structurings of something else that comes before them: i.e., the religious dimension that forms part of man. The underlying foundation is religion as such. Every human being is a religious being by nature. He is neither atheist nor Christian by nature; he is pagan. This religious experience naturally takes form in expressions, symbols, rites, and ascetical practices which vary with man's race. Here we confront the question of the religious genius or temperament of peoples, which is quite different from the question of established religions. Christianity must take proper account of this distinction if it is not to be identified with the Christianity lived by a specific religious temperament. Finally we get the organization of this religious life. It is here that we can properly speak about religions. This work of organization is man's work, sometimes originating with some eminent religious personality. More often it is a collective endeavor.

Thus religions are ambiguous realities, and that undoubtedly explains the contradictory judgments passed on them. On one side of the coin, they express and present an important chunk of authentic religious experience. Pagan myths, for example, interpret God's revelation through the cosmos. This manifestation, which constitutes the covenant with Noah, forms the bedrock of natural religions; and it remains as a permanent dimension of man. God continues to manifest himself through the glittering of the stars, the darkness of night, the solidity of rocky crags, and the blessed gift of the morning dew. The acquisition of scholarly and scientific knowledge does not at all eliminate this symbolic and religious knowledge.

The sacralization of the fundamental rhythms in cosmic and human life, which forms the bedrock of pagan cults, is also deeply rooted in man's authentic nature. In particular, the fact that the essential moments of human existence (birth, love, death) are accompanied by God's blessing is thoroughly legitimate in itself. Christianity will repair these human realities, but it will not destroy them. Only an obtuse secularism, failing to appreciate their human and divine value, would attempt this.

Finally we find a variety of natural mysticisms. Undoubtedly this is one of the most impressive aspects of the richness in religions. Whether it involves elementary forms of participation or the loftiest summits of self-stripping, these mysticisms bear witness to man's great attraction for union and fusion with the divine. All the efforts of certain modern theologians, who speak of the death of God and try to tie these lofty summits of human experience to outdated cultural contexts, pass condemnatory judgment on themselves. For science and mysticism are equally fundamental processes, and neither should rule out the other.

So religions do present us with authentic values. But the fact that they are human creations in terms of their doctrinal and ritual structures means that they always end up in some deformations also. This is the truth underlying the complaints of some people about sacralization. But their criticism is only valid with respect to these perversions, not with respect to authentic sacralization. Thus it is absurd to say that every natural religion is idolatry. We are weary of hearing such senseless remarks from some modern theologians. But it is true that the feeling for the sacral character of nature, insofar as the latter is a hierophany, can degenerate into idolatry if man's adoration stops at the sign and never gets to the reality behind it.

The same holds true for magic. It is entirely wrong to apply the label of "magic" to every ritual act designed to obtain a supernatural effect. To do this is tantamount to accepting a purely sociological and psychological analysis of the religious experience. The rites of pagan religions in themselves are not magical rites. They can be used perversely in a magical way, with the aim of controlling supernatural forces through the power gained over them. But this is not the authentic nature of a rite.

Finally, pagan mysticism remains an uncertain quest. For the God it seeks lies outside its grasp. That is why the image it forms of this God is often deformed. It tends to confuse him with the immanent force that animates the universe, or else to project him into a realm of total inaccessibility. That is why the admiration evoked by the great sages of the pagan Orient is blended with confusion about the content of the message they have left behind.

GOD'S LOVE IN ACTION

Judeo-Christian revelation presents us with totally different data. Religion bore witness to man's quest for a God whose very transcendance hindered any encounter. The object of revelation is to inform us of the free decision whereby God, out of love, brought himself before man. Man himself could not bridge the chasm that separated the created and the uncreated. But God himself has bridged it. He came to seek out man, who was seeking him, in order to introduce man into his own inner life. This gesture of divine love is, properly speaking, salvation. Insofar as the word expresses man's yearning to share God's life, it is found outside biblical revelation; for this yearning is natural to man. But the biblical affirmation does not bear on the notion of salvation but on the fact that salvation has been granted. There we have the specific element of biblical revelation, which is not so much in the order of representation as in the order of actual happening.

Properly speaking, the object of revelation is that intervention of God in human history which is essentially the Incarnation of the Word and Christ's resurrection. It has to do with this happening first and foremost. The primary object of revelation is the reality of this happening with both its human and divine historicity; it is a divine activity, but it is inserted into the web of human history. Revelation is the good news that salvation has been granted.

Since revelation has to do with a real happening, it can only be known through testimony. This testimony is first Christ's and then his apostles'. Once the divine authority of this testimony is recognized, it is the object of the act of faith. Here, too, there is a radical difference from the world of religion in general. For the latter, the religious experience as such is the essential thing. Faith, by contrast, belongs to a different order; it involves the recognition and acceptance of an historical event. Thus faith and religious sentiment are not necessarily bound up with each other.

The Christ-happening is the essential object of faith, but it is prepared for by divine interventions to which the Old Testament bears witness. Moreover, in the Church the things effected in Christ are communicated to all believers through the sacraments. The object of faith is the ensemble of this salvation history: i.e., the history of God's wondrous deeds (*mirabilia*), which include the works of creation, liberation, covenant, sojourn, and judgment that were carried out at different stages of God's overall plan.

It is his creation that the Word of God comes to save. This is the great affirmation that has dominated theology since Saint Irenaeus. In this sense, the religious dimension of man is no stranger to salvation. How could it be, since it is one of the deepest dimensions in man? But religious man himself also needs to be saved. And since religious man is not an abstraction, since he takes on different forms in accordance with the religious genius of peoples, these diversities will be assumed by revelation and mirrored in the diversities of its catholicity.

ONLY JESUS CHRIST SAVES

Thus religion does not save; rather, it is a part of him who is saved. Only Jesus Christ saves. If any man is to be saved, he will be saved only through Jesus Christ, no matter what religion he belongs to. Now this affirmation poses a question. It is certain that all salvation is provided by Jesus Christ. But it is also certain that this salvation is extended to countless numbers of people who have not known Jesus Christ, either because they lived before him or because they never had a chance to know or acknowledge him. So it is proper to make a distinction between the objective action of salvation and the conditions under which this action can be appropriated.

The question can be put another way. We have made a distinction, as we should, between the essence of religion and the essence of revelation. But in concrete reality, every human being is involved in the drama of salvation from the start. For God's plan to summon mankind to share in his own life dominates the whole process of unfolding history. Scripture shows us that the very first human being was introduced to paradise right at the start; in other words, he was called to share in God's life. And when he fell from this participation, he became a sinner rather than a purely natural man. He remained involved in the drama of grace and sin. This implies that salvation is possible for him.

The question here is: What is required for salvation where there is no knowledge of the salvific activity performed in Christ? Saint Paul treats this question in his Epistle to the Romans when he states that the Jew will be judged by the Law and the pagan by conscience. In other words, every human being will be judged in terms of the knowledge of God that was accessible to him. But as we noted before, the religious dimension is a constituent element in human nature. Every man encounters God obscurely in the proddings of his conscience, in the manifestations of divine providence, and in the experiences of his own contingency.

It is in this perspective that religion, as a universal datum, can be presented as a first revelation, as cosmic revelation. It is the revelation to which the covenant with Noah in the Old Testament bears witness, and to which Saint Paul makes reference when he tells the Christians of Lystra about God's procedure: "In the past he allowed each nation to go its own way; but even then he did not leave you without evidence of himself in the good things he does for you; he sends you rain from heaven, he makes your crops grow when they should, he gives you food and makes you happy" (Acts 14: 15-16). In this perspective, religion expresses the interior attitude which renders man capable of sharing in the salvation given by Jesus Christ.

But in terms of this same framework, what are we to say about religion, not as a primary datum of human nature but in terms of the forms it has taken historically in the major religions? This is our real question here: What about religions as means of salvation? This question is much more complicated. If we talked about "means of salvation" in the sense that the religions are positively instituted by God, then the term would be inadmissible. That is why Vatican II's Declaration on the Relationship of the Church to Non-Christian Religions threw out the term "salvation economies" with reference to nonbiblical religions.

The various religions, as we noted above, are positive arrangements of the religious factor. They are human creations. As such they are part and parcel of a humanity which, left to itself, mixes truth with error. Their authority is not divine but human. As we noted above, there is always a large element of ambiguity in them. On the one hand, they are the forms through which the people of a given civilization normally express their religious experience. on the other hand, they also constitute a screen that deforms this experience and poses an obstacle.

Thus one is being overly optimistic when he espouses the view that these religions form the normal condition of salvation for those who do not know Christ. The outlook of the Church Fathers was quite different. Justin saw in pious pagans an expression of their fidelity to the Word they knew only obscurely; but he was pitiless in his judgment of pagan myths and cults, which he saw as the work of demons. The conversion of pagans does not involve simply helping them to move from the implicit to the explicit; it involves snatching them from the forces of darkness that are preventing them from gaining access to the authentic religion. The whole missionary tradition has always followed this outlook, regarding pagan religions as both stepping stones and stumbling blocks.

It is just as impossible to regard the pagan religions purely and simply as the ordinary means of salvation for those who have not known Christ. For they are tainted by sin, just as is everything else of man's that is not illuminated and guided by Christ. It would be a grave mistake for anyone to think that the members of these religions are so related to salvation that they need not feel ill at ease, and that consequently the missionary obligation is somewhat less necessary.

That is how we see the complex question regarding the status of non-Christian religions in a salvation-history perspective. We recognize the religious values in them; but we must not fail to recognize also that they are part of a world which is tainted by sin. Our missionary outlook would be falsified if we based it exclusively on the positive aspects of these religions. For that would lead us to see them as the ordinary means of salvation, and to regard membership in the Church as an extraordinary situation. Just the opposite is true. The problem of salvation in non-Christian religions remains obscure. We cannot begin from there to explain salvation through the Church; we must start from the opposite direction. That is why the missionary obligation vis-à-vis non-Christians retains all its urgency.

DISCUSSION

J. M. GONZALEZ-RUIZ   1. The word "religion" is ambiguous in itself. We must come to an agreement on terminology. Religion, considered as magic or idolatry, is the embodiment of demonism; but religion is also adoration of God. 2. Insofar as the quest for God within non-Christian religions is concerned, we must start from the gratuitousness of God's revelation. The initiative always belongs to God; man's response comes second. For it is God who seeks out man. When Daniélou says that "religion is a permanent dimension of human nature," we must make a distinction between man in history and human nature. Historically speaking, God has never stopped seeking out man and man has never stopped responding. Religiousness, whatever form the response may take, is part of the human historical phenomenon.

J. M. SETIEN   The Christian religion, viewed as a sociological fact, is as ambiguous as are other religions. Thus if we want to establish the object of the Church's missionary activity vis-à-vis non-Christian religions, we must begin with a "religious" critique of Christianity.

A. SANTOS   The modern judgment on the value of pagan religions is really in contrast with the judgment of the Old Testament and Saint Paul, particularly in his Epistle to the Romans. The scriptural judgment is negative. How then do we explain the contrasting judgment today?

A. SEUMOIS   In talking about non-Christian religions, it is useful to distinguish between religious systems, the values contained in these systems, and the religious life lived in the atmosphere of these religious systems. If the religious way of life in these religions is authentic, it can only be supernatural and redemptive—hence Christian or, if you will, paleo-Christian. Since Genesis 3:16 there is only one single possibility of salvation for men, the supernatural and redemptive salvation through Jesus Christ; and hence there is only one authentic religious life dependent on this divine economy. The "non-Christian" religions are of a natural or "cosmic" order insofar as they are systems. They are the product of man and tied up with the development of various cultures. But their religious ground derives from the natural religiosity of human nature as illumined and elevated by primitive revelation; it is thus paleo-Christian. It is in this sense that Augustine and other Church Fathers affirm that the Christian religion has existed from the beginnings of humanity. Non-Christian religions are natural, cultural instruments; and in this sense they are providential for living the revealed paleo-Christian values. They are a useful and helpful milieu. In it is operative pre-Christian prophetism, which is the way that the Christian religion carried on its salvific activity before Christ, and which perdures until the satisfactory promulgation of the New Testament Church. As for the varied elements contained de facto in non-Christian religions, there may well be many that are false. But there can also be authentic religious values, which are to be judiciously examined and appreciated in terms of man's natural religiosity or in terms of New Testament Christianity.

A. M. HENRY   We must spell out the specifically novel aspect of Christianity vis-à-vis non-Christian religions. We must also spell out the notion of "enthusiasm for God," of which Daniélou spoke, because it exists also in certain non-Christian religions. It may not be at all peculiar to Christianity. Finally, we hear it said that the non-Christian religions are simply inventions of man's religious genius. Is that entirely exact? Can one really say that they are simply that, not involving any divine intervention or any interior help from the Holy Spirit at all? On the other side of the coin, can one say that there is no effort or inventiveness on the part of the human religious spirit in cases where the inspiration of the Holy Spirit is at work, such as in Christian revelation? Are not matters much more ambiguous and complex?

G. DELCUVE   Daniélou states that man is naturally religious. Is that true? In any case it is a much contested statement today. We have abundant evidence indicating that a person can live happily without religion. Moreover, it would be good to spell out the notion of "enthusiasm for God" in a Trinitarian sense: i.e., the enthusiasm of the Father for the Son and vice-versa.

J. FRISQUE   I agree with Delcuve's reservations about the statement that man is naturally religious. Moreover, if non-Christian religions are the creations of man's genius, then we must define what the Jewish religion is. Is it an exceptional creation of this same genius, or is it something else entirely?

J. MASSON   As far as the notion of "enthusiasm for God" is concerned, I think it means "doing God's will." But what is the will of God? How does one put "enthusiasm for God" into practice? In particular, does God have a plan with regard to non-Christian religions? And what is this plan? Moreover, it seems that we are establishing a juxtaposition between non-Christian religions on the one hand and the Christian salvation economy on the other. I feel that the Christian economy envelops the non-Christian religions. Thus it would be easier to view the interior dynamism of these non-Christian religions as a channel of salvation-grace. The plan of creation and the plan of redemption cannot be separated. We must not separate what God has united.

C. G. ARAVELO   The secularists say that desacralization is one of the objects of missionary activity. I should like to know what the import of that affirmation is?

D. S. AMALORPAVADASS   First of all we must realize that Christianity, as a religion, should itself be examined critically; for then our approach to other religions would be more sympathetic. Moveover, it seems to me that one question is central to our discussion: The relationship between the natural order and the supernatural order. We say that religions are means of salvation, and this raises questions: How does Christ save religious human beings in and through non-Christian religions? How does Christ's salvific grace reach religious people through the intermediary of religious systems that are actually lived? It seems to me, in effect, that we must carefully distinguish between religion as an abstract system and religion as a system that is actually lived out. Take Hinduism, for example, which I am more familiar with. The system as actually lived by people has evolved enormously under the impetus of actual events: e.g., political independence, contacts with the modern world and technology, and the like. We can no longer talk about it in terms of the abstract system of classical Hinduism. Christianity's mission to Hinduism can no longer be saving individuals as religious people; it must be a salvation-mission to the system that is actually lived today.

D. GRASSO   It is said that non-Christian religions are means of salvation. This is true in a sense, because there exists in them some supernatural values, some seeds of the Word, as Saint Justin affirmed long ago. But Vatican II adds that these values must be purified, elevated, and saved. That is why I should prefer to say that these religions are "paths to Christ," who himself is the one and only "path to salvation," instead of saying that these religions themselves are "paths to salvation." Christ is the expectation of the nations, as Vatican II points out.

O. SEMMELROTH   The non-Christian religions are means of salvation to the extent that one considers them not only as creations of man's religious genius but also as bearers of something analogous to revelation through the work of God's grace in them. *Lumen gentium* (LG) says that salvation is not ruled out for those who, through no fault of their own, do not come to a knowledge of Christ but live uprightly, *non sine gratia Dei.* When one Council Father tried to introduce a *modus* spelling out the necessity of revelation for salvation, the pertinent commission replied that this idea was already included in the phrase *non sine gratia Dei.* Thus in non-Christian religions we find a salvific activity on God's part that is analogous to revelation. They are means of salvation for non-Christians.

K. MÜLLER   Yes, outside the Church there is an authentic knowledge of God effected by grace. But there is a difference between these non-Christian religions and the Church. The former are frameworks where man can obtain knowledge of God. The latter is where we find the plenitude of salvation and grace.

A. CAMPS   We do well to give a positive value to the non-Christian religions. But someone has said that religion does not save, only Christ does. In setting up an opposition between religion and Christ on this score, one entertains a conception of religion (including the Christian religion) that is much too sociological. There is a unity between religious living, religious experience, and religion. If one sets up an opposition between them, one is focusing exclusively on the sociological and psychological structures of religion. We cannot set up an opposition between religion and Christ, because even in Christianity we win Christ's salvation through religious experience and religious living, not just through structures. Moreover, the question as to whether the non-Christian religions are integrated into the salvation economy, as posed by Masson, seems to go beyond the bounds of strictly scriptural argumentation, in my opinion. It is a concrete question pertaining to our day.

I. DE LA POTTERIE   We must clarify certain notions and their interrelationships. First, there is the notion of "religion" and of "idols." Today we all too readily set up an opposition between religion and faith. People contrast external religious structures, which are to be condemned, with faith or interior religion. All the external structures are classed under the heading of "idols." When Saint John (1 John 5:21) tells his flock to guard against idols, he is talking about any and all deviations from Christian truth: the anti-Christs false prophets, etc. He is talking about deviations from the faith, as understood by Qumran and the Old Testament. Thus, for the New Testament, "idols" does not mean the external rites but any impurity in living the Christian faith. So this term should not be restricted to institutional or external aspects of religion, which can sometimes be deformed; it should be applied first and foremost to deviations from the faith. In this way we can get beyond the false opposition set up between religion *qua* institution and religion *qua* interior faith. Moreover, the notion of "enthusiasm for God" is not a vague notion, as some of the previous remarks seemed to suggest. Without citing the text, Daniélou referred to Second Corinthians (2 Cor. 11:2): "The jealousy I feel for you is God's own jealousy: I arranged for you to marry Christ so that I might give you away as a chaste virgin to this one husband." The notion of "enthusiasm for God" has been Christologized once and for all. It means "winning men for Christ."

H. DE LUBAC   Daniélou reminds us that salvation is given by God. I would add that Christianity gives us a specific idea of salvation that is not the one given in non-Christian religions.

A. VANNESTE   In a certain sense one could say that the novel aspect of Christianity is that it has none. Christianity is the full measure of everything that is true and good in all the other religions. It carries out and explicitates fully what is valid and authentic in these other religons.

(Note: Here, as in most of the discussions, the reporters recorded mainly the criticisms voiced about a paper and disregarded remarks approving what was said.)

D. S. AMALORPAVADASS

The Apostolate to Non-Christians

CHAPTER SIX

The topic proposed here specifically is the apostolate to non-Christians. But our treatment of it cannot ignore the two topics that have been treated in the preceding papers: i.e., the aims and ends of missionary activity, and the role and value of non-Christian religions.

So let me begin by giving a brief summary of the two preceding questions, thus indicating the foundations upon which my more practical topic is based.

REVELATION AND SALVATION IN NON-CHRISTIAN RELIGIONS

With Saint Paul (1 Tim. 2:4-5) and the recent Council, we can take as our point of departure God's universal and efficacious will for man's salvation. Even today the gospel is far from having been preached everywhere, and the vast majority of mankind lives outside the bounds of the visible Church. So God's universal salvation plan, revealed and progressively carried out in the course of human history, is older and broader than the Church; and it necessarily includes the non-Christian religions.

True enough, the Church holds a special place in this salvation history and it retains the means of salvation in their plenitude. But it can neither limit God's salvific presence nor completely drain off the salvific power contained in Christ's grace. His presence and activity, as savior and light, are universal. They were at work and efficacious before the foundation of the Church, and they are so today outside the visible Church.

On this basis we can draw the following conclusions:

1. Non-Christians are included in God's salvific will, and in the plan according to which it is realized.

2. In this respect, the non-Christian religions cannot be set up in opposition to the Church. They must be understood and evaluated with reference to the Church.

3. The universal and operative presence of Christ is the reality contained in the expression, "seeds of the Word," which was dear to the Church Fathers and was picked up by Vatican II (AG 11).

4. It is a fact that non-Christians are saved in their own religion and outside the bounds of the visible Church (LG 16; GS 22; AG 7).

5. Non-Christians are not only "saved"; they are also saved "in their own religion." In other words, it is in this framework that God's grace reaches them. Human beings do not live as isolated individuals but as members of a certain social group and a certain religion; and these two realities have an influence on the formation of the human person (AG 10). Thus God's universal salvific will means that his grace reaches men in their real-life situation, and consequently that their religions are paths of salvation for them that are foreseen by God.

6. However, we would not say that human beings are saved *by* their religions. The ambiguous character of these religions and their inherent defects as structures and signs prevent them from being "channels or means of grace." Thus it would be better to call them "habitats of Christ's grace and salvation."

7. In fact, even the Christian is not saved by the Christian religion as such. He is saved by God, by Jesus Christ who is the one and only savior. This doctrine of Peter and Paul (Acts 4:12 and 1 Tim. 2:4-5), picked up by Vatican II (AG 8), is also acknowledged by those who seem to be the most daring in this matter: "The good and *bona fide* Hindu is saved by Christ and not by Hinduism."[1]

8. Any explanation of *the way in which* this grace reaches men and they respond to it is pure conjecture, for it is a mystery of faith. But in the main part of this paper I shall try to present my opinion on this delicate point.

9. Thus the non-Christian religions are neither equal nor parallel to the absolute religion that was founded by God's positive institution. But neither should we talk about them as "*natural* religions," as if grace were simply ruled out in them; for this would place them outside the Christian salvation plan.

10. It would be a gross exaggeration, entirely beyond the teaching of the Council, to say that these religions are the "ordinary" or "normal" path of salvation for non-Christians, while the Christian religion is an "extraordinary" path of salvation for them.[2]

So we can sum up. These religions have a place in God's salvation plan because they contain authentically spiritual and supernatural values, which are the fruit of God's active presence. Divine grace reaches men and saves them in the framework of these religions. As the conclusions of the Bombay Theological Session put it: "Every man and every religion is under the influence of grace. But Christian universalism is founded and centered on Christ."[3]

MOTIVES AND GOALS OF MISSIONARY ACTIVITY

A certain decline in missionary zeal must be accepted as a fact. Many find the cause of this in the "new" ideas concerning the presence of grace in non-Christian religions. These ideas may well have been presented in a way that lacked tact and prudence; but the problem remains nonetheless. That is why the conciliar document, without denying the traditional motive for missionary activity (i.e., the desire to save individuals), went on to provide the missionary élan with a deeper motivation and a broader field of action.

By virtue of the population explosion alone, the Church is becoming more and more of an unimportant minority and we cannot expect this trend to reverse itself. So if we judge missionary effectiveness in terms of numbers, we are faced with utter bankruptcy. But the Church, this tiny band scattered far and wide, has a universal mission: it is to be the leaven, raising every level of human existence, be it social, cultural, or religious.

While concerning ourselves deeply with the salvation of the individual, we must also probe more deeply into the motivation that underlies our missionary activity more basically. That motivation can be expressed in three words: *eschatology, universality, mission work*.

The final period of salvation history began with Christ's Easter, and everything is moving toward the "last day" of his return. In the meantime, God's plan for the world is to be fully carried out. His sovereignty is to be proclaimed, made plain and recognized by all peoples; they are to be reunited in peace and made disciples of Christ. The universality of God's sovereignty demands universality in our missionary activity; in other words, the Good News must be proclaimed everywhere and at every level of human life. The witness of our missionary activity prefigures, prepares, and hastens the dawning of the last day.

Thus we can express the overall vision in these words: Trinity-Incarnation-Church-Mission work.

The love which flows out from the unity of the Trinity and becomes visible in Christ is supposed to reach all men through the real-life witness of all the members of the Church. This witness simultaneously summons man to communion (AG 2-6). Thus the mission of the Church forms part of the never-ending tide that flows out from the "fount of love," whose highest source is God the Father.

Missionary activity is therefore one of the "profoundest necessities," deriving from the catholicity of the Church and the power of life and growth contained in Love itself. This primal motive is first reinforced by Christ's commandment, and then by the realization of man's frailty in this sinful world. How could we love human beings and not offer them all the means of salvation that are at work in the Church? Finally, it is reinforced by the conviction that if we wish to reveal man to himself, the only complete means of doing this is to reveal Christ to him.

Thus the necessity for mission work remains unchanged. But there has been a change in the missionary approach sought by the Church. Indeed we must say that theological studies into the salvation of non-Christians should reinforce these motives rather than diluting them, as Vatican II noted (AG 7).

TOTAL VISION AND CONCERN FOR WHOLE GROUPS

Up to now we have been concerned mainly with saving individuals (or even "their souls"), as if the salvation of individual persons were the principal or sole object of God's salvation plan. But it is not a matter of the human soul alone. It is a matter of the whole man: "Man himself, whole and entire, body and soul, heart and conscience, mind and will" (GS 3). And the important task does not relate even to whole human beings viewed as "individuals without any mutual bonds" who are separated from each other by time and space. It relates to them as social beings who are members of groups: "These are formed into large and distinct groups by permanent cultural ties, by ancient religious traditions, and by firm bonds of social necessity" (AG 10). In short, it relates to human beings who belong to social, cultural, and religious ensembles.

What is more, the whole human race and all creation is to be brought back into unity. The Church is supposed to assemble all the nations from the four corners of the world in order to make of them one single family, one single People of God, one single body of Christ, and one single temple of the Spirit (*cf.* AG 7; LG 9 and 13; GS 32; PO 1). Consequently the first concern and the most urgent task of the Church's apostolate is to have a vision that takes in the historical and cosmic context. The Church should be present in all the nations. And in each nation she should be present within every societal grouping, thus penetrating all the social, cultural, and religious complexes.

The catholicity or universality of the Church does not mean simply that the plan of God or the mission of the Church seeks the salvation of all men, or that the Church is to spread through the whole earth. It also and primarily means that the entire world, such as it is, is to be oriented toward the salvation summons addressed to it; that salvation is to be inserted into the very course of history; that grace is to penetrate the structures of the created world; and that salvation should be attainable in the very midst of this world. God's intervention in history—and in particular his overture to the world in the historical events of Incarnation and Resurrection—has made the whole world a salvation locale. It has transformed world history into salvation history, and time into a real occasion for man's encounter with God.[4] Teilhard de Chardin's intuition about the unity of mankind and about the unity of humanity and the universe in Christ is close to this view: "The essence of Christianity is nothing more and nothing less than faith in the unification of the world through the Incarnation. As I see it, the whole history of the world is simply a vast phenomenon of Christification." And the universal Church is nothing else but humanity saved together in Christ, the sign and instrument of salvation in the midst of a creation that has been called to salvation from the very beginning, the leaven immersed in a dough that ought to be entirely transformed.

In the framework of this total vision, salvation is to be effected first and foremost at the level of whole groups, without forgetting about the salvation of individual persons, of course. If this concern to transform and save whole groups is absent, then we will focus our efforts exclusively on the salvation of individuals and we shall reduce the apostolate to a numbers game. Salvation will be centered around the idea of possessing something for oneself alone and enjoying the security of such possession.

Such an approach will also lead us into discouragement when we note the small number of Christians among the more than two billion non-Christians today. And Christians will continue to be a decreasing minority on the numbers chart. Concern for individual conversions will cause us to evaluate the success or failure of our mission in terms of numbers and statistics, of annual reports on the number of conversions and baptisms. We shall develop a spirit of world conquest, a crusade mentality, a spiritual imperialism. We will seek to dominate souls and drag them into the Christian camp. The Church's relations with the world and with other religions will be a tissue of pessimistic evasions and negative oppositions, of sterile confrontations and rivalries, of arrogant condemnations and contemptuous pity; or, at best, they will come down to passive coexistence. By contrast, what we need is a charity that is universal, compounded of concern for all creation and of active "pro-existence" amid the world and its religions; and this charity must find expression in cordial collaboration and humble service. The Church should be present everywhere as the sign, the witness, and the instrument of God's plan for humanity, and as "a lasting and sure seed of unity, hope, and salvation for the whole human race" (LG 9). Here is where we should recall the images of the light of the world, the salt of the earth, and the leaven in the dough; they all suggest a universal influence coming from within.

We are not making a case for collectivism or depersonalization. We are simply trying to point out the dangers of a religious individualism and a spiritual egotism that are contrary to the spirit of the Church and detrimental to her apostolate. Concern for the salvation of the individual ought to be reinstated within a concern for the salvation of the universe:

> The human race is one . . . and we are members of the same body. Now the life of members comes from the life of the body. How, then, can there be salvation for the members if, *per impossibile*, the body itself were not saved? . . . It becomes increasingly clear that in such a doctrinal context the Christian's watchword can no longer be "escape" but rather "collaboration" . . . There is but one end: and it is only on condition that he aims at it together with all men that he will be allowed a share of the final triumph, that he will find a place in the common salvation: *in redemptione communi.* The city of the elect does not welcome profiteers.[5]

Finally, our methods and activities must be adapted to each situation or set of conditions (AG 6), so that they can penetrate the whole mass and the varied groups of which it is composed. In this connection we would heartily recommend the mass media; i.e., the social communications media (*cf.* IM).

AN HISTORICAL PERSPECTIVE AND COMMITMENT TO HISTORY

A sense of history and an historical perspective are not unnecessary luxuries for those engaged in the apostolate, because they must be in touch with the dynamic realities of human evolution and enter into the thrust of man's adventure in history. And if this is required of every apostle and missionary, how much more necessary it is for those whose apostolate is situated in the midst of the great religions of the world: e.g., Hinduism, Buddhism, Confucianism, and the so-called "mystic" religions of the Orient that predominate in Asian countries.

The absence of this historical sense and perspective has at times led to a defective missionary approach. Often in the past, and even today, we have looked at the devotees of non-Christian religions in the Orient as if they existed outside history. We often separate them from their culture and their religion, situating them within a static world and an "immobile history" and picturing them as living in a cultural and religious void. When we go to evangelize them with this outlook in our head, we may well believe that we must start from scratch and fill up an empty void. We may feel that we are supposed to jog them out of slumber, to introduce them to a civilization that is indigenous or imported, and to diffuse a new culture and a new religion. This approach amounts to ignoring or destroying what is there already and importing something new. Our missionary effort becomes an act of condescension and spiritual colonialism. Whatever good we might do, our mission becomes a process of humiliation and alienation for these peoples, a process of substituting cultures and religions.

This outlook and approach may have its roots in the general opinion that most of the oriental religions lack a sense of history, in contrast with the historical outlook that has characterized the currents of thought, art, politics, and economics in occidental countries. In the classical notion of Hinduism, for example, time can be considered as a mirage. The events of world history and man's life can be seen as transitory realities bound up with interminable cycles of birth, death, and rebirth. In short, we have a wheel that keeps on turning without ever advancing; thus time is bereft of creative activity and finality. It is assumed that man cannot at all control the mechanics of these happenings. On the contrary, he is their victim. He yearns for liberation from these endless cycles, seeking to discover the unity and identity of his being in that of the Absolute. We have a circular movement that has no goal, that possesses no ultimate meaning, and that does not lead to any consummation.

If we compare this view with the Christian conception of history, the contrast becomes evident. Not only is Christianity an historical reality with an historical origin; it also possesses a sense of history and a theology of history. From its viewpoint, history advances in a straight line: it has a beginning, a middle, and an end. God is the beginning and the end of this history. He is part of it through his transcendence. He directs its course and intervenes in it. History is the unfolding realization in time of God's eternal plan, which is one of pity and love for all men. He guides this plan to good results, thanks to the dynamism and the direction he has injected into it through his act of creation and his successive interventions in it. The death and resurrection of Christ are the center and acme of this history. God is thus the author, master, and end of man's history. History is in fact a salvation history, a goal-centered movement with a dynamic orientation. To accept the word of God and believe in Christ is to enter into this meaningful, goal-centered movement. Hence the Christian's attitude toward the world is optimistic: The world is good; what is evil can be restored to goodness because God is actively present, and because Christ has vanquished the forces of evil and destruction. Thus man can play a meaningful and important role in the picture.

Now the classic Hindu notion of history, which we presented above, is judged to be too simplistic and inadequately nuanced today. So it is surrounded with doubts. It is true that certain classic traditions of Hinduism fit in with this notion, but we must show more consideration and better understanding if we want to apply it to modern India. The philosophers and religious leaders of modern India claim a sense of history for Hinduism. As Radhakrishnan puts it: "History is not a repetition bare of sense, but a creative process determined by the free activity of individuals."[6] There are new features in the cycles. The events are unique and new; what happens can never be repeated. Detachment and asceticism are not so much negative attitudes toward the world or means of evasion as they are requirements for an authentic and sane commitment to this world. "The goal that the ancient Indian scriptures propose to us as the real object of our human actions is *lokasangraha,* i.e., the maintenance of the race in its unity in the midst of its cyclic evolution. It is the perduring meaning of history as the sum total of our activities, whether we know it or not."[7]

This interpretation of Hinduism's sense of history, which proposes a goal-centered history and an optimistic attitude toward the world, is much closer to the Christian concept than the classic interpretation described earlier. At the same time it ties in with the needs and requirements of a developing nation that has only recently won its independence. Political leaders, social reformers, educators, and members of planning commissions in the "new states" give meaning and historical orientation to their national life and to international policy.

The confrontation of Asian and African countries, particularly India, with the Western powers since the end of the eighteenth century, and the introduction of Western-style education and administration, began the process of awakening national consciousness in these peoples; it revealed the historical situation in which they found themselves. The movements for political independence and the coming of this independence at the price of long, heroic struggles are clear proofs that this national sentiment has grown up. Today democratic government, development plans, popular and adult education, communications media, social reforms, economic progress, scientific discoveries, and technological progress are so many means with which these recently independent countries hope to create internal well-being, to play their part in world civilization, and to exercise a major role in the concert of nations. Some sector of the rural population may well be ignorant of all this, but the leaders and intelligentsia of these nations are resolutely committed to the adventure of history and are totally dedicated to the historical development of their countries.

Now if this is the case, how could the missionary Church remain insensitive to, or ignorant of, the historical drama of those to whom it wishes to proclaim the good news of salvation? What would salvation mean, if it were not tied up with the historical drama of these peoples? Adapting the gospel involves precisely that. The missionary may well judge that a necessary part of his mission is to awaken these peoples to a sense of history. But he must also remember that these people live in a specific historical period, a specific situation within their own historical process, and that they have a centuries-old history behind them whether they know it or not. If you ask a Chinese person how old he is, he could rightly reply: six thousand years old! A native of India could give you the same response. It is not a question of naiveté or chauvinism, it is a fact. Chinese people of every age have six thousand years behind them. They stand at the end of six thousand years of Chinese culture and religious tradition, waiting to enter an even more glorious and wondrous new era. Whether the *conceptual notion* involves cycles or a straight-line development, is goal-oriented or not, the *reality* of history is still there. The straight-line course of history has other dimensions as well. It embraces not only occidental Europe but also all the continents and peoples of the world. It is a drama that has been unfolding on a worldwide scale for millions of years.

In this great historical drama all humanity—nations and peoples, men and women, young and old—are hurtling toward a final consummation under the dynamic impetus of creation. They are gathering their energies and resources and committing their whole being to make a better life and to create a better future. They know well enough that this can only be accomplished by transforming the world, which necessarily involves transforming themselves as well. We must have the integral development of each individual and of all men, so that they can take control over the universe they are to renew. Viewed thus, the drama of history essentially comes down to the evolving development of humanity.

The Christ-happening takes place within the unfolding course of this history. It is designed "to bring everything together under Christ, as head, everything in the heavens and everything on earth" (Eph. 1:9-10). In the course of this history, too, the Church is set up as "the visible sacrament of this salvific unity" and "a lasting and sure seed of unity, hope, and salvation for the whole human race" (LG 9). It is supposed to reveal the Father's plan for all men, and to "bring all humanity with all its riches back to Christ its Head, in the unity of

His Spirit" (LG 13). Finally, in the course of this history, Christ's good news is proclaimed so that it may serve as a leaven in the very core of the world (AG 8). If Christ, his gospel, and his Church are to transform the world, give direction to history, and lead all this to its plenitude, then they must penetrate this process, this drama, this movement of history.

What we have said about humanity in general also holds true for each country, people, and nation. Whether he is a native son or a foreigner, the missionary must first enter into this history. He must relate himself to the past and future of his people. He must take part in their drama in all its dimensions, whether it is a matter of political independence, economic development, social reform, racial equality, cultural renaissance, religious updating, justice and peace, or international solidarity.

Entry into the movement of history and *fraternal solidarity* in this venture are not simply preconditions and preparations for the apostolate; they are *an integral part of it*.

MAN-CENTERED APPROACH

In this historical adventure, humanity and every people belonging to it tend toward certain goals and yearn for certain goods. They show a lively insistence on certain values, face up to certain problems, and find themselves in certain grass-roots experiential situations. Above all, they strive resolutely toward the full realization of their being and the complete transformation of this terrestrial city (GS 3).

In this historical adventure, every nation and individual knows its resources and potentialities. They come to an awareness of their role and responsibility, trying to take their place and play their role in the unfolding pageant of history and its obligations.

Of all the forces at work here, the one which plays a vital part in the adventure is *man*; and the realm of his activity is made up of temporal realities, of the facts and deeds taking place in the city of man. Thus both believers and unbelievers see man as the center and summit of all creation (GS 12). The missionary—or the Church—must therefore center attention on the world of human beings, "that world which is the theater of man's history" (GS 2). The human person is worth the effort required to preserve him, and human society is worth the effort required to renew it. For the missionary and the Church, the reference point and guiding mark is "man himself, whole and entire . . . " (GS 3).

If the gospel is going to reach each individual, and if the Church is to make entry into a given human grouping, it will only be accomplished through authentic sympathy for man and through total solidarity with the realities of human life. When a group of baptized Christians enters this human community, nothing human can remain a stranger to them. Their obligation is to see to it that "nothing genuinely human fails to raise an echo in their hearts" (GS 1). In a spirit of fraternal charity, they must realize that "the news of salvation" which they have received "is destined for all men." On their journey toward their Father's kingdom, united in Christ and guided by the Holy Spirit, the members of this group should experience their real, intimate ties with humanity and its history (GS 1).

In all this effort, the Church must speak a language that is intelligible to this generation. The language spoken by aware and committed people is tied up with the realities enumerated above; and it is in this language that communication can be established between the Church and them. Their language is an essentially human pattern of speech. It arouses in them deep desires and aspirations, it finds echoes in their hearts and resonates throughout their being.

We cannot complain that none of this has been done in the past. The only (or perhaps, the principal) reproach we can lodge against ourselves is that we have not taken man seriously, that we have not recognized God's presence in the secular world nor seen God's salvific work in human activities. Our concern was evangelization in the strict sense, i.e., the verbal proclamation of Jesus Christ; and all the rest was considered simply a means or a method, a preparation or precondition. We talked about temporal realities without lingering over them, and we hastened too precipitously to the gospel. And this was because we viewed anthropology as a psychological or pedagogical recipe, rather than as a part of our approach and hence an authentic task in our apostolate.

By contrast, a truly anthropological approach is centered on man taken in himself. We may well have better motives of a rational and spiritual nature, but man and the human should be enough to hold our attention at present. Christ does not come simply at the end; when we talk with human beings about their problems, difficulties, desires, and aspirations, we ought to see God at work in them.

To reach man, the word of God should be a human and meaningful word; for although it is transcendent, it reaches man by becoming immanent in him. A human word—and that is what the word of God is to be—does not come from outside like a bolt from the blue; it is not imposed by anyone. It is a word that comes from within, reaching man from within his real-life situation. It is a word which he comprehends in terms of his own language and his own thought-categories, which he discovers progressively in the course of his actual human experiences.

> If we are to interpret the Christian message, we must look at it from a vantage point where it has meaning for all men. In other words, we must see it from a vantage point where it provides an answer to the questions concerning the meaning and sense of human experiences. Thus God's revelation cannot have for us a meaning that is not, at the same time, a revelation of the meaning of our existence.[8]

As another writer puts it:

Little by little we find this conviction taking root in the awareness of the modern apostle. If man, his brother and contemporary, is to discover God at all, he will discover him only in man, in the midst of his questioning about himself. There will be no real communication with his contemporaries except in and through the mediation of the human . . . For his contemporaries, and in short order for himself as well, any faith in God that is not the ultimate meaning of solid human realities will be nothing at all.[9]

So we must take man seriously, and without any preconditions. We accept him in his otherness. We respect his liberty in the liberty of God whose grace brings it about. We must discuss his problems unhurriedly, staying with him as long as is necessary and moving at his pace.

We should be capable of all this on a purely human level. This is not to say that we would be against the religious level or Christian ideas. But the latter levels will be meaningful to man only after he has exhausted the human import of his aspirations and problems, and the human means of fulfilling them. Once we have exhausted the human level, of course, we would spontaneously pass on to other dimensions, such as the religious and the Christian ones. With such an approach, the latter would not seem to be parallel or in conflict; rather they would seem to be tied together in a continuing progress toward plenitude. Moreover, they would no longer come as explanations imposed from without but as a discovery from within.

When we reach the religious level, the same restraint is in order. We must not rush ahead to reach the level of Christian thought. We cannot do violence to man's conscience, to the pace of his thinking and growing, or to his freedom of action. It is a progressive discovery, a step-by-step journey, a gradual takeoff from the ground. The pace may vary, but it should not be a sudden leap. The latter is possible when explanations come from the outside. But in a discovery process we must lead the other party from the human to the religious, and from the religious to the Christian, without him even noticing the transition from one to the other.

Finally, we must not be saddened or frustrated by the thought that we are not engaged in the apostolate so long as our commitment is confined to the human level of temporal activities. It is true that we must journey the whole route from the human level to the Christian level. But the apostolate does not begin only when we reach the latter level, or only in the framework of the Church, or only with specifically religious acts. As soon as we are truly committed and begin to serve people, even on the human level, we have begun our apostolate. And the journey will move at its own pace to reach the point where Jesus Christ is desired and summoned; at that point he will appear in all his plenitude, as the Way, the Truth, and the Life. Christ will be the revelation of God only if he is also the revelation of man (AG 8).

It is with these dispositions that we dialogue and collaborate with man. We seek to find the meaning of his life and his activities, the means of fulfilling his aspirations and resolving his problems, and the light that will guide him in overcoming his difficulties and carrying out his plans (GS 3,4,11). To succeed in this, we must learn how to decipher the authentic signs of God's presence and activity in the events and upheavals of this world.

THE UNFOLDING PROCESS OF AN INCARNATION ECONOMY

One of the most serious complaints against Christian missions in Asia and Africa was that the missionaries lived in isolation, founding Christian communities which were ghettos separated from the majority of the population. They made their faithful Christians strangers to their own country, to its needs, its traditional culture, and its age-old religions. They cut them off from its societal and national life, imposing an alien religion on them by threats, pressure, or the lure of liquor. Instead of acting to foster national unity and the integration of heterogeneous elements, Christians became a divisive factor, forming a state within the state and serving as the political and cultural agents of foreign powers. Their imposing institutions, the weight of their material resources, and their great influence with the colonial powers opened the door to suspicion, fear, and jealousy. Their negative attitude toward local cultures and religions caused them to be regarded as enemies, as an invading force bent on destruction.

National leaders might heap praise on Christians for their services in the fields of education, health, and social work. But at the same time they felt dominated. They reacted with jealousy, constantly seeking ways of keeping Christians within certain limits and sometimes harassing them. In short, no matter what services may have been rendered to the country by Christian missionaries, the general impression was and still is that they are strangers to its culture, religion, and national life. The garlands showered on us by national leaders and our good relations with high-placed officials and other people should not delude us; we are not desired, and we are not judged to be an integral part of the country. What we missionaries think of ourselves and what others think of us are two different things.

On the other hand, we must not think that all the accusations against us are just, that missionaries and Christians have not made any effort to integrate themselves into the country and act from within it. Striking examples of this effort can be given. But the general approach was from without, and the Church did not evolve from within human groupings as shaped by cultural, social, and religious factors.

I do not want to insinuate that the interior approach was never followed in the past. Nor do I claim to be proposing anything new. But I should like to stress certain aspects of an approach from within, and to point out their consequences for the peoples we seek to evangelize.

Presence   Let us suppose that a Christian or a group of Christians is sent to a certain place. They live in a village or in the neighborhood of a city. Members of the Church, they are conscious of their mission and feel obliged to carry it out in this particular place. They also know that through them the Church is supposed to be present there: "The Church must be present in these groups of men through those of her children who dwell among them or are sent to them" (AG 11). So their first concern will not be to preach the gospel forthwith and to invite people to conversion, faith, and baptism, for that is not their first task. They should instead devote all their efforts to becoming one with these people, to integrating themselves into the community, to winning the acceptance of the group and being considered real members of it. Why? Because "the Church must become part of all these groups for the same motive which led Christ to bind Himself, in virtue of His Incarnation, to the definite social and cultural conditions of those human beings among whom He dwelt" (AG 10).

So long as they are or seem to be unknown aliens and strangers, so long as they appear to be a marginal group or a pressure group that is not integrated into the community, they have not yet begun their mission. And indeed they are not even prepared to begin it, for they lack the spirit of the Church. We ought to do everything from within. And others should see what we do from within their own human groupings, with all their cultural, social, and religious ties.

Authentic presence is fashioned out of shared living, sympathy, and deep solidarity. It is not an institution. It is not a presence imposed by structures and buildings, by personnel and resources. It is a presence fashioned humbly by living together in the same conditions of life. It is not a presence of strangers, observers, reformers, do-gooders, or teachers (however much they may be needed); it is a presence of fellow journeyers, fellow citizens, friends and brothers. It is not a presence surrounded with an aura of superiority, but a presence based on equality, committed to the same drama of life, and intimately tied up with the history of the community. It is not a presence limited to certain individuals or neighborhoods, but a presence embracing whole groups and communities, whether they be civic, political, economic, social, cultural, or religious. It is not a presence restricted to the "Christian" and the "Catholic," or to confessional institutions; it is a presence readily opening out to secular structures and pathways, to temporal agencies and institutions, to all the currents of national life both at home and abroad. It is not a presence defined in territorial or geographical terms, it is a presence embracing human beings in all the realities of their surrounding milieu. In short, it extends to their living conditions, their fields of activity, their desires and aspirations, their problems and difficulties, their joys and hopes, their sorrows and trials, their tragedies and triumphs (GS 1-2). It is, in a word, a presence from within rather than a presence from without, a universal presence of total solidarity and authentic sympathy on a clear level of equality, particularly with regard to the poor and afflicted (AG 12). It is here that we find a meaningful form of reciprocal presence and mutual belonging.

Authentic human presence in a group gives rise to relationships between the Christian community and the human social group. These relationships are lived and nourished by communion, dialogue, cooperation, witness, the proclamation of the gospel, and service.

Communion   Christian presence must be animated and nourished by respect and charity, by the charity with which God has loved us (AG 11-12). This charity must be authentic and spontaneous, disinterested and generous, unlimited and universal. It should well up from the heart and find expression in practical action. It should be found not only in the relations of Christians to others but also in their relations to each other. Christianity is not primarily or essentially a philosophy, a moral code, or a doctrinal system. It is, first and foremost, a living web of relationships and a communion between persons, taking in God and other human beings. The love of Christians for other men should flow from the love which God has poured into their hearts through his Spirit and which unites them to each other. This relationship of brotherly love does not just nourish the communion of Christians with the human groups in which they have become incarnate; it also bears witness to Christ and his Church. "By this love you have for one another, everyone will know that you are my disciples" (John 13:35).

Dialogue   The relationship between God and men during the course of salvation history has been one of dialogue (*cf.* the encyclical *Ecclesiam suam*). Dialogue renders eloquent proof of our solidarity with human beings, and we must have it if we are to know them. Thus it is a precondition for, and a form of, service. Compared with the old system of adaptation by concession, it is a new form of missionary action. The conciliar decree provides the general lines of approach for such dialogue:

> Let Christians . . . acknowledge themselves to be members of the group of men among whom they live. Let them share in cultural and social life by the various exchanges and enterprises of human living. Let them be familiar with their national and religious traditions . . . Christ Himself searched the hearts of men and led them to divine light through truly human conversation. So also His disciples, profoundly penetrated by the Spirit of Christ, should know the people among whom they live, and should establish contact with them. Thus they themselves can learn by sincere and patient dialogue what treasures a bountiful God has distributed among the nations of the earth (AG 11).

The object of such dialogue may be human situations and problems, and man's values and aspirations—be they human, religious, or Christian. All have their own importance, and they lead into one another.

Cooperation   Dialogue is not limited to mutual acquaintance and understanding, to social or cultural contacts, or to an exchange of ideas and experiences. It can take the form of cooperation in certain activities which are, in fact, the best means of dialogue. Let me cite several sectors in which such cooperation is required and appreciated: education; efforts to eliminate famine, hunger, and disease; economic development projects; efforts to promote social justice, moral values, and freedom; the cause of world peace and international understanding (AG 12).

Up to now this type of work has been carried on primarily under the auspices of the Church's institutions. These institutions have a right to exist and have evident advantages; but more and more we should give expression to our service through other agencies and institutions. The activities conducted under our own banner create an impression of wealth, world power, and dominance; and they seem to be in competition with lay organizations. Thus the Church seems to be an ingrown community. Cooperation with other agencies would show how disinterested our service is, open the ecclesial community to the world, make her a power in transforming the world, and give her more opportunities to bear witness on a much vaster scale (AG 12).

Witness   We cannot examine the matter of witness in a theoretical way, independently of what we have already said. Witness takes every shape and form. We bear witness with everything we do and say, with everything we are (AG 11). However important the proclamation of the gospel may be, we cannot minimize the importance of living witness, embodied in our participation in development projects, civic and political life, and every joint effort. This witness gives consistency to our missionary activity. Its value does not reside solely in being a preparation for the proclamation of the Good News, or being a sign that accompanies and confirms that word. It has a value of its own, because Christians committed to the work of development with their fellow men are in a good position to reveal the religious source and character of their commitment. Simultaneously their whole life in the world becomes an eloquent witness to the reality of God, and a manifestation of his sovereignty over all creation. Such witness can be as clear and eloquent as the oral proclamation of the gospel: "Closely united with men in their life and work, Christ's disciples hope to render to others true witness of Christ, and to work for their salvation, even where they are not able to proclaim Christ fully" (AG 12).

Proclamation of the Gospel   Even then, something essential remains to be done. It is something indispensable, without which the process of evangelization would not be complete. It is the *kerygma*, the verbal proclamation of the good news of salvation in Jesus Christ (AG 15). Some time or other, the explicit proclamation of the gospel has its rightful place in the process of carrying out the Church's apostolate (1 Cor. 9:16). "Wherever God opens a door of speech for proclaiming the mystery of Christ, there should be announced to all men with confidence and constancy the living God, and He whom He has sent for the salvation of all, Jesus Christ" (AG 13).

Service   We have said much about presence, communion, dialogue, witness, and the proclamation of the gospel. All of this is to be carried out with humility and self-effacement, in a spirit of service or "ministry" that follows the example of Christ, who came to serve rather than to be served. The Church should appear as an entity living for the world and at its service.

Within the framework of this kind of presence, Christians will be able to "acknowledge themselves to be members of the group of men among whom they live" (AG 11). And the latter will be able to recognize them as such. If this happens, and if people begin to see the deeper meaning of things from within, they can reach the point of discovering that Christ belongs to them too. They will feel more and more at ease with the Christian community and Christ. They will realize that Christ has come to visit them through the Christian community in which he is incarnate, to take on flesh in another human group, another people, a new cultural and religious sector. Christ's incarnation in a given people or human community is not a matter of figures and statistics; it is a process of transformation from within, due to the leavening effect of the gospel. It is the way in which the nations become disciples of Christ, the goal of mission work. To achieve it, no effort is too great in terms of recruiting and deploying personnel, channeling resources, and expending our energy. There is sufficient motivation here for the missionary to persevere and advance in his vocation and to devote himself entirely to the Church's cause.

DIAKONIA IN THE SERVICE OF NON-CHRISTIAN RELIGIONS

Christ came to save and gather together the whole earth (Acts 1:8) until the end of time (Matt. 28:20). He came to save not only human beings but all man's efforts and works, not only the religious individual but all the religions of the world. Everything is summoned to salvation. Everything tends toward Christ, the author of salvation. Everything, including the world's religions, is to be included within the Christification of the universe. The drama of history is oriented toward Christ, whether men know it or not. The unfolding process of history, which modern man yearns for so longingly, is really to progress "toward and in Christ."

The same holds true for religious complexes. Man's concern during the course of this evolution in history includes religious problems as well as human ones. The fulfillment he seeks is not confined to the human plane; it also embraces the religious and Christian plane. Thus the religions of the world and every aspect of religion have, so to speak, a vocation to salvation. In their quest for direction and fulfillment, they are implicitly turned toward Christ. Like the whole thrust of history, they tend toward Christ. Their systems are to be imbued and transformed by the leaven of the gospel. They are under the universal sovereignty of God and subject to his judgment, be it condemnation or salvation.

The Church, the universal sacrament of salvation, just as Christ is, is to include the religions of the world in its perspective on history. It must regard them as one of the complexes to which it must be present. It must see in them a stage in the anthropological process, a stage where it can give loftier meaning and greater fulfillment to man's aspirations. It must consider them as a locale for its incarnation. It must realize that its worldwide *diakonia* is also meant to be on the level of these religions. Now this being the case, what *diakonia* do these religions seek and what *diakonia* can the Church render? The answer is a *diakonia* of salvation, in accordance with the salvific mission of the Church.

Here again *attitudes and approaches* to the religions of the world are vital and decisive on the part of the community, if the service of the Church is to be adapted. Several points are worth mentioning:

1. We must not forget that our *diakonia* is to be humble, partaking of Christ's *diakonia* on behalf of the Father and the world. We are not supposed to serve these religions with an air of disdain and superiority. Our service is to be essentially humble and forgetful of self. There is an even deeper reason why we should approach these religions with great humility, delicacy, and respect. Every human being, insofar as he is a person, is a mystery of freedom and of willing and of interior divine activity. We must always approach such a "mystery" with respect and tactfulness. The world's religions are not empty rooms to be furnished by us, nor holes to be filled up, nor refuse heaps to be eliminated. We realize that God is present in these religions too. They form part of God's universal salvation plan, and they are subject to his eschatological sovereignty. They are components of the covenant with Noah, and they have received cosmic revelation. Their elements and structures are touched by Christ's saving grace, and they are bound up with Christ, the universal sacrament of salvation. Through the "seeds of the Word" that these elements contain (AG 11), the Holy Spirit summons all men to Christ (AG 15). The Spirit was already at work before Christ's glorification, within these religions and the world. Now "sometimes He visibly anticipates apostolic activity, just as He unceasingly accompanies and directs it in different ways" (AG 4). All this comes down to saying that God is present, with his grace and truth, in these religions and their adherents (AG 9, 11; GS 92; N. AE 2).

2. We must not regard world religions as virgin territory which we are the first to work upon from scratch, nor as a *tabula rasa* which we are the first to write on. We must realize that we are entering an area already occupied, where others have worked ahead of us: i.e., God and the men inspired by him. Christ's words to his apostles should serve as a warning to us and teach us humility: "Look around you, look at the fields; already they are white, ready for harvest! ... For here the proverb holds true: one sows, another reaps; I sent you to reap a harvest you had not worked for" (John 4:35-38). Yes, the "seeds of the Word" have already been sown on this earth by God. We are supposed to do the rest, not alone but together with others.

3. We must remember that those we approach are waiting for us, even though they may not be aware of it. Along with their adherents, these religions—with their structures, elements, rites, and religious acts—are animated by God and thus in a state of expectation. This is evidenced by their manifold efforts, including the religious efforts by which men grope for God in order to find him (even though he is not far from any of us—*cf*. Acts 17:28). "These attempts through the kindly workings of Divine Providence may sometimes serve

as a guidance course toward the true God, or as a preparation for the gospel" (AG 3).

If our service is to be adapted to our audience, it must be shaped by the needs, aspirations, and desires of those we seek to serve. Sometimes these religions, like men in general, are unaware of their real needs. Then it is our task to make them aware of these needs, whether they adhere to a religion or not. Christians should do their best to ensure "that modern man, overly intent on science and technology of today's world, does not become a stranger to divine things. Rather, let them awaken in him a fiercer yearning for that truth and charity which God has revealed" (AG 11).

Now once we do approach them with the necessary attitude and the proper spirit, what is our *diakonia* role vis-à-vis these religions? *The diakonia involves several tasks and several stages*: becoming incarnate in their religions; purifying and transforming them; and finally, leading them to their fulfillment and consummation by leading them into the *pleroma* of Jesus Christ. The models for these stages and tasks are the mystery of the Incarnation, the paschal mystery of death and resurrection, and the mystery of consummation, ascension, and parousia.

PRESENCE AND INCARNATION

The Incarnation involves *being present* to the world and *taking it on*. Everything is to be taken on in order to be saved (AG 3). Christ took upon himself our whole nature, except for sin. In like manner, the Church is to become incarnate in every culture and religion, gradually penetrating them like the leaven in the dough until it becomes one with them. This incarnation spirit should be translated into authentic sympathy, an esteem for the human and religious values found therein, and a desire to assimilate their forms of thinking, expressing, praying, and worshipping. That is what the Church urges upon us: It encourages its sons to engage with prudence and charity in dialogue and cooperation with the followers of other religions and, while giving witness to Christian belief and living, "to acknowledge, preserve, and promote the spiritual and moral goods found among these men, as well as the values in their society and culture" (N. AE. 2).

PURIFICATION AND TRANSFORMATION

The second stage is that of *purification and transformation*. Its model is the mystery of Christ's death and resurrection. Every religion and every individual must go through this death to resurrection in order to be saved. The gospel that we proclaim illumines everything, shedding light on religious doctrines and practices and pointing up their values.

When one encounters Christ, one is subjected to judgment (John 3:17-20). Christ is the supreme norm of existence, of an existence for God and in God. Thus when other types of existence make contact with this supreme norm, their real value is examined and confirmed. Every encounter leads to a judgment. Christ does not judge anyone. But in his light and presence, in his words and deeds, men feel that their whole being and existence is being judged (AG 8). It is an extremely delicate and even dangerous task. For it involves judging a religion by the standard of the gospel and testing a culture in the fire of God's word. It involves separating the wheat from the chaff, truth from error, openness to others from self-absorption, grace from sin, real values from false values.

Thus judgment must be glimpsed from within, in the light of Christ, who illumines everything. To do this we must examine religions from within, and that is why incarnation precedes this stage. Hinduism—indeed, every non-Christian religion—must go through a "passion of the spirit," a "noetic crucifixion," in order to arrive at Christ's resurrection. Thus this process of judgment is made up of rupture and continuity, of rejection and assumption, of death and resurrection. It can also be regarded as an act of liberation or redemption: "Whatever truth and grace are to be found among the nations . . . [missionary] activity frees it from all taint of evil . . . Whatever good is found to be sown in the hearts and minds of men, or in the rites and cultures peculiar to various peoples, is not lost. More than that, it is healed, ennobled, and perfected for the glory of God . . . " (AG 9).

The signs of Christianity are instituted by God himself, endowed with meaning and efficaciousness, and animated by the presence of Christ himself. Thus the sacraments are actions of Christ. They signify the various happenings in salvation history, all of which are God's interventions in human history to save men and which find their acme in Christ's paschal happening. They mystically renew these same realities to save those who have faith in them today. By virtue of God's institution and Christ's presence, recalled by the words, and according to the dispositions of the recipients, salvation is communicated to them through these signs. Their efficaciousness does not come simply from the signs, but from Christ's activity.

Now if the sacraments are the ordinary means of grace and salvation in the Church, what are the means provided by God for the salvation of non-Christians in their own religions? First of all we must say that even though grace and salvation are gratuitous gifts of God, he normally acts through the physical and historical order. In other words, he makes use of means that are natural, normal, and ordinary. What is the value and efficaciousness of these signs in world religions? For example, are the rites, the *samskaras*, the moral rules, or the doctrinal teaching of Hinduism salvific?

Secondly, even in Christianity the signs are not efficacious in themselves. They become so through the person who is touched by faith and who gives them meaning and efficaciousness. This task is fulfilled by the words that are pronounced when the sign is acted out. In other religions the signs are natural signs, in the sense that they are created by man and signify human activities, the process of reproduction, the manifestation of natural phenomena, the cyclic course of nature; in these activities the gods themselves are caught up, so to speak. In general, these rites are closed in upon themselves and magical. They will be salvific only if they become prophetic, only if they relate to a person situated beyond themselves, only if they open out to transcendence and pave the way for divine interventions. They must be signs of a being (a person) who is good, free, and transcendent; who approaches man to save him. But these religions do not even have the notion of creation or person, at least not of creation understood as the primary intervention of God in history.

If we consider religions (e.g., Hinduism) as religious structures and systems, we find that their elements are ritualistic, immanent, and closed in upon themselves. The same holds true for their mysticism.[10] But if we consider Hinduism as actually lived out by men and women, then these practices do seem prophetic, open, and guiding their devotees toward communion with a person: God. In this respect they can be salvific.

This is very evident in the *bhakti-marga*, the practice of loving devotion to a personal God, such as the cult of Siva, Vishnou, and their avatars; Rama, Krishna, etc. If we go into the temples and the centers of pilgrimage, if we observe the *puja ceremony* of cultic worship, if we experience the expressions of *bhakti* (piety) and the ecstatic experiences of the worshippers in the presence of their God, if we hear the moving cry for pity and pardon and the authentic acts of adoration, renunciation, and love, then we would be astonished to hear that such religious expressions could be regarded as superstitious, magical, or purely natural rites. By contrast, take a look at certain Christians attending their devotions (e.g., novenas and litanies) or receiving the sacraments (e.g., confession). You might well feel that they are living in a world of rites whose meaning they do not understand. You might well feel that there is little reference to Christ, little or no real faith, and merely the expectation of some magical or mechanical results.

It is true that at times, even in the Church, we seem to have ambiguity, a mixture of paganism and faith, of self-absorption and opening out. But there is an essential difference between the signs of salvation in the Church and those in other religions such as Hinduism. In Christianity the signs are salvific by nature (*per se*), because they are prophetic and dynamic; but in real life they can, now and then, become ritualistic and magical. In Hinduism, by contrast, they are not salvific *per se*, for lack of internal prophetism, dynamism, and an opening to transcendence; but in real life, for some individuals and in specific cases they do become prophetic, open to a personal God, and responsive to his intervention and summons. The source of difficulty is thus the system itself, insofar as it cannot be baptized.

FULFILLMENT AND CONSUMMATION

Finally we have the stage of *fulfillment and consummation*. Christ did not come to destroy but to bring to perfection. He came to lead all cultures and religions to their end goal and consummation. The newly planted churches can "take to themselves in a wonderful exchange all the riches of the nations which were given to Christ as an inheritance" (AG 22). They can "borrow from the customs and traditions of their people, from their wisdom and their learning, from their arts and sciences, all those things which can contribute to the glory of their Creator, the revelations of their Savior's grace, or the proper arrangements of Christian life" (AG 22). They can "reflect attentively on how Christian life may be able to assimilate the ascetical and contemplative traditions whose seeds were sometimes already planted by God in ancient cultures prior to the preaching of the gospel" (AG 18). They can integrate their various prayer forms and cultic expressions into the Christian liturgy. They can assimilate the spiritual literature of other nations. When all this has been done, then we can say that all religions have been consecrated to God and have thereby attained their fulfillment and consummation in the *pleroma* of Christ.

The task is an immense one, but it is part of our *diakonia* to the cultures and religions of this world.

In my introduction I alluded to *the way in which divine grace might reach non-Christians within their own religions*, and the way in which men make their fundamental option in life. Here we find the best *diakonia* that the Church and her members could possibly render to the religions of the world; and they must not fail to do so.

Before spelling out what this service might be, let us make a brief comparison between the signs and means of salvation contained in Christianity and those which are presumably found in other religions.

How does the grace of God reach us in the Church and save us? It does so through words and signs, through the gospel and the Eucharist (AG 5,9). They are differing aspects of the one fundamental and primordial sacrament, i.e., the Church and ultimately Christ. In short, we are saved by our participation in the paschal mystery, which is proclaimed by word and represented by the sacraments, of which the Eucharist is the chief one.

Now some might find this inadequate. Some might say that certain elements of Hindu literature and some of its traditional formulas can be judged to be prophetic and salvific. But what is even more true for the most part is the lack of magisterium or competent authority to distinguish the authentic from the false and the prophetic from the ritualistic in this ambiguous potpourri. Moveover, God's interventions cannot be verified historically in non-Christian religions as they can be in Christianity.

To conclude, the elements of Hinduism and other non-Christian religions cannot be *means* of salvation in themselves as the Christian sacraments can be. But in certain cases we can presume God's possible intervention, to which the devout person opens himself. In such a case, "it is through the sacraments of Hinduism, through the message of morality and good life, through the *Mysterion* that comes down to him from Hinduism, that *Christ* saves the Hindu normally."[11]

We can also give an explanation based on the "fundamental option" advanced by traditional theology. This also holds true for those who follow no religion: so-called nonbelievers, humanists, atheists, Marxists, etc. If grace touches them, how does it do so? Through the "fundamental option" that each man is supposed to make in his life, whether it be in the framework of his religious tradition or in the framework of secular life. A person can close himself up in egocentrism, reject existence, and thus reject "others" (God and man). Or he can open out to disinterested love, to an acceptance of existence, and hence to an acceptance of others (God and men). We find an opening out to all, a commitment to the various facets of life, a spirit of service, an unreserved acceptance of others as such. And at the core of all this we find an act of faith, a response to God's summons, a "yes" or "amen" to God's intervention in his life and in human history. So this person is saved thereby.

Let us examine the case of Hinduism more closely. There is always a cult of a personal God in Hinduism—perhaps less in Buddhism and Confucianism. True enough, and *advaita* philosophy with its mystical character has inspired and dominated all the religious traditions of India. It teaches that there is one single being that is infinite and eternal and that is immanent in nature and the human soul; we experience it in the depths of our being. But there is also the *bhakti* current, which has developed remarkably throughout India. It teaches that the ultimate reality is a personal God in real contact with the world and the soul. This God is love. He has pity on his worshippers and sends them his grace. And they in turn surrender their souls to impulses of devotion and self-abandonment. The *advaita* system may dominate at the philosophical level, but the *bhakti* system is the religious current of the people for the vast majority of Hindus.

For a century and a half a renaissance has been going on in Hinduism. A reform movement has taken shape, seeking purification and rejecting magical, mythological, and superstitious elements. Christian expansion in India was both the reason and the source of inspiration for this reform. Hindu worship and living customs have been gradually influenced by Christianity. We now find a clear tendency toward prophetism and toward a real, personal relationship between the personal God and his worshippers, while the ritualistic aspect is diminishing. There is a certain forward thrust in Hindu worship, and life is moving ahead. Hinduism is in a process of organizing itself. Programs of religious instruction have been set up through the temples, monasteries, and ashrams, especially through the Ramakrishna Mission. So there is progress. Exaggerated mysticism or ritualism is balanced by the growing prophetism or by the *bhakti* current.

In addition to the discovery of a personal God, a need has developed to confront the challenge and assault of technological culture and the demands of a developing country. Service to others and commitment to temporal tasks have appeared on the scene as an integral part of religion.

This revival and progress can be attributed in part to the dynamic element of Hinduism, and in part to its confrontation with Christianity. The leaven of the gospel has been active in recent years. It has not just saved certain Hindus by converting them to Christianity. In some way it has also saved Hinduism, by making it a little more prophetic and hence a little more salvific.

The *diakonia* expected of the Church in this area is precisely that of carrying on in the same way and of serving as a factor for openness in Hinduism, its rites, and its doctrines. It must help Hinduism to open out to a personal, transcendent God, to love and service for others. Any effort aimed at this goal in our relations with adherents of other religions will aid their salvation. We can work along these lines in our school classes on the moral disciplines, in our dialogues, in the various sectors of cooperative effort, and in the printed matter aimed at non-Christians.

SOBER OPTIMISM

Throughout this paper I have been generally optimistic in my attitude toward other religions and the value we give them. But we should not delude ourselves about all this, for then we would find ourselves in a bind. When we talk about making Hinduism more prophetic, this may seem very easy. But the reality is quite contrary. We recognize the power of God and the efficaciousness of his word. We believe in man's goodness. But we must not forget the tendencies of fallen man toward sin, the centuries-old restrictiveness and rigidity of religions, and the minimum traces of prophetism inscribed in their very nature. It is not just a question of clarifying ambiguities, eliminating impurities, and separating elements in the potpourri. The difficulty is not as clear when we consider persons rather than the religious systems and frameworks. The task of "saving Hinduism" and "making it prophetic and salvific" is not as easy as the phrases would have us believe. Hinduism requires a more radical *metanoia*: not just purification and completion but also rejection and breakaways. A new life is not possible without a real death. Thus Christ is a sign of contradiction, whether we wish it or not. The scandal of the cross cannot be avoided in any case. It is possible that Hinduism needs confrontation and opposition, that this might be a better way for it to discover Christ as its fulfillment and savior.

I should like to repeat some earlier words of mine here.[12] Our task is not to consecrate a Pantheon, a Church of all saints, in some ceremony. Nor is it to baptize, for example, the *Sankara* system into a Christian system of Indian philosophy. If we compare each Hindu system to a Hindu temple, and if we plan to build a Christian cathedral out of it, we would first have to demolish it completely. Then we would take the resulting rockpile, choose some blocks and reject others, add some stones of Christianity to them, and thus build our new cathedral. For the Indian metaphysical systems somehow lack cornerstones or keystones (e.g., the notion of creation) without which a Christian edifice could not exist. This is the way in which Johanns envisaged a Christian Indian theology.[13]

This leads us right into our conclusion. A real dialogue should begin, and perhaps remain for some time, at the concrete level of religious experience before moving on to the level of ideas, doctrines, and systems. The aim of dialogue between religions is not simply mutual comprehension but an exchange of religious experiences.[14] *Diakonia* to these religions should also start from this level. After having served there for some years, we might well find a point of entry for serving within their systems and doctrines.

Diakonia on the level of religious experience should not be restricted to an elite. It should become the concern of the entire Church, of the Christian masses. This calls for great and systematic efforts to train our Christians. But no effort is too great, no effort should be refused, when it is a matter of carrying out a mission that is the *raison d'être* of the Church.

NOTES

1. Raymond Panikkar, *The Unknown Christ of Hinduism* (London: Darton, Longman & Todd, 1964), p. 54.
2. Heinz Robert Schlette, *Towards a Theology of Religions* (London: Burns and Oates, 1966), p. 81.
3. In *The Clergy Monthly Supplement* (June 1965), pp. 238-39.
4. Hans Urs von Balthasar, *A Theology of History* (New York: Sheed and Ward, 1963), pp. 59, 66, 138-39.
5. Henri de Lubac, *Catholicism* (London: Burns, Oates and Washbourne, 1949), pp. 111, 120.
6. S. Radhakrishnan, *Eastern Religions and Western Thought* (Oxford 1940), p. 128.
7. Aurobindo, *The Human Cycle.*
8. Henri Bouillard, "Human Experience the Starting Point for Fundamental Theology," *Concilium*, Vol. 6, pp. 40-49.
9. J. Le Duc, "Catéchèse, Précatéchèse," in *Catéchèse*, No. 21 (October 1965), pp. 400-401.
10. D. S. Amalorpavadass, *Destinée de L'Eglise dans l'Inde d'aujourd'hui* (Paris 1967): "La mystique naturelle á la lumiére de la théologie catholique," pp. 315-24.
11. Panikkar, *op. cit.*, p. 54.
12. Amalorpavadass, *op. cit.*, pp. 302-03.
13. P. Johanns, *To Christ through Vedanta*, Light of the East Series (Ranchi, India), No. 4, Part I: Sankara; Introduction.
14. Bede Griffiths, "Approches des non-chrétiens: Rencontre avec l'Hindouisme," Part II, in *Informations catholiques internationales*, No. 221-222, August 1964, pp. 17-19; *Le Christ et l'Inde* (Paris 1967); *Christian Ashram* (London 1966); Swami Abhishiktananda, *La rencontre de l'Hindouisme et du Christianisme* (Paris 1966).

DISCUSSION

A. BOUCHARD   First of all, I should like to stress my interest in his synthesis of missionary spirituality, and to thank him in the name of missionaries. I am particularly pleased that he pointed out that the desire to extend Christ's Incarnation to all nations is quite adequate as motivation for the missionary.

T. TSHIBANGU   I should like to have an explanation of one expression that seems very unclear to me. "Men are saved *in* their religion and not *by* their religion." What does that mean?

Moreover, little has been said about African religions. They are studied very little in themselves, and we are generally inattentive to non-Christian African values. But one could well say that in these religions stress is laid on the unity of creation, on an intuition of the supernatural. One can also note the concrete, vital character of these religions; the character of continuity in movement since the start of creation; in a word, the historical character of these religions, hence the importance of historicity and tradition when one presents Christianity in Africa.

In general, these religions are hardly mystical or speculative at all. They are vitalist. There is some talk of a renaissance in the African religions, of a resurgence of sects. Among the intellectuals, for example, there is certainly a search for traditional religious values. This could be very important for the integration of these values into a Christian theology that would be more African.

A. CAMPS   The paper of Amalorpavadass seems to me to be very important for missionaries on the spot. But when he talks about reforms in Hinduism, isn't he talking about very limited reforms? What is their real influence? My impression is that he has exaggerated the importance of these reform movements in Hinduism.

D. GRASSO   I think that non-Christian religions are channels of grace. But that does not mean that they are "paths of salvation." They are only paths to Christ.

J. MASSON   It seems to me that in theory we have no difficulty in reaching an agreement. But should not our practical work be the publication of serious monographs on the non-Christian religions, in which we would lay stress on the concrete living-out of these religions and its status?

A. VANNESTE   We always define the non-Christian religions in relationship to the Christian religion. Does this not ultimately signify that we are not taking them very seriously? If we are to have a real dialogue with them, must we not allow the thought of these religions to have an influence on Christian thought itself, as was the case with Greek thought long ago?

G. DELCUVE   I should like to ask Amalorpavadass a question. On the one hand, he insists on the necessity of showing the continuity between non-Christian religions and Christianity. On the other hand, he stresses rejection and rupture, *metanoia*, as necessary things if these religions are to move on to Christianity. How does he see this pedagogical process?

H. DE LUBAC   In line with Camps, I should like to ask a question of the author. To what extent does the conception of time and the notion of history mark a considerable evolution in present-day Hindu thought? Is it a matter of the direct or indirect influence of Christian thought? Or does the explanation come from factors internal to Hinduism? In another vein, as a professor of the history of religions, I must pay homage to the firsthand work of the old-time missionaries with regard to the study of non-Christian religions: e.g., Buddhism. To encourage such monographs would be to pick up a rich missionary tradition.

CLARIFICATIONS AND REPLIES BY THE AUTHOR

First of all, I must thank you for your favorable reception of this paper, and for your questions and requests for clarification.

1: Timothy 2:4-5. I am not an exegete, and I would not presume to give a response. But I should like to explain how I understand this passage. If I understand correctly, salvation consists in coming to a knowledge of the truth; and the truth is none other than Jesus Christ. No one is saved without faith, and faith is the encounter or explicit contact with Christ. Knowledge of Christ is knowledge of the truth. Just as one can grow in knowledge of a person by starting with secondhand information and reaching personal acquaintanceship, so the religious non-Christian can grow in his knowledge of Christ. Thus the preaching of the gospel is still necessary for this man to grow in the knowledge of the whole truth. As John 16:13 says: "The Spirit of truth . . . will lead you to the complete truth."

2: Anthropological and mystical approach. It is true that there does exist a mystical tendency in India. Thus it constitutes an approach to Hinduism. I have discussed this subject in my book, *Destinée de l'Eglise*. In Chapter 15, I talk about "an encounter with Hinduism on the level of experiencing God." I spoke more specifically about "natural mysticism in the light of Catholic theology." But India is not just a land of mystics, so there are other rules of dialogue and other approaches. That is why Chapter 14 deals with the "conditions and levels of a dialogue with Hinduism." The whole first part of the book analyzes more deeply the religious situation of Indian society today, and my conclusions are that there are different strata in the Indian population. This calls for different approaches. But even in the case of mystics and mysticism, I do not think there is any problem in beginning with an anthropological approach. According to Yogulo and Yoghi, a mystic can begin where he chooses. He can even begin with idolatry, provided that he gets beyond that level. The point of departure can be anywhere. Thus the anthropological approach is not limited to any one of these levels—i.e., the human, the religious, or the Christian.

3: As far as African religions are concerned, my remarks may also hold true for them too. But I do not know if that is the case. That is why I excluded the African continent deliberately in my introduction. It is up to Africans and missionaries to Africa to see if my remarks are applicable. In the anthropological (man-centered) approach, the point is to exhaust the human level before passing on to the religious and Christian levels. In dialoguing with nonbelievers, for example, there is no common ground except the human one. This is the level that is sometimes passed over when we deal with other religions, or even with catechumens. Take the case of people who have faith or a religious sense. Even here I would not begin with the religious or the Christian, because one often notices that the human level is lacking in their spirituality or religious outlook. We sometimes find people who are very holy, but not human enough. They are saints but not "human beings." I want their faith to embrace everything that is human. When do we exhaust the human? I do not know. But if one takes an interest in man and stays with him without forcing him, the human level is exhausted at some point. It is not a matter of time but of rhythm and the pace of God's grace. I do not say that at the end of the human level, he will automatically move on to the religious or Christian level. But when one reaches the limits of the human after having tried to exhaust its meaning and resources, there is a possibility of raising a question as to whether there is not some meaningful "beyond." In other words, there is always a limit; and this limit gives rise to the possibility of going beyond it. There is a second hypothesis with regard to natural mysticism: Can concentration on the ego open up to transcendence? I do not know. But why exclude that possibility?

4: Camps expressed doubts that the reform movement was as strong as I seemed to suggest. I think that it is more important than it may appear to be. It is true that it is not obvious, especially in the villages where the people are illiterate. One must also realize that any reform in Hinduism progresses very slowly because there is no magisterium or organization as there is in Christianity. Even in Christianity one cannot implement reform there; I can mention the liturgy in the dioceses of India, which is totally pre-Vatican II. With all the means at our disposal, we cannot expand the liturgical movement quickly enough. With reference to the *bhakti* movement, Camps is correct in saying that it began in the ninth or the eleventh century. But he is wrong to think that it has disappeared today. It is becoming more and more vigorous, and it is spreading throughout India. Today it is the most widespread form of Hinduism. A philosopher may be an *advaita*; but when he comes to practice his religion, he has a god. He is able to reconcile the two.

5: The world religions are means of salvation, or Christ saves Hindus in their religion. There is a slight distinction. If Christ's salvific grace reaches Hindus, it does not simply fall out of the heavens. He must have other means. Since God created the physical and historical order, I think that grace must pass through Hinduism. Grace reaches them in the structure of Hinduism. I deliberately avoid the words "*by* Hinduism," or the phrase that "non-Christian religions are *means* of salvation," to distinguish them from the Church. For we consider the Church as the universal sacrament of salvation, and the sacraments are efficacious *ex opere operato*. Throughout I use the term, "habitats of salvation" rather than the term, "means of salvation." As for "channels" of grace, this can be identical with "means" of salvation. It is a question of terminology. Likewise I prefer to employ *channels* and *means* to avoid ambiguity.

6. Delcuve's question about rupture and continuity. From the start I feel that all continuity presupposes rupture, because there is a limitation. But I did not want to draw attention to the limitation. I wanted to point up the progressive evolution. Nevertheless, we should not forget that there is a

continuing rupture. It is this very tension between rupture and continuity that is the source for the dynamism of progress.

7. De Lubac's question on the evolution of the sense of history in Hinduism. My honest impression is that this evolution exists from within but, as in most cases, our energies are half-asleep. They need to be aroused. When they are stirred up from without, they become operative. With respect to Hinduism, it seems to me that the arrival of the British administration, the introduction of English language courses and Western literature, and the preaching of the gospel have been challenges and sources of inspiration for reform. They stimulated the internal dynamism of Hinduism to interpret itself differently, in accordance with the new situation of India today.

JEAN FRISQUE

The Role of Development in Missionary Activity

CHAPTER SEVEN

The topic proposed for your consideration here relates to a reality of enormous dimensions. It has to do with the contribution of the nascent churches of Asia and Africa to the aims and objectives of development work. The initiatives taken by these churches in the educational, medical, and social realms have been numerous, and there are many institutions in which this work has been implemented. Even the unobservant traveler cannot fail to notice this.

This is the reality I should like to examine here. What is the significance of this contribution to development work in terms of mission work? Is there merit and validity to the concrete forms taken by this contribution up to now? Is it true that the amount of effort and worry involved in this contribution so far represents an impediment to evangelization in the strict sense? These questions are not theoretical ones. They are being posed pointedly by men and women who are actively committed in the field.

WHAT DOES "DEVELOPMENT" MEAN?

Development cannot be the modern label that one sticks on a merchandise as old as the history of Christianity. For at the core of Christianity there is the new commandment; that is, the summons to display fraternal love without restriction. Since time immemorial the missionary effort has been accompanied by a desire to give food to those who did not have it; or, to put it another way, it has been accompanied by a desire to help man make progress, to help him reach a higher level of culture. Let us recall the example of Saints Cyril and Methodius, who devised an alphabet for the Slavic peoples that is still in use. We all know that there are countless similar examples to be found in the history of mission work.

But let me repeat: The contribution which the Church has never ceased to make to man's material and spiritual progress down through the centuries cannot

91

be characterized purely and simply as a contribution to development. Why not? Because development is irreducible to progress; it is much more than the latter. Progress is a purely objective reality, while development is a fully human reality that appeals to the liberty and commitment of each individual and every nation. As Paul VI reminded us in *Populorum progressio,* to speak of development is to speak of the authentic betterment of the whole man and of every man; and this betterment presupposes that everyone will take his own *active* role in building man's future. In short, development is a modern category tied up with the advent of a secular world—that is, a world wherein men discover that part of their mission is to invest their own resources in building up a world that is ever more humane and habitable for human beings.

What is more, in line with the way Paul VI used the term, development is a category that is broader in scope than current parlance would have us believe. For many people it refers simply to economic and social development, and not to the *integral* development of the whole man and every man; but it is obvious that all the aspects of development are intrinsically tied up with one another. In this broader perspective, development is a reality that concerns all peoples, whether they be rich or poor in economic terms. When we think about building a real human community, the most knotty problem of underdevelopment today seems clearly to be the problem of *underdeveloped awareness and conscience.* Is it not true that at the very moment when men and nations are being invited to live together, the course of events proceeds as if the human conscience were not equipped to confront the tasks facing people today and to commit itself with honesty and clear-sightedness to cooperation on a worldwide scale?

I stress this point here at the beginning because I have observed certain things on my travels. I have seen how ignorance or unawareness of this point can have grave consequences on our understanding of what mission work should be in today's world. Here and there in various parts of the Third World, Christian men and women of every category seek to make their own contribution to the development of their country. But more than once I have been surprised to find that they do not at all perceive the tieup that could exist between an authentic contribution to development and a necessary updating of missionary activity itself. In the remarks that follow we shall continue to bear in mind that our talk about development has to do with a reality that is eminently topical and relevant today.

Statement I: The People of God can contribute actively to development only if they accept a more fully rounded vision of their mission among men.

To understand this statement we need only refer to the work of Vatican II, more specifically, to the dynamism that animated its sessions from start to finish. Pope John XXIII, we know, saw it as an attempt by the Church to find once again her eternal youthfulness. She had lost this look to the extent that a chasm had been formed between her and the modern world. In the decades preceding the Council, numerous efforts had been made to restore dialogue with contemporary mankind. But the Church, as a body, experienced many difficulties in trying to take responsibility for such efforts; things continued to go along as if it were the Church of yesterday trying to address the people of today. The merit of John XXIII was that he realized it would take a shock wave throughout the Church to enable her to be truly reconciled with the modern world; only that would enable her to be *really present* once again to the men of our day. John XXIII saw the convocation of an ecumenical council as the privileged means to this end; for there can be no change in the Church except through the exercise of joint fidelity to the Spirit.

WHAT DID VATICAN II DO?

The master work of Vatican II is undoubtedly its dogmatic Constitution on the Church (LG). In its quest for self-identity, the Church recognizes herself as the People of God. The fundamental reality of the Church is made up of these men and women. They are committed to the common adventure of history with their fellow men; but their faith in the living Christ and the bond established with him enables them to be the leaven in the dough, the chief instrument for carrying out God's plan for humanity, in the very midst of this world. What does that mean? Negatively speaking it means that the Church is not primarily an institution, however venerable that institution might be. Positively speaking it means that the Church is a communion of persons in Jesus Christ. And that is as true when they are scattered among other men and committed with them to carrying out the tasks imposed by man's evolving history, as it is when they are assembled together by the ecclesial institution to penetrate more deeply into the mystery of Christ throught the proclamation of the Word and their participation in the Lord's body.

In defining the Church as the People of God, Vatican II implicitly recognized that the center of gravity for human existence was somehow shifted with the coming of the modern world. Let me explain. The man of yesterday was primarily a religious man, anxious to express his relationship with the world beyond in all things; hence the importance of sacred words and liturgies. If he was a believer, then the important thing was to do the Father's will, which the Church's authorities were charged to spell out down to its minutest details.

In a Christian society where almost all the members are baptized, obedience to the Father's will readily took the form of passive submission to the ecclesial institution. In contrast to this, we have the image of modern man. Need we remind you that he has been taking shape in the West for centuries already, perhaps going back as far as the twelfth century. He is a man who knows his own potentialities. He is a free and responsible man, who is convinced that he must take his own history into his own hands, and who feels obliged to transform the world in order to carry out that history. The primary language he understands is not religious language but *profane language,* that is, the language which expresses his work to him—the part he plays in constructing the city of man. Life's center of gravity is shifted from the realm of religious expression to the realm of profane expression; or, as we would put it today, from the realm of "rite" to the realm of "living."

Now it is clear that within the framework of a profane or secular civilization the exercise of one's faith in the living Christ cannot be separated from man's assent to the truth of his creaturely condition. Within such a framework, all the members of God's people are summoned to be active, responsible creators, on the basis of the fundamental fellowship to which baptism introduces them. Within such a framework, the mission of God's people is carried out primarily on the level of secular life, where the People of God find themselves dispersed among other human beings; for the evangelization of our contemporaries must necessarily meet them at the point where they are conscious of an obligation to take charge of their own destiny. This task can be shouldered by a Church which sees itself as the People of God; it cannot be shouldered by a Church that is passive consumers. This, in brief, is the awareness that dawned clearly with Vatican II.

DEFINING THE MISSION OF THE PEOPLE OF GOD

How then are we to define the mission of God's people *on the level of profane life*? It is here, we suspect, that the relationship between mission work and development intervenes as a question.

At the heart of our missionary responsibility lies clearly the task of evangelization: unveiling the good news about the salvation attained for all men in Jesus Christ. Specifically, evangelization is the reason behind the sending of the people. If the People of God are sent out into the world, just as Christ was sent by the Father, that is the only reason for it. But what does "evangelizing" mean? So long as the center of gravity for human life was situated in the realm of religious expression, evangelization was restricted to the explicit proclamation of Christ and his mysterious dwelling amid his own followers. Evangelization was an expressly religious act, exclusively tied up with the ecclesial institution. This ecclesial action was always accompanied by "works of mercy." But that was primarily intended to add a sort of "practical example" to the proclaimed message, or in some cases to lead people more readily to faith and baptism. Within such a perspective, the witness given by Christians in real life was only a "silent" witness in itself; it was nothing without the proclaimed message, because in itself it was only seen in terms of its moral overtones. What is more, it led to deeper understanding of the Word only to the extent that it clearly embodied the demands of the gospel.

If one remains within this perspective today, he is bound to see the relationship between mission work and development as a *competitive* one. For the work of evangelizing embraces only religious efforts in this perspective, and it is obvious that every contribution to development is a specifically secular act even though it may represent authentic witness in some cases. Thus contributing to development is an excellent thing, but alien to evangelization in the strict sense. So one is readily inclined to ask whether the time dedicated to development work by missionaries is not just time taken away from the work of evangelization. That is what I mean by a competitive relationship.

Are we to stop there? I think not. For we have not said everything about evangelization when we reduce it to an expressly religious act. With the appearance of the modern world we have learned to see the realm of secular life, henceforth given value by man, as a realm which itself possesses a *religious dimension* even if this dimension is not expressed there for its own sake. We do not have to "add" religious acts to secular life so that it will have a religious dimension it would not have had otherwise. If we consider things correctly, man's adventure in history is not simply a "temporal" adventure. When men strive to make the world more and more habitable for human beings, when they work for development and seek peace and brotherhood, they are not just putting their creaturely resources to work. They are also and above all committing the most secret impulse of their spiritual liberty, their decisive option in life, their way of envisaging the "absolute future" to which all men aspire. Man's adventure in history is a dramatic event insofar as men commit themselves to it in their condition as sinners. It will be completed successfully only if men respond to the initiative of grace in Jesus Christ. Attaining the state of sonship in him, and thereby being freed from the bondage of sin, human beings are simultaneously restored to their true condition as creatures. Henceforth they are capable of correctly employing all their resources in the service of a human future that is truly worthy of God's plan.

Having said this, we can readily appreciate that development is a human task with a religious dimension. Christ's unique mediation is thoroughly involved, as is the gospel which provides us with the explanation. When Christian men and women contribute authentically to the integral development of the whole man and of all men, they do not speak explicitly about God, Jesus Christ, or their faith. But their secular work, and the equally profane language that expresses it, allows people to get a *presentiment* of the ultimate Word which animates their lives and summons them unceasingly. This should be one of the major preoccupations of a theology of the Word today: to shed clear light on what I would call the *symbolic function of man's secular language.* It is not just secular life that possesses a religious dimension; the secular language which expresses this life necessarily refers to the religious dimension of existence as well. In concrete terms this means that the Christian, committed to the work of development with his fellow men, is fully capable of *revealing* the religious quality of his commitment. His whole secular life can be a witness, and this witness is necessarily a *spoken witness.*

Thus we should not reduce evangelization to a specifically religious activity of the ecclesial institution. It is that, of course, and it always will be. But it is also setting to work to carry out the *irreplaceable service* that the People of God are summoned to render to the world. Properly understood, this service is the realm where we build up an authentic witness, speaking already of Christ's lordship over all creation. Thus mission work and development work are no longer in competition. Quite the contrary is true. We would have to say that the first realm in which the evangelization of our contemporaries is carried out is that of the indispensable contribution of the People of God, dispersed among the peoples of the world, to the integral development of the whole man and all men. To convince oneself of this, one need only complement the thoughts of *Lumen gentium* (LG) with those of *Gaudium et spes* (GS). In short, one need only realize that Christ's unique mediation is fully committed to the historical evolution of humanity, and that it implicitly finds real room to unfold therein.

Statement 2: The People of God can contribute actively to development only if they re-evaluate the visage of the ecclesial institution and the missionary activity it exercises.

We have just seen that mission work and development are not juxtaposed activities in the realm of secular life. Instead they are two interrelated dimensions or levels within the single task of the People of God. But mission work is obviously a properly religious activity as well, that is, the activity *par excellence* of the ecclesial institution. So now we must face another question: Now that we have highlighted the mission of God's people in the realm of secular life, does this not lead us to re-evaluate the missionary activity traditionally exercised by the ecclesial institution?

HISTORY

During the early centuries of Christianity, the missionary effort readily stood out as the primary responsibility of the People of God spread out in the Mediterranean basin. The Christian communities everywhere vividly experienced what life in Jesus Christ was, and they were driven to unveil the riches of this life to those around them. Unconcerned about the political, economic, or social destiny of the Greco-Roman world, Christians felt responsible instead for its spiritual destiny. They spoke about Jesus Christ and lived in him with an infectious faith. They all felt sent to proclaim the good news of salvation at any cost. Mission work was thus a specifically religious activity for which the local Christian community felt responsible; but it was far from being institutionalized the way it would be later on.

With the conversion of the Roman Empire and the dawn of a Christian empire, missionary activity began to take on a new outlook. It tended to become more and more institutionalized, as did Christian life in general. This is easy enough to understand when one realizes that countless numbers of men and women flooded into the Church without having any real knowledge of the responsibilities imposed on them by baptism. The Church readily became a

Church of "clerics" and "religious," while the Christian people became a group of consumers. Only a minority felt any sense of responsibility, and it came to organize itself more and more. The clergy and the religious became professionals in the ecclesial institution, the people it could count on to perform the many tasks confronting it. There was no lack of work to be done. To keep our remarks to the Latin Church, the cultural situation of the West was such that one could not dream of preaching the gospel without humanizing as well. The specific activity of the ecclesial institution began to extend itself into an ever vaster network of Christian institutions that took the manifold aspects of human life under their wing. With this institutional bias, we gradually Christianized attitudes and behavior patterns without being concerned about an authentic personalization of the faith. Evangelization involved setting up a typically Christian society. In terms of efficiency, this method had many advantages. But it unfortunately led to certain habits that would be hard to slough off when circumstances required it. On the plane of missionary work, in particular, evangelization was accompanied by the setting up of Christian institutions which helped to Christianize life; in many cases their beneficial contribution was a powerful way of attracting people to the Church.

The serious shortcomings of this missionary method would surface with the advent of the modern world. As people began to become more and more aware of their own worth, and of the responsibilities they had to shoulder to construct their own future, they were less and less inclined to accept the guardianship of the Church institution. As they saw it, this protective relationship could only lead to an alienation of awareness and personal conscience. A paradoxical situation developed. At the very same time that this new awareness was surfacing in Europe and the Christian regime was beginning to suffer dislocation, the European colonial powers were lending active support to the Church's missionary activity in Asia and Africa; and this activity continued to develop along the lines that had now become traditional. The Church's tutelage was supported less and less in the Western Church, but government took advantage of its services in all the lands where the West was trying to impose its hegemony. For the colonial powers, the Church's traditional missionary activity represented a good way of expanding Western civilization.

TRANSITION

These facts are known to us all, of course. But I wanted to recall them here so that it would be perfectly clear that the traditional cast of missionary activity, which is still evident today in the churches of Asia and Africa, corresponds less and less to the needs of our day—and particularly to the needs of development. To be sure, throughout the course of its missionary efforts the Church has been concerned about the progress of humanity. And it continues to serve this cause today through its educational, medical, and social institutions. In this area all the Christian churches have worked along the same lines. But as I noted at the beginning of this paper, contributing to man's progress is one thing and contributing to development is another. To speak of development is to speak of a summons to personal responsibility and awareness. Development has come to have meaning only with the advent of the modern world, and it does not mix well with an outlook based on tutelage.

The People of God cannot contribute actively to development, and exercise authentic missionary responsibility in this field, without being led to re-evaluate progressively the traditional cast of the ecclesial institution's missionary activity. I say "progressively" because obviously such an important transition is not going to take place in a day. What is more, in many instances people's outlooks are not yet ready to shape an integral vision of development. Right now the essential thing is to deepen our sense of awareness and to accept the necessary changes as normal and desirable.

At the end of this transition, the ecclesial institution will be restored to its true reality. With the weight of Christian institutions taken off her back to a large extent, the ecclesial institution will be better able to do what she was created for. When Christians and future Christians are gathered together by the Church, they are so gathered to be initiated into Christ's mysteries. The proclamation of the Word should have a central place in this initiation. But the proclaimed Word is not a cold thing nor an intangible reality. It is meant to be the specifically religious expression of the gospel, which is alive in the heart of God's people and which can already be felt somehow in the realm of secular living. Never has such a religious expression been as necessary as it is today. We do not allow room for ourselves to be challenged by the ever-present intervention of Jesus Christ in the midst of the world, if the Word which expresses it is only felt by presentiment through the mediation of secular language. It is indispensable that this Word find its own expression in a religious language that preserves its ever-present vitality.

The ecclesial institution is not an *en-soi,* a reality wrapped up in itself. As Vatican II pointed out time and again, it must be in the service of God's people as they grow to full measure. It is the People of God, both when they are scattered abroad in the world and when they are assembled together, that is the esslesial Body of Christ; it is not the institution that is this. The service to be rendered by the ecclesial institution is an indispensable one. For the People of God cannot correctly live their faith in Christ without being religiously initiated into this faith in appropriate gatherings. They cannot bear authentic witness to the Risen One living among them and animating their whole life, if this witness is not accompanied by explicit proclamation of the Good News to all men of good will. But whether it is the voice of witness or the proclamation of the Word, it must be tied up with the actual life of the People of God that is ever animated by the spirit of the living Christ. To do this is simply to return to the gospel and to the way in which the primitive Church conceived its mission. And this return to essentials has always taken place when the Church was going through a period of transition.

Statement 3: The People of God can make their indispensable contribution to development only by rediscovering the profound bond that should exist between mission work and man's history.

It is a fact that in gradually moving away from the regime of Christendom, the ecclesial institution and Christians have run the risk of losing sight of the close relationship between mission work and man's adventure in history. In becoming more spiritual, the Church has lost something of its incarnational quality; and this could have had serious consequences for her understanding of her mission to men. Once again the conciliar perspective of the Church as the People of God has served to bring things into proper balance.

SPIRITUAL POWER AND TEMPORAL POWER

During the first few centuries of her history, the Church showed little interest in missionary strategy. By the end of the apostolic period, Christian communities were established in the principal towns and cities of the Mediterranean basin. This development took place naturally within the framework of the Greco-Roman Empire, and it took advantage of all the possibilities offered by the Pax Romana (the system of roads, for example). But Christians were a minority group within a highly cultured society; and they did not yet realize that there could be a tieup between the development of mission work and the political destiny of humanity. They were interested solely in the spiritual plight of the world in which they found themselves.

Then came the fourth century and the official conversion of the Empire to Christianity. Today we often find that we speak of that moment in Church history in purely negative terms. When we do, we forget an important element in that process: the dawning realization of contemporary Christians that their faith could have an impact on the political sphere itself. That was an important stage in the maturation of the Christian conscience, a stage that would leave its mark on later mission developments.

Let us just consider the Latin Church for a moment. What do we find? The void left by the barbarian invasions prompted the spiritual power, particularly the supreme pontiff, to take new responsibilities into its hands. Churchmen began to play an increasingly important role in temporal affairs. Step by step a real missionary strategy took shape, and it was intimately bound up with the political destiny of occidental Europe. To be sure, it would take centuries to strike a proper balance in the relationships between the temporal power and the spiritual power. The process had scarcely begun in the twelfth century. At that time the pope was practically accorded the right of tutelage over all spheres of human life, including the political sphere, by virtue of Christ's universal lordship which he exercised here below in a privileged way.

At the start of the Renaissance, political leaders began to reject this ecclesial tutelage over the political sphere in no uncertain terms. But even in 1493 we find Alexander VI making an important decision; he divided up the newly discovered non-Christian lands between Spain and Portugal. But certain habits had been formed, and the missionary expansion of the Roman Church would closely follow the growing hegemony of Europe over the entire world. In many cases, mission work would fall under the control of princes despite the efforts of Rome to safeguard the transcendence of its message. The disadvantages of this system would intensify as time went on. By the turn of the twentieth century, non-Christians would see missionaries as the most insidious agents of Western imperialism.

MISSION WORK AND MAN'S DEVELOPMENT IN HISTORY

I reiterate this history here, not to pass judgment but to draw an important lesson for us. In the last analysis, during the centuries of Christian dominance the missionary effort was animated by a desire *to be profoundly present to human history,* so that it might continually rectify this history in the light of the new commandment prescribed by Christ. If mistakes were committed, and we know they were sometimes serious errors, they were committed to the extent that the missionary effort did not take adequate note of the distance between the cultural universe of the white man and that of another specific culture. The catholicity of the Church was obscured at the same time.

In the future, of course, there will be no question of the Church exercising a right of tutelage over man's political destiny. But the People of God must not lose sight of the close relationship that should exist between mission work and man's history. Need we talk more about missionary strategy? Undoubtedly no. Or perhaps we can say simply that the missionary strategy for today and tomorrow should more and more be one of *service.* Humanity is groping to build its future under its own responsibility. The People of God are at work in this cause; and their contribution to this future, as we noted earlier, is indispensable.

The ecclesial institution should primarily lend an ear to this process. It should not assume guardianship over it nor draw profit from it for its own purposes. It should simply allow the People of God as a whole to play their role in it, to be the leaven in the dough, so that all things may gradually be recapitulated in Christ. The People of God should contribute actively to the development of the whole man and all men; they should try to realize how they can bear authentic, spoken witness to the risen Christ in this realm of activity. If they do this, they will readily rediscover the profound bond that exists between mission work and the historical evolution of humanity.

And so I need only conclude my remarks. The few statements I have made here hardly exhaust the topic. I am content to trace a few lines of thought for our reflection and to arouse some reactions. I personally expect that there will be more than a few reactions to what I have said. The period through which the

Church is passing right now has an element of crisis in it; but it is also full of promise. When I look closely at the events that are taking place in every corner of the world, and when I note the growing convergence of the initiatives taken by the People of God in various areas, I am inclined to feel that the time is close at hand when the Church, the Body of Christ, will once again be the first blush of youth for the world.

DISCUSSION

A. CAMPS   What is the difference between progress and development? Why do you say that the former is an objective reality and that the latter is a purely human reality?

J. DANIÉLOU   You set up an opposition between religious development and secular development, and you say that the latter has a religious dimension. To what extent does this full flowering of man involve a religious dimension, not only from the viewpoint of those who cooperate in it but also from the viewpoint of those who are its object? And also from the viewpoint of the object of development itself?

A. VANNESTE   One thing you say seems ambiguous to me. You say that the Church, not the ecclesial institution, should contribute to development work. But today the Church's contribution to development is made primarily through ecclesial institutions. How do we reverse this tendency?

G. DELCUVE   I should like some clarification regarding the indispensable service of the People of God to the world. Besides, is it correct to say that the Church loses its incarnational qualities in becoming more spiritual? Finally, it seems to me that much too strong an opposition is set up between profane language and religious language. A specifically religious language must exist. But the Church is supposed to show that the gospel also has a secular dimension, an import for human existence.

I. DE LA POTTERIE   To what extent is evangelization an expressly religious act, and to what extent can one say that it likewise involves a secular aspect? Moreover, it seems to me that too sharp an opposition is set up between the Church as institution and the Church as the People of God. The Church is an institution as well. That does not mean we must necessarily approve of all the concrete forms this institution has taken during the course of history.

J. M. SETIEN   I wonder whether it might not be necessary to make a distinction between apostolate and evangelization. Evangelization is specifically the proclamation of Christ. The apostolate represents work in the midst of the secular world, but it also has a religious dimension. Moreover, I do not understand very clearly the assertion that secular language necessarily reflects the religious dimension of existence.

H. DE LUBAC   It is good to highlight the advent of the modern world, its growing self-awareness and its secularization. But it seems to me that excessively sharp oppositions are set up in this paper: the Church as institution versus the Church as People of God; the religious passivity of the earlier centuries of Christendom versus the freedom and initiative of modern man; the assimilation between "secular" and "life" on the one hand, and "religious" and "rites" on the other.

D. GRASSO   If development is the betterment of man, then it must also be the religious betterment of man; for it is the latter that gives meaning and orientation to the former. The real contribution of the Church to development is her clarification of man's fundamental problems: his destiny and all the dimensions of his life. It is there that we perform the real work of evangelization.

K. MÜLLER   The secular institutions for development and the progress of peoples include the aspect of religious betterment. Would not the Church's role be to work to see that these institutions are convinced about man's integral development?

A. SEUMOIS   First we must distinguish between direct evangelization, which is the proclamation of the kerygma, and indirect evangelization or apostolate, which involves the intervention of institutions with a directly secular aim. Only the former has an expressly religious character. Next we would do well to make a distinction between the proper role of missionary personnel as such—directly consecrated to evangelization and the founding of new churches—and the role of the Christian layman acting as a citizen, whose proper role is the task of socio-economic development. This is his proper task as citizen. As a Christian, he must carry it out with the aim of shedding the light of the gospel on the civil and secular sector, on terrestrial society.

A. CAMPS   Sometimes the religious elements of certain cultures are an obstacle to development. The Church could play an important role in removing these obstacles. Besides, must we not talk about the work of predevelopment, even as we talk about the work of pre-evangelization? By that I mean helping other cultures to become capable of cooperating in their own proper development.

CLARIFICATIONS BY J. FRISQUE

1: If it is to be the primary field of evangelization, development must be understood in the sense of *Populorum progressio*. That is to say that it must be integral: it must embrace the whole man and all men. In this perspective, we cannot take it solely on the economic and social level. It is the concrete implementation of Christ's new commandment. Development is a secular task in which man expresses all that he is and all he can produce. He expresses all that his creaturely resources can produce. Now this work, taken in the concrete, engages the whole man and the radical option of his liberty. In this way he builds an authentic witness that speaks of Christ's universal lordship over the world. As such, it must be considered an explicitly religious act, as an evangelization in the strict sense. When we speak of development, we must exclude the term *pre-evangelization*. Moreover, this witness is given in a profane or secular language that provides a presentiment of the divine Word animating the Christian people. Obviously this assumes that this Word is preached as such: the spoken witness of deeds and the proclaimed Word are two authentic pathways of the one work of evangelization. The service rendered by the People of God in this domain is irreplaceable, because it puts to work the new commandment in all its unlimited scope.

2: As far as Christian institutions are concerned, their outlook is often one of tutelage rather than one of service. Up to now they have been addressed to a consumer-people who were not really evangelized. Now this outlook must give way to an outlook of service to the world. However, I am not against Christian institutions as such. If in a given country they have a role of real service, I see no problem with them. But if in another country they are resented-because they exert tutelage over the people, challenging the liberty and automony of responsible people in secular life, then there is no doubt that they no longer have a place.

3: As for the distinctions between "evangelization" and "apostolate," or direct and indirect evangelization, it seems to me that these distinctions are difficult to accept today. They no longer fit in with today's perspective, where activity in the secular domain on behalf of the world is already taken to be an evangelization. But I repeat: If development is an essential dimension of the revelation of salvation, it clearly supposes the proclaimed Word.

D. GRASSO

The Primacy of Evangelization in Missionary Activity

CHAPTER EIGHT

By the term "evangelization" we mean the proclamation of the gospel to non-Christians with the aim of faith and conversion, and with consequent incorporation into the Church through baptism. It is clearly distinct from pre-evangelization, which embraces the work preparatory to the proclamation of the gospel; it could be considered the goal toward which pre-evangelization tends. The conciliar decree *Ad gentes* (AG) treats it in number 13.

I propose to show here that evangelization thus construed has a primacy in missionary activity, that it represents the missionary's most important activity and conditions all his efforts; in other words, that it is the reality toward which preceding work tends and from which subsequent efforts spring.

Given the short space available, I shall treat this topic in schematic fashion, touching upon its essential points.

CHRIST'S MANDATE

The primary and fundamental reason for the primacy of evangelization in missionary activity is embodied in Christ's mandate to preach the gospel to every creature (Mark 16:16; Matt. 28:16-20). Before he ascended into heaven, he entrusted his mission from the Father to his disciples: "Go out to the whole world; procalim the Good News to all creation. He who believes and is baptized will be saved; he who does not believe will be condemned" (Mark 16:15-16). So that his mandate might be carried out faithfully, Jesus promised his own aid right up to the parousia, when he will come to judge the living and the dead. The only mission of the apostles, and hence of the Church in the world, is this: To preach and baptize, to proclaim the gospel and administer the means of grace. Everything else in its mission flows from this aim in one way or another.

Moreover, this was likewise the mission of Christ, which the Church carries on. He made his debut in public with these words: "The time has come . . . and

104

the kingdom of God is close at hand. Repent, and believe the Good News" (Mark 1:15). When people tried to keep him in one town too long, he resisted their efforts: "I must proclaim the Good News of the Kingdom of God to the other towns too, because this is what I was sent to do" (Luke 4:43). Even in front of Pilate he does not hesitate to affirm that he was sent into the world to bear witness to the truth (John 18:37); it is the truth that he has heard from the Father (John 15:15) and that he makes known to the world—to his disciples in particular.

The whole gospel is subordinated to this proclamation of the truth. The author of the fourth Gospel makes this quite clear. The miracles of Jesus are in the service of his message. Everything serves to help Jesus explain the nature of the kingdom he has come to proclaim to man, of the good news that is the object of his preaching. There is nothing astonishing in this. He is the Incarnate Word. His mission can only consist of proclaiming and making manifest to men the salvation-plan that the Father conceived before the world existed.

IN THE FOOTSTEPS OF THE APOSTLES

The apostles follow Christ's lead completely. Their chief concern is to remain faithful to the mandate they have received. From the very start of their activity, they feel that they are essentially "ministers of the word" (Luke 1:2). When the Holy Spirit descends upon them, they begin to announce Christ; and they continue to do this until death seals their lips.

When the growth of the Church and its internal problems do not allow the apostles to reconcile their preaching with works of charity, they do not hesitate to give up the latter and give preference to the former: "It would not be right for us to neglect the word of God so as to give out food" (Acts 6:2). Deacons will take over such functions while the apostles, faithful to Christ's mandate, will concern themselves with prayer and the ministry of the word (Acts 6:4).

The same holds true for Saint Paul. He is hounded by a knowledge of his obligation to be a preacher of the gospel (1 Cor. 9:16). For him evangelization is not a motive for pride; it is a duty stemming from Christ's mandate. Preparing to set out for Jerusalem, with a presentiment of the death that awaits him there, he is still at peace inside: "I have not hesitated to do anything that would be helpful to you; I have preached to you and instructed you both in public and in your homes, urging both Jews and Greeks to turn to God and to believe in our Lord Jesus" (Acts 20:21-21); so he is prepared to face the risks that await him in the Holy City. When he awaits death in a Roman prison, he is comforted by this thought: "The Lord stood by me and gave me power, so that through me the whole message might be proclaimed for all the pagans to hear" (2 Tim. 4:17).

For Saint Paul, the preaching of the gospel does not just hold first place in his own life. It also holds first place among the Church's ministries and the charismatic gifts that the Spirit confers on the community of the faithful. He says explicitly that Christ did not send him to baptize, but to preach the gospel (1 Cor. 1:17), thus indicating that the ministry of the Word takes primacy over that of the sacraments. He says the same thing with regard to the charismatic gifts. When he enumerates them in First Corinthians (12:8-10), we find the gift of healing and the power to work miracles among them. But he is most desirous of the gift of prophecy, which is specifically tied up with the proclamation of the gospel (1 Cor. 14:1). His reasoning is that the person who prophesies is one who speaks to men and edifies them (v. 4), while the person who speaks with the gift of tongues, preferred by the Corinthians, edifies only those who are gifted with understanding it. It is also interesting to note that the gifts of healing and working miracles are social in nature too; they benefit others and help to build up the community. Yet the Apostle does not give them primacy. This indicates that there is a hierarchy among the social gifts as well. First place goes to prophecy, tied up with the proclamation of the gospel to instill or deepen faith. The gift of faith is the greatest gift that the Spirit can give to the community. Even in terms of earthly recompense, Saint Paul urges that particular attention be paid to those "who are assiduous in preaching and teaching" (1 Tim. 5:17).

EVANGELIZATION AND FAITH

We might well ask ourselves why the New Testament accords primacy to evangelization. Saint Paul himself gives us the answer, basing it on the very nature of evangelization as the vehicle for faith: "So faith comes from what is preached, and what is preached comes from the word of Christ" (Rom. 10:17). If there is to be salvation, he notes, there must be faith; we must invoke the name of God. That is why there must be evangelization. Through it we communicate faith, which is necessary if we are to please God at all (Heb. 11:6). The primacy of evangelization among the ministries of the Church is grounded on the primacy of faith in the supernatural order. Evangelization and faith are on the same level of importance. It is impossible to please God without faith; and faith is impossible without proclamation.

Obviously this does not mean that preaching the gospel is the only pathway to faith. But it is the ordinary pathway, the one established by our Lord Jesus Christ for the spread of his message. Since we know that this message is spreading gradually, we must conclude that there are other pathways known only to God. Through these other pathways he accords faith to those who do their best to live according to their conscience (AG 7).

Despite the existence of these other pathways known only to God, the Church must make every effort to see to it that faith comes to all men through the ordinary pathway established by Jesus Christ. These other pathways also existed in Saint Paul's time, but he still saw his missionary duty as his primary one (1 Cor. 9:16). We can say that this is the very aim of the Church: to proclaim the gospel so that man will be able to make his choice for or against salvation.

GROWTH

But there is more to it. Evangelization has primacy among the Church's ministries because it is the factor behind her convocation and development. Faith is the first step toward justification, which involves incorporation into the Church.

The New Testament presents preaching as a reality that obliges men to take a stand in regard to salvation, to accept or reject it. It establishes a dividing line between those who are called to constitute the society of the saved and those who, by virtue of their bad dispositions, are excluded from it (Mark 4:11-12). According to Saint Paul, the proclamation of Christ by the apostles is a fragrance leading men to life or to death (2 Cor. 2:15-16). It is through the gospel that men are born in Christ (1 Cor. 4:14). It is through preaching the gospel that we develop the divine life conferred on us by baptism. Saint Paul himself affirms the necessity of continually begetting his Christians until Christ is formed in them (Gal. 4:19). This must go on continuously until the full measure of Christ is attained (Eph. 4:13). Thus the Word of God establishes our first contact with Christ in the missionary proclamation of the gospel. It must go on from there to abide in the faithful, so that it may unfold all the richness of Christ.

The Church consequently cannot develop herself or realize her universality without preaching the gospel to every creature (Mark 16:16). Evangelization is the great factor behind the catholicity of the Church, as *Ad gentes* clearly recognized: "Acting out of the innermost requirements of her catholicity and in obedience to her Founder's mandate, the church strives to procalim the gospel to all men" (AG 1).

CONCRETE APPLICATIONS

This doctrine concerning the primacy of evangelization has direct and immediate repercussions on the Church's missionary activity. Right from the start, the specific task of the Church in the world is not temporal, social, or economic in nature, but religious. The gospel, we know, is a leaven designed to transform man's whole life and his relations with God, other Christians, and the world. The Church carries out this leavening work through two fundamental functions instituted by Christ: the hierarchy and the laity. The former carries out this work by preaching the gospel, the latter by bearing witness to its meaning in their own lives. This is the way in which the Church contributes to the progress of peoples. The Church civilizes man by Christianizing him, that is, by proclaiming the gospel and making it the motive force behind man's whole life.

This has great importance for the missions. The participation of the Church in the progress of peoples, in the development of Third World countries, is not an end in itself. When the case calls for it, it strives to work out the preliminary steps leading to evangelization, as *Ad gentes* (AG 11-12) notes. Dialogue and pre-evangelization are in the service of evangelization. This likewise serves to point out the limits of this term, which is so commonly used today but which can be so equivocal in meaning.

Undoubtedly this can create serious difficulties for missionaries when nations see evangelization as an attack on their internal unity or as a spiritual form of colonialism. The danger is there, and it urges us to use prudence; but it cannot deter the Church from her mission. The same accusation was hurled at the Church when it began to expand in the Roman Empire. Celsus accused Christians of being lacking in patriotism and loyalty to the empire. They were not deterred by these accusations; and when it became necessary, they gave up their lives for Christ. That was how the gospel became the real leaven of classical culture, pointing up the authentic values it contained and begetting Western civilization. That is precisely what the gospel is summoned to do for other cultures today. It must transform them from within, eliminating their negative features and developing their positive potential. The proclamation of the gospel does not destroy the pluralism of man's cultures. But it does reconcile them with the unity of the human conscience, which is based on the fact that all men everywhere have a common origin and a common destiny.

Vatican II expressed this idea quite clearly in its missionary decree:

> Missionary activity is closely bound up too with human nature itself and its aspirations. By manifesting Christ, the Church reveals to men the real truth about their condition and their total vocation. For Christ is the source and model of that renewed humanity, penetrated with brotherly love, sincerity, and a peaceful spirit, to which all aspire. Christ and the Church, which bears witness to Him by preaching the gospel, transcend every particularity of race or nation and therefore cannot be considered foreign anywhere or to anybody (AG 8).

Let me add another observation. Evangelization, the proclamation of the gospel, is not just the primary duty of the Church in propagating the kingdom of God; it is also the real contribution which the world expects of her in this era of development and progress. The Western and Westernized world is rife with confrontation and revolt, and it is often global in scope. Today's young people no longer accept the world that their elders built with enormous effort and sacrifice. Our affluent world of consumerism is rejected by young people, not so much because it has failed to bring about social equality, but because it is a world without a real soul.

What is the soul-food that it lacks, without which we cannot be happy despite all the progress achieved already? For us Christians, the answer is clear: the gospel. The modern world has taken shape without paying any attention to the gospel, and now it is suffering the consequences. People's revolt today is, at bottom, a refusal to accept a world in which the spiritual dimension of man is not given its rightful place. We are not concerned here with placing the blame on the right people; we just want to point out how matters stand.

The developing countries of the Third World must avoid this mistake. So our contribution as Christians must be centered around the gospel. In giving them the gospel, we will spare them the harsh experience that we are now going through. And we are the only ones who can give them the gospel. Governments may devise aid plans and lavish capital investments on them; we cannot and should not follow the same tack. The Church's mission is a different one. She is supposed to form men's consciences, to show them the truth of their condition and their overall vocation, as mirrored in Christ their prototype (AG 1 and 8).

So evangelization does have primacy in the missionary activity of the Church: Not only because Christ's mandate impels her to preach the gospel to every creature; not only because this is the only way in which she can achieve her universality; but also because that is what the world expects from her at this critical moment in history.

DISCUSSION

J. M. GONZALEZ-RUIZ   Many questions remain before us after this excellent paper. Is evangelization to be subordinated to development? To the betterment of man? What relationships exist between human betterment and evangelization? Is the gospel only a purely spiritual message? Is evangelization without ties to human, social, political, and cultural realities? Does not evangelization involve a value judgment on all human realities as well?

G. DELCUVE   We would all agree that evangelization has primacy in mission work. But we are still left with the question: What is involved in proclaiming the gospel? Is the gospel really a piece of "good news"? Is it, as Paul suggests, something that offers advantages and a response to contemporary man? Does it accord with his overall vocation? It is not enough to announce the mystery of faith. We must also proclaim its meaning for men of today. It is in this sense that the gospel is the source of man's integral development.

A. SANTOS   Grasso's paper is not so far up in the clouds as some seem to suggest. It simply affirms certain things, without claiming to be exhaustive. Its theme was the primacy of evangelization, not a definition of evangelization. Evangelization is not only kerygmatic preaching but also pastoral work, not only the spoken message but also the message in print and other media and the message embodied in deeds.

A. M. HENRY   For me, the primary thing we must discover is "how" we are to evangelize, not "that" we must evangelize. The latter fact is obvious. Christ spoke out and proclaimed the Good News, but he also acted; he preached in actions. Today we might well ask what we ourselves are doing. What does the "good news to the poor" signify when the major fact and scandal of our time is underdevelopment? What are we to say to peoples who are practically grovelling in the dirt?

T. TSHIBANGU   It seems to me that Grasso's paper answers a basic question being asked by many missionaries: Which is primary, evangelization or aid to development? Have we perhaps given too much emphasis to the latter? Speaking primarily of Africa, I would say that the developing nations need an added dose of soul-food, of God's Word. The important thing is that there be a tieup between our preaching of the Word and our witness in deeds.

H. DE LUBAC   I am in complete agreement. Our efforts at charitable witness should not tempt us to forget the ultimate aim of such work: i.e., the Word of God. The preachers of the gospel are "prophets of meaning" in a world that has sometimes lost sight of its meaning and destiny. The gospel reveals to man the truth about his overall vocation; and this truth holds for all nations and places.

C. G. ARAVELO   It seems to me that no dissociation should be made between the Word of God and development. We need only show how one comes from the other, how one influences the other.

CLARIFICATIONS BY THE AUTHOR

1: Evangelization is not subordinated to human betterment. They are two interrelated dimensions. Man's betterment cannot be envisioned without the development of his religious dimension. It is the gospel that provides us with its meaning, insuring that development is man's betterment rather than his degradation.

2: I am in complete agreement with Delcuve. I was not trying to explicitate what evangelization is; I was simply pointing out that it does have primacy. It is obvious that it must involve proclaiming the Word and bearing witness in deeds, etc.

3: On the other hand, I do not at all agree with Henry when he says that everyone in the Church is convinced about the primacy of evangelization. Obviously if a man is dying of hunger, I am not going to begin by talking about the gospel. I will try to relieve his wretched state. But this notwithstanding, the fact remains that in the work of the Church and her mission, the primary concern should be to proclaim the Word of God.

A. M. FIOLET

Toward A Theology of Development

CHAPTER NINE

The lively course of ongoing history in the Catholic Church received new impetus from Vatican II. Since the Council it has been marked by a deeper cognizance of its own real nature, and this thrust has produced a serious crisis for the missionary vocation in the Church.

For centuries the Church saw herself as a hierarchical institution of salvation which, by virtue of the mandate from Christ, was to be the mediatrix between God and man in a world of sinners. It was to dispense truth and grace to humanity in God's name.

A dualistic conception of the world placed God in heaven and man on earth. It depicted the proclamation of truth and the mediation of grace as the word and action of God descending vertically from heaven to earth, as an import from the outside. Operating from this outlook, the Church proclaimed certain divine immutable truths and precepts, and it administered specific, immutable instruments of salvation. Under the direction of a central government, all this was done in a uniform manner for every country in every age.

This dualistic conception of the world frustrated the missionary vocation of the Church by weighing it down with a false equation. It wrongly identified God's salvific action with the administration of God's word. In reality the latter borrowed concepts and terms from occidental philosophy, and it found expression in a liturgy shaped by occidental culture. For this reason, the gospel of Christ remained an exotic plant for non-Western peoples. It was an alien element superimposed on their conception of the world and their culture. With the sudden and rapid socioeconomic development of the new nations in Africa and Asia, the Western Church felt the keen edge of this frustration; it came to feel that development aid was a discriminatory activity competing against mission work.

During the sessions of Vatican II, the Church once again discovered that she

111

was the People of God on pilgrimage through this world. Theological reflection oriented itself once again around the Old Testament notions of *diaspora* and *paroikia.*

The Covenant: God with Us

Revelation, as God's self-revelation, did not shoot into terrestrial reality from outside like a meteor. Humanity never heard heavenly voices coming from another world. God's word and salvific action were not forced on man as some overweening force. Man did not experience divine revelation as a natural force to which one must bow in discomfort. He never met up with God.

Israel encountered Yahweh for the first time when national feeling sprang to life during its oppression in Egypt. In the shock produced by the miraculous exodus from mighty Egypt, these slaves without rights learned to experience the presence of Yahweh through the explanations and tutelage of the prophets. God turned natural forces and the nations into his shock troops, using them to turn his covenant into a reality. He was a cosmic sovereign operating on behalf of his people. In this unexpected turn of events, Israel discovered that she was a chosen people; she lived this election as a covenant that God was going to accomplish in her life as a nation from that moment on. Israel's questioning study of her own ongoing history feeds a faith in God that becomes ever richer and more complete.

In Israel—the chosen people who will serve to bring blessings on all the nations of the earth (Gen. 12:3)—men learned to know God because they experienced his presence through concrete human situations and historical events. Slowly and gently God, once unknown, joined up with mankind on the road, just as he did with the wayfarers to Emmaus. At the start his presence was unnoticed, for he seemed to be completely caught up in their conversation. Little by little, and ever more clearly, he gives orientation to the conversation (Abraham's vocation) and points it in a definitive direction (the Exodus). It was in Israel that this recognition was first celebrated, as humanity came to know God in the signs he worked in its real life. Often murky and constantly deformed, human history gradually became salvation history, that is, the history of God's arrival and salvific indwelling *in* human history. A long road lay ahead for humanity before the Son of God would dwell with us as a brother in this world, teaching mankind to discover and live the total dimensions of God's salvific action throughout his creation.

It is by reflecting on this destiny—that is, on the covenant and on Christ as its fulfillment—that the believer grasps the meaning of his existence and the orientation of his history. Through the man Jesus, Emmanuel or God-with-us, he becomes aware that his existence is a salvation reality, a life in communion with his Father.

Thus the unique feature of Israel's faith is its experiential knowledge that the God who forms a covenant with his people is, at the same time, the God of all creation and all peoples. Each individual and all peoples exist because God wills to incarnate his covenant within them.

God's salvific activity embraces all terrestrial reality and all human history. That is why terrestrial reality and human history form the locale of an encounter with God. Is it not evident that he summons creation to existence unceasingly? The initiative comes from Yahweh always and exclusively. For man exists only through the grace of his love, which invites him to give a response in his own life.

With this prophetic interpretation of her life as a nation and of her history as a covenant that Yahweh formed with his whole creation, Israel professed that the transcendent, salvific activity of Yahweh is *immanent to the world and universal.*

YAHWEH'S TRANSCENDENT PRESENCE

The ever-present importance of the Old Testament is that Israel, surrounded on every side by animist and pantheistic beliefs, professed her belief in the absolute transcendence of a Yahweh who was actively present everywhere. It is he who summons his whole creation to existence; it is he who makes it active. He is so far beyond man's limits, so much the wholly Other that man, enslaved in the power of sin, finds himself stripped naked before him; he can do nothing but offer him feeble, inadequate responses or resistance. Indeed it is through the sinful infidelities of his nation that the believing Israelite, turned back into himself, lives the experience of divine transcendence with deep intensity. God for him becomes a consuming fire (Heb. 12:29).

But the religious outlook in Israel never lived the absolute transcendence of Yahweh as a theophany of the absolute and supreme being coming from another world. It experienced the immanent presence of Yahweh acting in this world. Israel knew of no separation between soul and body, heaven and earth, the natural and the supernatural. Thus it could not be tempted to seek communion with God in mortification of the senses or in escape from terrestrial realities. Its faith was situated entirely within the boundaries of terrestrial realities. The Hebrew lived God's presence and his intimacy with Yahweh in the varied events of everyday life, in the unexpected turns of his nation's life, in the overwhelming sorrow of the exile and the unexpected joy of repatriation. His faith did not diminish his concrete responsibility with regard to his social milieu or his contacts with fellow Israelites.

This faith was not nurtured by abstract truths, but by the material benefits of salvation that had to be fought for in the vicissitudes of human life. They were, at the same time, signs of Yahweh's compassionate presence. Israel's faith made it live out its total commitment to the nation's prosperity as a messianic promise, and its clan solidarity as a concrete expression of Yahweh's love (Lev. 26:3-13). For this reason, the interpretation of God's revelation to Moses ("I am who I am": Ex. 3:14) as a revelation of the transcendent *"esse a se"* is a Greek perversion of the biblical salvation message. For it really is talking about the total though veiled immanence of Yahweh's transcendent existence. The point of the biblical testimony is that Israel will learn to know Yahweh only through its faith-inspired interpretation of its own existence and history. In this way, and only in this way, will Israel come to know the loving nearness of Yahweh, his protecting presence, as communion with God, as covenant. Yahweh's reply to Moses means this: If you want to know who I am, look at what I will do with this people. For this reason, Israel lived its existence as a "passover," as Yahweh's act of passing over the blood-sprinkled doorposts of the Israelites in Egypt (Ex. 12). "To exist," for Yahweh, is "to exist in communion with" his people.

For this reason Israel was never taken up with the speculative question of God's existence. Yahweh and Israel's existence as a nation form one reality (see Isaiah 45:14-18). God's grace was not given to a people already existing; the very existence of this people is grace. Human existence has religious dimensions. The Old Testament knows no distinction between nature and grace. Israel exists *because* Yahweh bestows his grace on it. And it is precisely this national consciousness that is the permanent basis of Israel's continuity and the source of its national and social prosperity. When Israel forgets God, her enemies gain the upper hand and the harvest goes up in smoke (Joel 1:10; 2:27). Freed from all the theophanies, from all the divine forces that intervene from without, Israel divested nature of its myths, desacralized history, and made human society profane; for in themselves these terrestrial realities are the immanent revelation of the transcendent God. Israel's faith is the fruit of the concrete events that go to make up her history. It is not a divine message dropping straight down vertically from heaven.

The figure of the expected Messiah is modified continually as Israel's social structures evolve: king, prophet, servant of Yahweh, son of man. Israel's ethics derived from its concrete condition: a nomadic people in the process of becoming a sedentary people. Israel did not receive revelation as some voice pronouncing truths and precepts; instead it did so by conceiving the whole of created reality as the work of Yahweh, who carries out the covenant in history.

ISRAEL'S VOCATION

This prophetic interpretation taught Israel to see its own real-life experience as God's salvific activity, and its own history as salvation history. But it also taught Israel to see that Yahweh was not a national God whose salvific activity was limited to them. God is the creator of heaven and earth, the Lord of all peoples and nations. He works out his salvific design in Israel in order to reveal to all nations that their existence has a covenant dimension. It was primarily through her sinful infidelity, which inevitably led to the exile, that Israel was forced to learn from experience that Yahweh was not linking his salvific action to Israel's national grandeur in the mere fact of election; this covenant embraced every terrestrial reality and all human history. It did not involve the nation of Israel, but the authentic Israel: that is, the community of true believers who live out the sacramentality of terrestrial reality by interpreting their existence as communion with God (*cf.* 1 Kings 8:41-43: the prayer of Solomon at the inauguration of the temple; Isaiah 45:1-25: the vocation of Cyrus). The election of Israel involves gathering this people of God from among all the nations. This election is not a personal privilege that can exert a monopoly over God's salvific activity; it is a total openness to accepting salvation for the benefit of others.

SALVATION THROUGH ISRAEL

By virtue of her vocation, which is to spotlight God's universal salvific activity in the midst of all the nations, Israel knows she is not a citizen who establishes permanent residence in this world. But neither is she an alien (*xenos*) lost in this world, even though she is en route to a different world. Israel is a nation composed of people from outside (*katoikos*); she has a task and a mission designed to benefit all the nations. For by virtue of their vocation, these people know that Yahweh, through the covenant made with his chosen people, intervenes continually and decisively in the history of the nations among which they live.

Wherever they live, they live with the unshakable religious conviction that the history of their people is ultimately the salvation history that Yahweh is carrying out with the nations; and they live with this conviction even when the destruction of their existence as a nation is imminent. Their sojourn in Egypt and their entrance into the promised land, their exile in Babylonia and their return to Palestine: all these events must be framed within the same religious perspective. Israel is the chosen people *in* which and *through* which God is already setting up his future kingdom in the world. And it is precisely as "outsiders" that they are to remain ever open to the salvation plan that God is already working out among the nations (1 Chron. 29:10-19; Ps. 37:13; Heb. 11:9-13; Romans 4:20-24).

In the diaspora, Israel lived with an awareness of her apostolic vocation: "For if he has scattered you among the nations, there too he has shown you his greatness. Extol him before all the living . . . our Master . . . God for ever and ever" (Tob. 13:3-4).

In its proselytism, Israel was supposed to bear witness to God's universal salvific action among other nations. In its status as a dispersed people, it was supposed to be a missionary community of believers. But when this missionary élan during the diaspora led many proselytes to convert to the Israelite religion, the Israelites forgot their vocation. They succumbed to temptation and terminated their fundamental mission to other nations, keeping the grace of election for themselves. Their proselytism degenerated into an imperialist outlook as they tried to incorporate all the nations into Israel. Due to this sectarianism, they were no longer working in the service of God's universal salvific activity.

God with Us through Jesus Christ

By ushering in the notion of God's transcendence, Aristotelian and Platonic dualism made the Christian forget his roots in the Old Testament. Greek thought is dominated by the dualism existing between divine realities and human realities; God is in heaven and man is on earth. This philosophy provoked an opposition between matter and spirit. And, in Christian terms, it provoked an opposition between the natural and the supernatural, between human liberty and grace, and between general and special revelation.

In the present-day process of secularization, the Christian is becoming more and more aware that his life and thinking are victimized by this dualistic conception of reality. He finds himself less and less able to believe that there is an opposition between God's world and man's world. He cannot live his life over against God, over against an unfamiliar supernatural world, over against unsuitable truths and precepts that come from this supernatural world, over against an authority that comes from without. He cannot continue to live in two worlds, where God constantly threatens his human authenticity and fetters his personal responsibility.

By opposing man to God and isolating God from man, this conception has turned man into a rebel who longs to free the world in which he lives from God's paternalism. If a church no longer sees itself as being in the world, if it sets itself up in opposition to this world by presenting a message that is incompatible with real life, then it creates a situation whereby Christianity and man's vocation to make the world a true home for all men must move ever further and further apart. There we have the most deep-rooted cause of the present-day atheistic process of secularization.

Modern man no longer bothers to pray to a God who stands in opposition to this world. For such a God he cannot bring himself to die to the things of the world in order to win some nonterrestrial heaven. If the Christian message of salvation does not say clearly that redemption through Christ has to do with the salvation of *this present world* and with *man's concrete, physical existence*, then the Church is not longer a fit dwelling place for modern man. By that very fact, terrestrial reality as a whole is neglected as if it were the milieu of the atheist. But God loved the world so much that he gave his only son (John 3:16); so Christians have an obligation to testify, through their way of life in this world, that its redemption has been accomplished in an exemplary way through the person of Jesus Christ. They cannot proclaim a redemption that inspires them to abandon this world or to regard this life as an abomination.

Reflecting on the faith of Israel, today's Christian is beginning to rediscover terrestrial reality *as a covenant* that God fashions continually with his creation; and he is also beginning to draw the practical consequences from this rediscovery. He knows that he should not picture God's transcendence in some outer space, for God reveals himself solely within the limits of terrestrial reality. He can do nothing with a revelation made up of truths, commandments, and graces coming from some "beyond." He has never heard any heavenly voice explaining the realities of faith to him. The course to follow has always been the same: he must engage in the difficult task of questioning his own existence. He has never met God face-to-face. God has never given him any precepts other than those he could discover in carrying out his daily work as a human being or in dealing with the other human beings that make up his social milieu. He can no longer picture grace as aid coming from the beyond to take the place of his own personal effort. He knows that Scripture should never be separated from salvation history as the source of God's immediate word. God is the author of Scripture because he is the author of salvation history. Scripture is the faith-based vision of writers who were inspired by the presence of a God at work in history; this God revealed himself working for the benefit of all nations in Israel, his chosen people, and he revealed himself fully in the man Jesus. For this reason Scripture, as the faith-inspired interpretation of Israel's history and Christ's life, is the definitive norm for comprehending terrestrial reality and human history with the eye of faith.

Faced with the vital questions posed to him by the non-Christian and the post-Christian, the Christian himself can no longer accept the older notion of a God who speaks and acts from outside and then breaks into his creation. Such a message will not convince any nonbeliever. The Christian must proclaim the "death" of this extraterrestrial God, for he cannot make room for such a God without damaging his own personality.

For the Christian of today, the possibility of communion with God and the determination of his moral obligations do not operate beyond and above the limits of concrete terrestrial reality. For him revelation has another meaning. It means starting with Scripture as the normative testimony of God, who effects salvation through the people of Israel and the human life of Christ. It means going on to discover thereby the concrete obligations and responsibilities of his personal existence, and to interpret world history as *salvation history*. He seeks to conceive the obligations of his technical, economic, social, cultural, and political activity as so many elements that go to make up communion with God. He seeks to explore the ultimate depths of a life lived in communion with other human beings, his brothers, and to live this life in its totality as communion with God. It is here, and here alone, that the transcendent God reveals himself to him, that he learns what God demands of him and receives "the power" (John 1:12) to reply to the divine summons in his life.

This conception sees divine revelation as the faith-based interpretation of the salvation happening, and the latter is our day-to-day life lived on the basis of God's word. Such a conception turns the Christian way of life into a dedicated, never fully finished task.

To begin with, the Christian knows that human nature is prone to evil; he also knows that in man's personal life and in society, sin obscures terrestrial reality as the place of an encounter with God. The painful experience of sin destroys any and every utopia based on simplistic humanism or superficial evolutionism. The happenings of each day remain the battlefield where man struggles to find God. He knows he cannot readily distill God's salvific activity from the events of human history and the realities of this world; he will discover it only painfully over a long period of time.

Secondly, the Christian realizes that his faith-based interpretation of terrestrial realities as salvation happenings is always determined historically by the contemporary conception of man and the world. And now that our conception of the world is undergoing profound modification once again, he knows he is summoned to reformulate what he believes and professes both for himself and for others. And even if these attempts at renewal undermine many certitudes that seemed to shelter him from danger before, he is not panicked by the murkiness around him. For he continues to find solid support in this certainty: God wills that he exist and that the world around him exist, so that he may communicate with man in a covenant. The fragility of "unshakable" certitudes does not frighten him because he is dealing with the *human way of conceiving* and formulating God's constant salvific activity in creation.

It is easy to keep one's distance from the contemporary attempt at renewal in matters of faith. One may dub it as a humanism that is closed in upon itself, that chases God from his creation in order to give man the central place. But in so doing, one strikes at the very core of the Christian salvation-message. For this message proclaims that God himself gave man the center stage in creation; he gave it to *the man Jesus.*

This outlook considers revelation as the climactic event of terrestrial salvation. It rightly finds its inspiration in a new, higher evaluation of the salvific import to be found in the mystery of the Incarnation. In Jesus, in this man who is the son of the Father, it was revealed to us that there is an ultimate reality involved in our communal life with other men, and in our efforts on the technological, social, cultural, and political levels to make the world truly habitable for all. That ultimate reality is an encounter with the Father through the power of *his Son's redemptive, fraternal humanity.* In living our human existence, subject to the power of the evil one, did he not live it as communion with his Father? His grace does not free us from our "being-in-the-world." It frees us so that we may be truly human men. In Christ, who is the Word of God made man (John 1:1-3), the word of God that signifies and effects salvation is pronounced over our human existence and over all terrestrial values; and this began with the prophetic interpretation of human history in the Old Testament.

Adopting this perspective, we might well read once again the Christological hymns to creation that are to be found in Colossians (Col. 1:15-20), Ephesians (Eph. 1:3-14), and the prologue of John's Gospel (John 1:1-18). If we do, we will note in them the cosmic pro-existence of the man Jesus, and his humanity in the service of all. Wherever human existence is truly a "being-in the-world," wherever human values are truly lived out, there is manifested the mystery of God's "being-in-the-world." "They are the ones he chose specially long ago and intended to become true images of his Son, so that his Son might be the eldest among many brothers" (Romans 8:29).

Christ is the firstborn of all creation. Responding to the summons of his Father in his life as a human being, he became the firstborn of all the dead (Col. 1:15-18). Through his obedient "being-in-the-world" (Phil. 2:6-11), he gave men the power to become children of God (John 1:12). The whole of creation and human history is the scene where the divine plan is played out: "to bring everything together under Christ as head, everything in the heavens and everything on earth" (Eph. 1:10). Through Christ's passion and resurrection, his "being-in-the-world" became an offering of human values for all men: peace, justice, brotherly love, and communion. In this *shalom,* the kingdom of God was established henceforth in this world. Now we can glimpse what our human community can and should become in him: the new earth.

God's Salvific Will and the Church's Missionary Vocation

On the basis of this same outlook, I should like to draw some conclusions about God's cosmic salvific action insofar as it relates to the missionary vocation of the Church.

1. God's salvific activity embraces the whole inhabited earth (the *oikumene*) and all of human history. For to be a human being means to be called to the covenant. Human existence *is* grace. Mission work cannot claim that it is supposed to bring the grace of Christ to nations as a value superimposed on the intrinsic value of being a human being.

2. The Church, as a salvation institution that lives on a mandate received from the Lord, should not identify itself with the kingdom of God. Why? Not only because it too awaits the eschatological consummation of the kingdom but also, and even more so, because this kingdom is already being fashioned in this world wherever man is trying to live a truly human existence. Missionary activity must be keenly aware of the salvific awareness among all peoples.

3. The Roman Catholic Church should not identify itself exclusively with the Church of Christ, excluding or ruling out other Christian communities. Christ is the head of the body, which is the Church (Col. 1:18). Even though Christians are divided from each other, the Church of Christ is one; they cannot annul this unity.

For this reason, all the Christian communities who seek to be faithful to Christ are the Church of Christ in one way or another, even though they may be so differently in certain respects. Division has impoverished all the churches. They live out different aspects and values of God's revelation in Christ, to the exclusion of others. Now that Vatican II is over, the Roman Catholic Church knows that, as a result of this sinful division, it is not the Church of Jesus in all its plenitude; that it needs the other churches to become so. Catholic mission work would be a watered-down salvific instrument of the Lord, if it administered the word of God and the sacraments as if it alone were the Church.

In carrying out their missionary mandate, the divided churches of the West should realize that the useless introduction of historical disputes into situations where they are inappropriate jeopardizes this task. In their missionary activities, these churches should use all means possible to bolster the real unity of local Christian communities. This means that the churches should cooperate with each other as much as possible from now on, despite everything that divides them.

4. In the New Testament, the Church is conceived primarily as a local church. Based on the word of God, it seeks to live out the societal life of the people among whom it dwells as a salvation-happening, in which God effects his redeeming presence through Christ. Making use of the ethnological, cultural, and social forms proper to these people, the Church attempted to give a contemporary, native response to God's salvific activity.

The Church is a community of faith in dialogue. It does not open its doors solely to the charismatic and prophetic gifts of all its own members; with respect it approaches Christians of other denominations and non-Christians, their way of life and their way of thinking, as well as the religious and philosophical conceptions that guide them. Through this dialogue with other Christians and the non-Christians in its society, the local church deepens its own understanding of the faith and creates the auspicious situation for carrying out its evangelical mission.

5. Mission work is the service that one local church renders to another local church so that it can be the sign and instrument of God's salvific action in its own area. Its service of assistance should respect the primary responsibility of the local church which needs this assistance. The task of the missionary cannot be to wander from one end of a new nation to another, proffering a monologue made up of truths and precepts. The missionary must realize that his culture is different, that his conception of man is different, and that he cannot therefore import his Western interpretation of God's word into the native culture as some alien element.

The assistance he gives to the local church is a service he renders to the nascent nation. Starting with the Word of God, it should lead these nations to comprehend their specific situation in its ethnological, social, economic, and political context. The service of the missionary, then, should lead first and foremost to the formation of a corps of native preachers and leaders. These native people, endowed with prophetic sensitivity to God's salvific activity in their own concrete situation, will try to find out how their own people can give a truly indigenous response to God's salvific activity.

6. In this general framework it becomes obvious that mission work and development aid have one and the same roots: i.e., the evangelical message of God's kingdom in the process of becoming. They are not two realities in

competition with each other. Together they are designed to serve the new nations which are seeking to improve themselves.

If mission work is not accompanied by development work, or if it ignores the latter, then it deprives the nascent nations of the possibility of fashioning their own cultural and social institutions in which they might formulate their own indigenous and contemporary response to God's saving activity. The local church that asks for assistance must beware of the heterogeneous elements introduced by the assisting local church; in like manner, the assisting church should help the young church to examine things critically on the basis of God's word, and to beware of the neocolonial aspirations and political abuses woven into aid to developing countries. The local Christian community should be the first to express its unfavorable reactions when the assistance threatens to degenerate into an attack on the dignity of the individual or the rights of certain groups.

7. Now suppose that the local church wants to be sure that its search for a sound updated response is inspired by the spirit of Christ and not by a factionalist national sentiment. Then it should verify its own response as authentic and legitimate by comparing it with the interpretation of God's word in the universal Church, by which I mean here, the community of all the local churches together. In Galatians, Saint Paul attests to the importance of this duty. He explains that his preaching of the gospel in the local churches is verified by the church of Jerusalem: "They recognized that I had been commissioned to preach. . . . So Cephas and John, these leaders, these pillars, shook hands with Barnabas and me as a sign of partnership" (Gal. 2:8-9). Every local church needs this sign of partnership extended to it by the universal Church as a sign of communion, if it is to be able to function fully as an instrument of God's salvific activity among its people. The assistance of the missionary Church should initiate a constant dialogue between the indigenous churches and the universal Church. The Roman Pontiff is the center who authenticates and legitimizes this dialogue, which in turn enriches and serves as a corrective within the bosom of the universal Church.

DISCUSSION

H. DE LUBAC   The underlying historical affirmations in this article seem to me to be false or arbitrary; in particular, the opposition set up between the history of Israel and Aristotelian-Platonic dualism, with an almost total neglect of the New Testament. It is not true that in the past the Church was wholly inspired by the dualism that is caricatured here. We have always spoken of God as being simultaneously transcendent and present in the world. Since Christ, the

Church has always prayed the same Our Father: "Your will be done on earth as it is in heaven." and the Church has always fought against dualist heresies. Obviously there have been excesses, but they were never accepted as doctrines of the Church. I refer, by way of example, to the outlook which saw Christian ascesis as an escape from the world.

J. DANIÉLOU   I am disturbed by Fiolet's statements. It seems that everything has been reduced to man's betterment in history. What is the specific nature and import of Christ's salvific activity and the Church's mission in the betterment of man? And I should like to pinpoint a fundamental ambiguity in this paper. Is it a matter of total secularization, in which·God would be the immanent motive force behind the world in its process of development? Or is it a matter of a process of humanization that would be a participation in God's transcendent life? The question is most important.

I. DE LA POTTERIE   I must echo the feeling of malaise engendered by this paper. 1. Fiolet stresses the dualism of Greek thought as the source of all evil, not just in this paper but in a book of his recently published in Dutch. I would echo the questions posed to him by a Protestant minister in the book's preface. Is it true that the dualism is essentially and exclusively Greek? Does the gospel message not have a vertical impact on human existence? If it does, then is it not dualistic in relation to this existence?

2. Insofar as immanent revelation is concerned, it seems to me that it is untenable to assert that God revealed himself solely through Israel's reflection on its earthly history. For then one denies the biblical experience of theophanies that brought benefits to the people of God. By contrast, the experiences of the prophets (their summons and vocation), Christ, and Paul point to their personal encounter with the transcendent God. Christianity is precisely the synthesis of verticalism and horizontalism in the person of Christ, the God-Man.

3. Finally, with regard to the total salvation of man, it is obviously directed at man in his earthly reality. But if it is truly total, then it winds up in the beyond. Otherwise it would make no sense.

J. M. SETIEN   I should like to make a few remarks on the conclusions of the paper. In the first, the author affirms that human existence is a grace. What does this statement mean? What depth would there be to human existence in communion with God's salvific activity, outside of communion with Christ's death and resurrection? It is certainly true that grace is everywhere. It is true that man's existence in history *has* grace. *But it is not already grace.* Conclusion 5 states: "Mission work is the service that one local church renders to another local church so that it can be the sign and instrument of God's salvific action in its own area." But how do we define the instrumentality of one local church toward another local church in this respect (i.e., as an instrument of God's salvific action)? Conclusion 7 also requires clarification. What exactly is the part and role of the pope, as the center of the Catholic Church, in the exchange between churches which are not even Catholic.

D. GRASSO   I should like to know what this paper contributes to missionary activity. Would it not be better not to evangelize peoples that are naturally religious? It seems to me that we must, on the contrary, stress the extraterrestrial aspect of man's salvation, the vertical dimension of this salvation.

D. S. AMALORPAVADASS   The approach involving terrestrial values is very important. In Asia, the transcendent aspect is clear; but one must stress the terrestrial aspect in order to arrive at a balanced synthesis. That is why Fiolet's paper seems very topical to me.

A. SEUMOIS   The paper is not clear. In the last analysis, it does not touch upon the question alluded to in the title: "Theology of development." Moreover, one cannot start with the Old Testament to work up a theology of development that is valid in the economy of the New Testament. One must start with the mission entrusted by Christ to his Church. Personally, I find it impossible to approve such a paper. [Seumois insisted that his opposition to this paper be recorded officially.]

CLARIFICATIONS BY FIOLET

There is not enough time for me to reply to all the questions brought up. So I shall concentrate on one. The chief problem that I pose in my paper is not primarily a theological one. I should like to stress that we are dealing with a religious crisis faced by many Christians today. Their question is: How can I find God? How does God come into the world and into my life? Has God spoken to man directly, or has he spoken through other men in a human way, particularly through Israel and Jesus Christ?

Behind these questions lies a particular outlook: the concept of God's transcendence. First of all, we must affirm that every Christian accepts God's transcendence by faith. But today many Christians are trying to free themselves from a very specific conception of God's transcendence, which holds that God is in heaven and man is on earth. In short, they are trying to free themselves from every sort of dualism. But even if they reject dualism, they do not deny the duality of their human existence. Every human being is created in the image of God; or, as Saint Paul puts it, "after Jesus Christ, the image of God, according to which all men have been created." Within our sinful human existence he lived, for us and in our place, his existence as the Son of God; and he gave all men the power to be sons of God.

Thus we should rethink the dogma of Chalcedon. At Chalcedon the Church declared that in Christ there was one person and two natures: a human nature and a divine nature. But the Church said nothing about the relationship between the human nature and the divine nature. We must ask ourselves whether we may not have unconsciously introduced a certain dualism between these two realities in Christ: his existence as man and his existence as God. If we have, then Christ becomes a dual person, living separately in his Father's world and in our human world.

The main purpose of my paper was to rediscover the meaning of the New Testament gospel by first trying to understand the message of the Old Testament in itself. This is a very important task if we are to carry out the Church's missionary task among non-Western nations. And I am very pleased that Amalorpavadass agrees with me on the usefulness of this exploration.

ARNULF CAMPS

Missionary Activity and Borrowed Structures

CHAPTER TEN

The development of the Church's missionary activity has been conditioned by diverse historical circumstances. Mission work has ever operated to set up some sort of relationship between our religion, Christianity, and other religious beliefs. Moreover, Christianity is a religion that has borrowed its external shape, by virtue of its contacts with occidental civilization over the course of two thousand years. Let me just mention a few salient features. The occidental *gestalt* of Christianity includes a clearly defined social organization (territorial division into dioceses and parishes), a specific form for the liturgy (the Latin liturgy of the Roman rite), a distinctive theological system (scholastic theology), and a corresponding organization of the sacerdotal ministry (historically linked with celibacy).

It is through the intermediary of its missionary activity that this occidental *gestalt* of Christianity made contact with nonoccidental cultures and religions. What is more, the way in which this contact took place was conditioned, in large measure, by historical circumstances. In the meantime, Christianity had acquired rather fixed opinions and judgments on other religions and cultures. In general, this contact took place in a colonial context; this made it very difficult for Western missionaries to arrive at a deep understanding of the spiritual and cultural values of other peoples. It also made it difficult to recognize the personal worth of the individuals professing other religions and cultures.

We must also note that this encounter took place in a specific spiritual context. Western Christianity had formed a categorical opinion about salvation, asserting that the latter was possible only within Christianity and that other forms of religious belief, with their whole framework of religious behavior, were riddled with falsehood in that respect.

---

[1]Papers 10, 11, and 12 were discussed at the closing public session. See Appendix, pp. 148ff.

These historical circumstances account for the fact that a specific missionary tactic developed over the course of the past few centuries. The tactic was called adaptation. Many theologians devoted books to the question.[1] A characteristic feature of this conception is indicated in the way the following question is posed: What concessions can the European structure of Christianity make to other cultures and religions? European Christianity, being the norm, was to be safeguarded and kept intact as much as possible. Concessions would be allowed only when confronted with difficulties that seemed insurmountable for non-Christians. In the latter case, the laws of cooperation would have to be taken into account.

To this end, certain distinctions were made between what was essential and what was accidental in Christian doctrine. The essence of Christianity was to be preserved intact, and that essence was considered to be anything insuring the unity of the Church: e.g., the Latin liturgy, scholastic theology, and the social structure of the Church. Concessions were allowed only in accidental matters: e.g., certain devotions, certain types of artistic displays, and modes of dress. A theology and practice of adaptation, based on such principles, could scarcely pose such questions as the following: What place was to be given to other beliefs and cultures in the economy of salvation? Which of their values were to be safeguarded? In short, it was a system of superficial adaptation that dealt only with details.

Then we had a change in the historical context on which this theology and pastoral effort was based. Missionary activity no longer takes place in a colonial context because it must take account of the natural thrust toward positive assertiveness among other religions and cultures. The spiritual context, in turn, underwent a radical development. Westerners could no longer consider other religious beliefs as being totally false pathways in the economy of salvation. We recognized that if non-Christians did have a chance for salvation, then it depended on their social system and religion, for man is eminently a social being *even in religious matters.* Our knowledge and awareness of other religions and cultures has also improved greatly, so that we can no longer hang on to outdated opinions.

Western Christianity itself has evolved in its awareness of its own foundations. No one today considers the Latin liturgy as an integral part of the essence of the Church. On the basis of the reform promoted by Vatican II, the vernacular has been introduced into the liturgy. The Council also opted for a more solid adaptation of liturgy and theology to the wise principles of other religions, whose existence could not be wholly without the seal of divine cooperation. The birth of different theological schools within the occidental Church has also contributed to a relativization of scholastic theology. We see new features in our ecclesiastical structures: episcopal collegiality in communion with the pope; episcopal synods; diocesan and parochial councils; the ever-increasing importance accorded to the role of the laity. These new features will have an impact.

The two partners present in missionary activity, other religions and Christianity, are in a process of evolution. Then we also have nonoccidental Christians living within the framework of a Westernized Church in Asia, Africa, and Latin America; they are no longer satisfied with the present situation, and they are tending to assume a leadership role that is more and more pronounced within the universal Church.

Thus the theology and tactic of adaptation, peculiar to an epoch now gone by, no longer fits the real-life situation of the Church. In the light of these new problems, it is not surprising that some theologians and missionaries are looking for new solutions. One group talks about non-Christian religions as being anonymous forms of Christianity.[2] Another group sees them as signs and precursors of Christianity itself.[3] Still another group regards Christianity as the *locum tenens* for other religions.[4] All agree in affirming that other religions have a positive place in the economy of salvation. Salvation is possible for non-Christians within their own religion insofar as a real encounter with Christianity has not taken place.

The encounter between Christianity and other religions is viewed as an episode in the general economy of salvation, and it must be carried out in a spirit of dialogue. Dialogue indeed is the new form or feature of missionary practice, as opposed to the old system of adaptation. The two interlocutors should have an open mind and heart. They should be prepared to discover what the God of universal history has effected in the ensemble of humanity's nations, races, and religions. That is what Vatican II stipulated in the Declaration on the Relationship of the Church to Non-Christian Religions (N.AE.). As the Council suggests, this dialogue should seek to bring out everything that truly derives from God, regarding it as an enrichment of the whole thrust of the salvation economy.

So there we have a new way of approaching the question, a way that can give rise to new structures within the non-Western churches. No longer can we engage in a superficial adaptation of the accidental elements of Western Christianity to non-Western religions. Under a new form of Christianity, we must re-create everything that is positive in other religions. Missionary activity will no longer be the bearer of borrowed structures. Instead it will stimulate the full flowering of the Church, and it will no longer be an exotic plant in the cultural and religious milieu of other beliefs.

Some practical conclusions force themselves on us. First of all, missionaries must devote particular attention to the period of pre-evangelization. We have reached a stage in missionary activity where we are trying to discover other religions for the sake of a new and better religious future. This means that there must be in-depth study of other peoples' language, culture, and religion, so that we may uncover the genesis of world salvation history in these religions and cultures. We must explore it with a positive attitude, and in such a way that other peoples can be induced to pursue the present-day history of salvation in accordance with God's will and the expression it takes in Christianity. We must reveal to non-Christian peoples the dynamism of the salvation economy, without neglecting the richness of their own religion.

Secondly, bishops' conferences within the boundaries of the various major sociocultural realms should agree to set up a more deep-rooted program of adaptation, in accordance with the wishes of Vatican II: "Thus it will be more clearly seen in what ways faith can seek for understanding in the philosophy and wisdom of these peoples. A better view will be gained of how their customs, outlook on life, and social order can be reconciled with the manner of living taught by revelation. As a result, avenues will be opened for a more profound adaptation in the whole area of Christian life" (AG 22). This program cannot be carried out without help from a pastoral research center in each sociocultural region. We must encourage the creation of such centers, and entrust them to competent personnel.

Thirdly, with the assistance of the bishops' conferences and the regional research centers, bishops should display a lively interest in initiating experiments for the sake of better adaptation. In the passage cited above, Vatican II expresses its support of greater adaptation in every area of Christian living. Far from remaining a dead letter, this problem should be given serious attention. We should, as quickly as possible, undertake studies in the realms of liturgy, theology, and new church structures. Experimentation is the only way, since we cannot determine the final goal in advance. These experiments should deal with more thoroughgoing adaptation with regard to the formation of liturgical ministers and the norms of life to be followed by them (the celibacy question). To repeat once more, the norm should not be equated with the tradition and history of the occidental Church. It should be identified with the Christian life adapted to the special genius and character of each culture.

These experiments will show us the road to follow. But it is also true that they must be conducted under the direction of bishops' conferences and regional pastoral centers.

NOTES

1. See, for example, J. Thauren, S.V.D., *Die Akkomodation im Katholischen Heidenapostolat* (Munster, 1927); O. Dominguez, O.M.I., "Theologia adaptationis et praxis missionaria," in *Scientia Missionnum Ancilla* (Nijmegen-Utrecht, 1953); T. Ohm, O.S.B., *Machet zur Jüngern alle Völker* (Fribourg i. Br., 1962).
2. See, for example, K. Rahner, S. J., "Das Christentum und die nicht-christliche Religionen, " *Schriften zur Theologie* V (Einsiedeln, 1962).
3. See, for example, P. Schoonenberg, S. J., *God's World in the Making* (Pittsburgh, 1964).
4. See, for example, R. Schlette, *Die Religionen als Thema der Theologie* (Fribourg i. Br., 1963).

T. TSHIBANGO

The Mission and Responsibility
of Newly Formed Churches

CHAPTER ELEVEN

In very clear terms, Vatican II set forth the essential tasks that are incumbent today on the young churches that have been fashioned by missionary activities in the modern age. The recommendations and instructions of the Council are set forth in three documents in particular: *Lumen gentium* (LG), *Ad gentes* (AG), and *Nostra Aetate* (N.AE.).

In these recommendations and instructions we pick up two facets: (1) the general declarations of the Church, expressed as early as *Lumen gentium,* on the nature of "local churches" within Catholicism, and the young churches fashioned by missionary efforts as one form of these local churches; (2) three aspects of the tasks and responsibilities that are incumbent on these young churches today.

These three aspects can be set forth as follows: (1) the members of these young churches have a duty to participate in the general missionary work of the universal Church; (2) these churches have a duty to contribute to the institutional and disciplinary organization of the universal Church; (3) these churches have a duty to make a doctrinal contribution as they grow to spiritual and ecclesiastical maturity.

In this article, I shall first try to determine exactly what the Church demands. Then I shall examine concretely the role and tasks that the young churches are asked to carry out today. Finally, I shall simply indicate the indispensable ways and conditions for the young churches to carry out their mission successfully.

The Church's Recommendations and Demands

Before determining the tasks specific to newly formed churches within the universal Church, we must consider a very clear and precise passage in *Lumen*

For discussion of this paper, see Appendix, p. 163.

gentium. It talks about the universality or catholicity of the one People of God, which should be made real within the diversity of individuals and nations, in accordance with the historical and sociocultural conditions specific to them.

The passage first speaks about the communion of all the faithful, dispersed throughout the world, in the one People of God:

> Among all the nations of earth there is but one People of God, which takes its citizens from every race, making them citizens of a kingdom which is of a heavenly and not an earthly nature. For all the faithful scattered throughout the world are in communion with each other in the Holy Spirit, so that "he who occupies the See of Rome knows the people of India are his members" (LG 13).

Between the different members we should find a mutual exchange of gifts and services:

> In virtue of this catholicity each individual part of the Church contributes through its special gifts to the good of the other parts and of the whole Church. Thus through the common sharing of gifts and through the common effort to attain fullness in unity, the whole and each of the parts receive increase. Not only, then, is the People of God made up of different peoples but even in its inner structure it is composed of various ranks. This diversity among its members arises either by reason of their duties, as is the case with those who exercise the sacred ministry for the good of their brethren, or by reason of their situation and way of life, as is the case with those many who inter the religious state and, tending toward holiness by a narrower path, stimulate their brethren by their example (LG13).

Then comes the passage that justifies the diversity of the different parties in the Church:

> Moreover, within the Church particular Churches hold a rightful place. These Churches retain their own traditions without in any way lessening the primacy of the Chair of Peter. This Chair presides over the whole assembly of charity and protects legitimate differences, while at the same time it sees that such differences do not hinder unity but rather contribute toward it. Finally, between all the parts of the Church there remains a bond of close communication with respect to spiritual riches, apostolic workers, and temporal resources. For the members of the Church are called to share these goods, and to each of the Churches these words of the Apostle apply: "According to the gift that each has received, administer it to one another as good stewards of the manifold grace of God" (1 Peter 4:10; LG 13).

Gustave Thils[1] makes a very apt statement apropos of this passage: "In her structure and daily life, the Church should sincerely and concretely embody legitimate diversity and variety of every sort, out of respect for the Spirit and the manifold variety of his gifts. There are diverse spiritualities and rites, diverse languages and institutions, diverse doctrinal categories and philosophical systems. But this wondrous diversity would end up in chaos if it were not cemented by the essential identity of the Spirit, the faith, and the fundamental ecclesial structure."

NEWLY FORMED CHURCHES

Ad gentes explicitly discusses the missionary spirit in the Church, and the present situation and future prospects of newly formed churches. When we examine this document, we find that the Council took pains to stress its first and most fundamental recommendation to missionaries. That recommendation is the formation of authentic Christian communities in mission lands. The missionary's whole effort should be to strive to set up Christian communities that are solidly implanted and organized in the mission lands and that are provided with all the spiritual and material resources necessary for growth and development:

> Let missionaries as God's co-workers (cf. 1 Cor. 3:9), raise up congregations of the faithful who will walk in a manner worthy of the vocation to which they have been called (cf. Eph. 4:1), and will exercise the priestly, prophetic, and royal office which God has entrusted to them. In this way the Christian community becomes the sign of God's presence in the world. . . . This congregation of the faithful, endowed with the riches of its own nation's culture, should be deeply rooted in the people. Let families flourish which are penetrated with the spirit of the gospel and let them be assisted by suitable schools. Let associations and groups be organized through which the lay apostolate will be able to permeate the whole of society with the spirit of the gospel. Finally, let charity shine out between Catholics of different rites (AG 15).

This whole section serves as an introduction to Chapter III, and we are struck by the fact that a whole chapter of the decree is consecrated to particular or *local* churches. It spells out the conditions indispensable for their existence, and the duties incumbent on them.

It is no accident that a whole chapter was devoted to the life of local churches established by missionary activity. I participated in the meetings that preceded the drafting of the text, and I know the Council was concerned with the primacy and urgency of establishing authentic churches in mission countries, churches that would be characterized by their own distinctive features and that would be summoned to enrich the universal Church with their own distinctive gifts and treasures. We took great pains to examine and spell out in this chapter the conditions required for fostering the newly formed churches as well as the tasks and responsibilities incumbent on them.

For our present purposes, I shall begin by citing two passages that deal generally with the participation of local churches in the work of spreading the Christian faith. The first passage recalls the missionary vocation of the whole Christian community, wherever it may be:

Since particular Churches are bound to mirror the universal Church as perfectly as possible, let them rightly realize that they have been sent to those also who are living in the same territory with it, and who do not yet believe in Christ. By the living witness of each one of the faithful and of the whole community, let the particular Church be a sign which points out Christ to others (AG 20).

The second passage puts strong stress on the obligation of these churches to carry out a missionary apostolate beyond their own frontiers:

In order that this missionary zeal may flourish among their native members, it is very fitting that the young Churches should participate as soon as possible in the universal mission work of the Church. Let them send their own missionaries to proclaim the gospel all over the world, even though they themselves are suffering from a shortage of clergy. For their communion with the universal Church reaches a certain measure of perfection when they themselves take an active part in missionary zeal toward other nations (AG 20).

But what seems even more important and significant to me is the contribution on the doctrinal level that the Church expects from these newly formed churches. Here we really do have something new. The Church is summoning these churches to contribute their treasures to the building of the universal Church, once they have become solidly implanted as ecclesial communities.

I shall cite this important passage in its entirety. It alludes to the maturation process of a newly formed church, the results expected from its deeper exploration of Christian thought and living, and the organizational conditions favorable to fruitful results:

The seed which is the Word of God sprouts from the good ground watered by divine dew. From this ground the seed draws nourishing elements which it transforms and assimilates into itself. Finally it bears much fruit. Thus, in imitation of the plan of the Incarnation, the young Churches, rooted in Christ and built up on the foundation of the apostles, take to themselves in a wonderful exchange all the riches of the nations which were given to Christ as an inheritance (cf. Ps. 2:8). From the customs and traditions of their people, from their wisdom and their learning, from their arts and sciences, these Churches borrow all those things which can contribute to the glory of their Creator, the revelation of the Savior's grace, or the proper arrangement of Christian life.

If this goal is to be achieved, theological investigation must necessarily be stirred up in each major socio-cultural area, as it is called. In this way, under the light of the tradition of the universal Church, a fresh scrutiny will be brought to bear on the deeds and words which God has made known, which have been consigned to sacred Scripture, and which have been unfolded by the Church Fathers and the teaching authority of the Church.

Thus it will be more clearly seen in what ways faith can seek for understanding in the philosophy and wisdom of these peoples. A better view will be gained of how their customs, outlook on life, and social order can be reconciled with the manner of living taught by divine revelation. As a result, avenues will be opened for a more profound adaptation in the whole area of Christian life. Thanks to such a procedure, every appearance of syncretism and of false particularism can be excluded, and Christian life can be accommodated to the genius and the dispositions of each culture.

Particular traditions, together with the individual patrimony of each family of nations, can be illumined by the light of the gospel, and then be taken up into Catholic unity. Finally, the individual young Churches, adorned with their own traditions, will have their own place in the ecclesiastical communion, without prejudice to the primacy of Peter's See, which presides over the entire assembly of charity.

And so, it is to be hoped and is altogether fitting that Episcopal Conferences within the limits of each major socio-cultural territory will be so united among themselves that they will be able to pursue this program of adaptation with one mind and with a common plan (AG 22).

The strongest statement in this passage is not only clear and unambiguous but also rather bold and daring. It talks about the obligation of these churches to subject the data of revelation and tradition to fresh theological scrutiny.

This passage goes even further than the one in *Nostra aetate* (N.AE.) which tells us to deal respectfully with the valid spiritual values to be found in the religions and customs of the people who belong to these newly formed churches. There the Church also exhorts its members to engage in prudent, charitable dialogue and collaboration with those who adhere to other religions. It tells them to bear witness to the Christian faith and way of life, but also to recognize, preserve, and foster the spiritual, moral, and sociocultural values of their own people. *Ad gentes,* however, goes even further and talks specifically about a theological effort as well.

Now *Ad gentes* does urge reflection on theological matters, aimed at subjecting the works and words revealed by God to a fresh scrutiny in the light of the tradition of the universal Church. But, *a fortiori,* the reconsideration and re-examination of liturgical institutions and other juridico-social dispositions should not pose any problem to the ecclesiastical organization. Here one should be able to effect in the newly formed churches what was once accomplished in the Eastern churches, considered in terms of their relationship with the Latin Church. They maintain their own distinctive character with respect to discipline and church government. Vatican II takes away any trace of doubt on this matter:

History, tradition, and numerous ecclesiastical institutions manifest luminously how much the universal Church is indebted to the Eastern Churches. This sacred Synod, therefore, not only honors this ecclesiastical and spiritual heritage with merited esteem and rightful praise, but also unhesitatingly looks upon it as the heritage of Christ's universal Church. For this reason, it solemnly declares that the Churches of the East, as much as those of the West, fully enjoy the right, and are in duty bound, to rule themselves. Each should do so according to its proper and individual procedures, inasmuch as practices sanctioned by a noble antiquity harmonize better with the customs of the faithful and are seen as more likely to foster the good of souls (OE 5).

From the conciliar passages cited above we can easily extract the essential tasks of the newly formed churches in the work and proclamation of today's universal Church.

The Role and Duties of Newly Formed Churches

First of all, there is the demand made upon the faithful who belong to these newly formed churches. By deepening their religious and spiritual life, they are to bear witness to their faith in God and Jesus Christ. They are also to give evidence of charity toward other men by engaging in the work of evangelization and participating in the task of building up the world in which they live.

The great missionary encyclicals of Benedict XV, Pius XI, and Pius XII laid particular stress on the duty of participating in the work of evangelization, in the strict sense of the term. From Pius XII to Paul VI, more and more stress has been laid on the duty of participating actively in the growth and development of mission countries, which de facto are the very same countries now considered to be underdeveloped.

Above and beyond the efforts in their own nations, vocations to foreign missionary work are already beginning to show up in mission lands. We already see some individuals deciding to leave their homelands into order to preach the gospel in distant lands. This was evident two years ago in Africa, for example, when an appeal was made to the African clergy for missionary volunteers to Guinea. Moreover, in the last few years, African priests and religious have joined international missionary congregations. Some have been sent to exercise their apostolate in regions quite distant from Africa. But these leanings toward foreign missionary work should be encouraged among the members of the newly formed churches only to the extent that they do it willingly and knowingly, and that they have considered the needs of their own country and the conditions underlying effective work in the new mission territories.

Now we have already seen that the conciliar Church sees the major role of the newly formed churches to be one of contributing to the institutional management and doctrinal progress of the Church. These two aspects are being explored anxiously today.

Speaking in general and basic terms, we can say that the newly formed churches offer the advantage of not being encumbered by excessively frozen institutional or doctrinal traditions. Thus they are relatively free to create new forms of ecclesiastical management and to elaborate new doctrinal outlooks; and these new features would enable us to move out of our present difficulties and impasses and to progress in our comprehension of God's revelation.

Others here at this meeting have treated explicitly the different features of the original contribution that can be made by the newly formed churches. For example, there is their way of conceiving and handling relationships between the different members that make up the People of God (e.g., clergy and laity). There is the matter of the liturgical organization of Christian worship. And there is the contribution these churches can make to the needed adaptation of ecclesiastical structures and laws.

As far as I am concerned, the most important and urgently needed contribution they can make relates to the area of proper understanding and doctrine—however paradoxical and premature that may seem.

A PERIOD OF "GROWTH"

No one would deny that the Church today is in a state of general crisis. Each one of us can bear witness to this crisis, and some keen observers have analyzed and spelled it out well. Everywhere we hear the same question: "Where are we going, anyway?"

De Lubac puts it this way: "It would be useless to deny that, for the past few years, we have seen growing signs of a spiritual crisis such as the Church has rarely experienced. The Modernist crisis at the turn of the century affected only a few regions. It was confined almost exclusively to intellectuals, and it did not truly affect Christian awareness as a whole. Today's crisis is the inevitable repercussion from our rapid progress and from the upheavals of every sort that followed the World War in 1914."

Karl Rahner writes: "We are truly in a period of transition from one epoch to another." Even before him, Teilhard de Chardin spoke simply of a transitional age, seeing the whole process in the more general perspective of human evolution. Congar treats the present crisis in great detail, referring particularly to the crisis in the realm of doctine:

> Today we find ourselves in a difficult situation. Everything seems to be in doubt, or about to be put in doubt. There is the general atmosphere of modern theological currents, the contact with unbelievers, the revival of questioning in biblical hermeneutics, and the problems posed by the scholarly sciences—particularly those that deal with man. All these things oblige us to re-examine positions that were once held securely. It is not just that new problems are being posed. Among large segments of the Christian people we find a shift of interest. They are moving from decision-making by the Church imposed authoritatively from above to decision-making by personal conscience on the basis of Christian experience in the world of men. That all this involves an element of disquiet is too obvious for any of us to doubt, for we can feel it personally. We might well ask: "Where are we going? Where will we be in twenty years?"[2]

We sometimes get the impression that in today's Church one can affirm anything whatsoever and justify anything whatsoever. In the past few years, the Holy Father himself has increased his warnings and cries of alarm. He has made statements about the present overall state of crisis and also warned against the theological deviation that is evident everywhere to some extent.

To confront this situation, a world episcopal synod was convened in Rome in 1967; it was meant to consider the problems of faith in our present day. A second synod was convened the following autumn. It apparently tried to tackle the situation produced by the disturbing attitudes that are to be found more and more among both clergy and laity with regard to the traditional positions of the Church and the magisterium.

ORIENTATION OF NEWLY FORMED CHURCHES

Considering this generalized state of crisis, one would like to call a halt in many instances insofar as the newly Christianized countries are concerned. One would like to tell them not to follow blindly the currents of thought and debate that are evident in the older Christian countries; not to adopt the changes and modifications (e.g., in the area of liturgical reform, ecclesial dispositions, and new doctrinal problems and positions) that are often launched too rapidly. One would like to see a momentary breathing space, even longer if need be, so that they will have time to find a secure and assured orientation.

Just ask yourselves these questions. Should the young Christian churches blindly follow all the ideas that sprout up in older Christian countries? Should they follow all the calls to action that are issued day after day, without subjecting them to a personal critique or referring them to local doctrinal and sociocultural conditions? These young churches must take their own position, for their own sake and for the sake of making some contribution to the universal Church. For they must help to put things back in order; they must help us to discover and implement new principles of thought and action.

The members of these young churches do not seem to be concerned with many of the forces that operate on older Christian churches. They do not feel deeply caught up in the great ideological currents that underlie thought and reflection in the Western church. Consider the case of the Council Fathers and the few experts who came from mission lands. During the conciliar sessions, they found themselves hard-put to identify themselves with one or another of the factions into which the Council was divided. Were they "progressivists" because they were "existential" about doctrine, or were they "conservatives" because they were "notional" about doctrine?

Faced with the present crisis in the Church, we might well reiterate the remark that Jacques Maritain made in a different but analogous context: "The problem that confronts modern society is primarily a problem of understanding." If understanding is achieved, then everything is achieved; if our outlook is off the track, then our whole life-orientation is off the track.

THEOLOGY AND SCHOLARLY SCIENCE

I personally would add here: There is a generalized crisis in today's Church, and in large measure the blame must be placed on theology and its status as a scholarly science. Are the underlying principles of theology adequate for the present situation, if we consider them in the framework of the general development of the scholarly disciplines? Are they capable of responding to the questions asked by human beings and Christians today, if we consider the factors that have transformed the conditions for thought and action in the contemporary world?

Everyone agrees that the epistemological base of theological science must be re-examined today. Vatican II itself recognized this, particularly in section 62 of *Gaudium et spes* (GS 62). This passage focuses on the harmony that must be established between culture in its broadest sense and Christianity:

> Although the Church has contributed much to the development of culture, experience shows that, because of circumstances, it is sometimes difficult to harmonize culture with Christian teaching.
>
> These difficulties do not necessarily harm the life of faith. Indeed they can stimulate the mind to a more accurate and penetrating grasp of the faith. For recent studies and findings of science, history, and philosophy raise new questions which influence life and demand new theological investigations.
>
> Futhermore, while adhering to the methods and requirements proper to theology, theologians are invited to seek continually for more suitable ways of communicating doctrine to the men of their times. For the deposit of faith or revealed truths are one thing; the manner in which they are formulated without violence to their meaning and significance is another.
>
> In pastoral care, appropriate use must be made not only of theological principles, but also of the findings of the secular sciences, especially of psychology and sociology. Thus the faithful can be brought to live the faith in a more thorough and mature way. . .
>
> May the faithful, therefore, live in very close union with the men of their time. Let them strive to understand perfectly their way of thinking and feeling, as expressed in their culture. Let them blend modern science and its theories and the understanding of the most recent discoveries with Christian morality and doctrine. Thus their religious practice and morality can keep pace with their scientific knowledge and an ever-advancing technology. Thus too they will be able to test and interpret all things in a truly Christian spirit.

Next it offers a special recommendation to the theologians:

> Through a sharing of resources and points of view, let those who teach in seminaries, colleges, and universities try to collaborate with men well versed in the other sciences. Theological inquiry should seek a profound understanding of revealed truth without neglecting close contact with its own times. As a result, it will be able to help those men skilled in various

fields of knowledge to gain a better understanding of the faith. This common effort will very greatly aid in the formation of priests. It will enable them to present to our contemporaries the doctrine of the Church concerning God, man, and the world in a manner better suited to them, with the result that they will receive it more willingly.

Thus, in one respect, the awareness shown by the Council regarding Christianity's confrontation with the present day is very much alive. On the other hand, I feel obliged to offer some observations on this whole matter. The conciliar text does indeed face up to the situation created by the confrontation of Christian doctrine with secular science. But, as I see it, it only partially responds to the demands of our contemporaries. For it stresses only the necessity of adapting our way of expressing religious truths to the contemporary world, and of learning how to grasp and understand the conclusions of modern scholarly sciences. It points out that theological scholarship can acquire greater depth by its contact with the spirit of modern scholarship; but I think it should have gone further and said that theology, noting the course of the modern scholarly spirit, must be willing to change its conception of its own status as a scholarly science.

The incomplete vision of the Council is also to be found among theologians. To take one example, let us examine the viewpoint expressed by Congar in his present studies. Congar certainly acknowledges the crisis in contemporary religious thought. He also acknowledges the principle of taking account of the perspectives of modern philosophy and science in order to revitalize theology. But when all is said and done, he feels that the contribution of modern philosophic disciplines is only a secondary one, ancillary to theology itself. The latter essentially does not have to change its status, which is grounded on the Aristotelian and Scholastic conception of scholarly science.

We find this basic position of Congar in the way he divides up theological activity between the realm of "datum" and the realm of "construct." But we do not find it only in his work. It crops up, in an even more accentuated form, in the work of Jacques Maritain.

Now it seems to me that we must tackle these things in an even more serious and radical way. Consider the doctrinal aspect of the present crisis. Doctrines, formerly presented as being theologically absolute, are being called into question; the developing course of scholarly science and reflection presents them as things which are not absolute. The unease also stems from the fact that certain problematic issues have perdured up to now because we have continued to regard certain principles as essential long after we should have freed ourselves from them. And it seems to me that these difficulties are fundamentally rooted in the traditional conception of theology.

The situation would change if we seriously accepted the fact, once and for all, that the status of theology changes with the evolution of general attitudes and conceptions regarding scholarly science. As I have already stressed elsewhere, the positive disciplines are making progress in an intellectual climate where positive thought is regarded as the ideal mode of knowledge; this has created conditions in which we must pose the question of theology's status as a science in new terms. And the question we must ask ourselves is: What value can traditional (i.e., Scholastic) theology retain for our contemporaries?

The modern procedure of scholarly science is experimental, inductive, and positive. The very result of scholarly science is considered to be really and perpetually progressive. So once and for all, theology must be seriously considered to be a fundamentally positive science.

Whatever one may think, such an attitude does not come easy. The natural tendency of the mind is to think that what will show up is already preformed in what is, that every undertaking will lead to results that have already been conceived or that can be conceived here and now. In such an outlook, the new result is a clearly forseeable outcome of past data.

Couldn't theologians take advantage of the modes of investigation and types of understanding that modern epistemology is constantly elaborating and perfecting? Wouldn't this benefit theology? Couldn't theologians then move on to rework—methodically, systematically, and thoroughly—the epistemological basis of sacred science? Couldn't they say that it is an authentic scholarly science, but interpret "science" in the modern sense of the word? Doesn't the modern interpretation of this term offer rich prospects in many respects, including but going beyond the Aristotelian notion of scholarly science?

Here I am pleased to cite some observations made by Lonergan, for they are strong, crystal-clear, and very much to the point.[4] "Considered in terms of the conditions that mark modern times," notes Lonergan, "theology seems to be behind the times." It must be updated. Lonergan explores with acute insight the origin, extent, causes, and areas of theology's retardation as a science. The important factor resides in the epistemological foundation that supported older theology.

Lonergan observes that theology has already changed from being "deductive" to being "empirical" in large measure. There has also been a change in mental outlook. Once we had a rigid dogmatism, echoed in the formula: *semper tenuit atque tenet sancta mater Ecclesia.* The findings we obtain today on some question seem to be merely a provisional summary of the present state of research.

After analyzing the whole question carefully, Lonergan concludes that we must *revitalize the very foundations of theology.* If theology is to revitalize itself, it must have a new bedrock foundation and critical position. The process of change must be thoroughgoing, shunning compromise completely; we cannot put new wine into old wineskins. One type of foundation is appropriate for a theology that seeks to be deductive, static, abstract, universal, and equally applicable to all in every time and place. But quite a different type of foundation is needed when theology moves from the deductive to the empirical, from being static to being dynamic, from the abstract to the concrete, from the universal to the historical totality of individual facts, from invariable rules to intelligent adaptation. To sum it up in one sentence: Lonergan states quite precisely that the question of foundations comes down to the whole question of a science's *methodology.*

It is methodology that produces the conclusions, laws, and principles accepted today; it is methodology that will produce a revision of these conclusions, laws, and principles tomorrow. The foundation that gives support to the man of science is, in the last analysis, his scientific method.

In its work, then, theology must change its clothes and become a truly positive science. In short, it must seek to make constant reference to reality; it must be capable of the same material precision as the other positive disciplines; and it must move toward results that can never claim to be absolute and finished but must rather be open to further illumination and interpretation.

The newly formed churches would seem to have a major, if not a determining, role in the fostering of this new conception of theology. Take Africa, for example, I personally am convinced that African epistemological tendencies fit in quite naturally with the most advanced tendencies of modern epistemology. There is the whole thrust of the African mentality, which fits in with contemporary developments in the thought of Western Europe, even though this may seem odd at first glance. The current of concretist and vitalist philosophies evinces deep sympathy (e.g., existentialist philosophy and some strands from the philosophy of Bergson). We have some conclusions arrived at in the critique of the sciences (e.g., those of G. Bachelard), some recent notions on the interpretation of history and its objectivity. We have the whole realm of the human sciences, which were once rejected by traditional Western thought. Today they are having great success and are forging ahead. We have depth psychology. We have philosophical critiques of the image, the symbol, and the myth, these being considered as valid forms on their own level for expressing certain realities. We have the critical reflections of men like Ricoeur and Gusdorf.

Here I should like to stress the references that are being made to the intellectual and spiritual position of Bergson's philosophy. It is being given special mention as one which could open the way to a revitalization of theology. We have the attempts of Edouard Leroy at the turn of the century, and the hopes expressed quite recently by Etienne Gilson. More than once, philosophers and anthropologists have tried to highlight the tieups between Bergsonian philosophy and the thought modes of so-called "primitive" peoples (including the Black African). These tieups are based essentially on the following characteristics observed in both: the realism of their vision of the world; attachment to the concrete in the processes of knowledge and speculative reflection—the privileged faculty of the primitive being spontaneous, noncritical intuition, that of Bergson being critical and (ideally) supra-intellectual; a philosophy concerned with life; *élan vital* and vital force; finally, practical optimism toward life, which is neither naïve nor the dupe of appearances.

In the West, the critique of knowledge is moving into a post-Cartesian and post-Kantian era. In common with African epistemological tendencies, the new European epistemology tends to be "unitary" in spirit, while at the same time being positive, concrete, and concerned with "concrete rationality." Such a spirit tends to develop a doctrine that seeks to be positive always, that advances step by step, that accepts relativity and hence fallibility. These features are absent in the thrust of traditional theology.

Now if this is truly the case, then the universal Church faces an important task. She must foster this new type of theological reflection and effort in the newly Christianized countries, encouraging it and giving it the means to find expression. It is also a major responsibility for the newly formed churches. They must make the necessary effort to initiate and spread this new conception of theology. In the African sociocultural community we must create conditions favorable to the elaboration of a theology which will constitute a real, effective contribution to the Church's quest today.

The newly formed churches must help us to liberate men's minds and hearts from the unease and anxiety of the present day. And they must proceed to do so on the basis of revitalized principles, going back to the source of the questions that still remain unanswered. Some questions seem to be insoluble; they remain unresolved from day to day. In other instances, our inability to face up to new questions bears witness to the impasse created by our unwillingness to give up certain invalid and inept principles. In both cases we beat about the bush and do not move ahead. So we must change our perspective and pose in different terms the old and new questions that cannot be solved by our present principles.

Let me just cite some of the major problems of this sort: (1) the problem of religion and the problem of God; (2) the rleationship between nature and the supernatural; (3) miracles; (4) the relationship between grace and freedom; (5) the problem of sacramental reality; and (6) the nature of the Church (spirit and institution), and the related questions on today's agenda: papal primacy and collegiality, infallibility, etc.

Let me also just mention the larger tendencies in the matter of interpreting and comprehending revelation: the symbolization of spiritual realities and their import; and the demythologizing of our expression of divine revelation.

All these questions constitute basic problems that call for close attention from theologians and the deep concern of the ecclesiastical magisterium. But we cannot simply agree to re-examine these questions, to pose them in new ways, and to reject the terms in which they have reached us so far. We must also be willing to acknowledge *at the start* that the outcome will probably be unforeseen and may even be disconcerting. Every scholarly discipline, of its very nature, must be open to unforeseen results that cause shock waves.

Such an attitude is not easy to come by. The natural tendency of the human mind is to think that the future outcome is already preformed in the present reality, that any given project leads to already foreseen results. In such an outlook, the new result is but a foreseeable consequence of past data. This outlook rules out the real progress of scholarly knowledge and the world from the very start. And the reality it foresees can be carried out at once.

We must not be afraid to encourage exploration in new directions. We must recognize the law of continuity in human evolution, and we must accept the legitimacy of moving beyond what has already been attained as a sure possession. When we calmly encourage such exploration, when we accept the fact that we must integrate new results into the body of older knowledge, then we shall move on to a new and richer doctrine.

Indispensable Conditions

In trying to sum up what the newly formed churches must do to carry out their proper role in the Church, I would underline the basic importance of these two tasks: (1) They must set up adequate institutions and structures; (2) they must utilize people who are properly prepared for the new forms and conditions of the mission effort.

To achieve these results, we need only implement the recommendations formulated in *Ad gentes*. (First and foremost, we must call for *coordination* of episcopal conferences and other ecclesiastical institutions and associations *on a regional level*. This does not yet seem to have been done effectively in mission lands.)

It is especially important that, in addition to study and training centers, we encourage research and information organs on the regional level: e.g., specialized periodicals on *theology, liturgy,* and *pastoral work.* They will make a contribution to research work, to the elaboration and growth of doctrinal domains, to the organization of cultic worship, and to the apostolate in general.

As far as the training and formation of personnel is concerned, we need only refer to the apt observations and recommendations in *Ad gentes*. It covers the spiritual, intellectual, and moral formation of missionary personnel. Now, a few years after Vatican II, we can take stock and see how much of this has been implemented.

Above all else, we must create conditions that favor the full flowering of religious and spiritual values, by seeking to *establish Christian communities that are inventive and creative.* Sound values will develop naturally in Christian communities that are truly alive. They will enrich and even save the universal Church. Theology, liturgical forms, and distinctive disciplinary practices are rooted in the life of a given community; they are branded with the integral experience of this community, finding nourishment and sustenance in its substantive life.

NOTES

1. Gustave Thils, *Syncrétisme et catholicité* (Paris: Casterman, p. 82.)
2. Yves Congar, *Situation et tâches présentes de la théologie,* pp. 58-59.
3. Bernard Lonergan, "The New Context of Theology," a paper delivered at the International Theology Congress held in Toronto (August 20-25, 1967).

J. M. GONZALEZ-RUIZ

Mission Work
and Freedom of Conscience

CHAPTER TWELVE

If we are to frame a sound "mission theology" within its proper context, we must first spell out what the "task of evangelization" means.

The gospel is the concrete proclamation of salvation for the individual and for human history, made by Christ to mankind. It is an *eschatologizing* message rather than an *eschatological* one. Why? Because it gives a specific *élan* to the pace of human and cosmic evolution. This *élan*, operating from within and on the basis of its own internal dynamism independent of evolution, confers its power on history and transforms it into a "goal above and beyond everything else." In the symbolic language of the Bible, this goal is "the kingdom of heaven."

This salvation message has a *cumulative* rather than an *evasive* import. By this I mean that salvation is not an aristocratic goal. It does not seek to save the individual (or his main feature, the soul) by taking him out of his spatial and historical context and setting him in a higher, definitive context. On the contrary, evangelical salvation embraces the whole of man, in his worldly context and his difficult ascent through the web of history: "The human person deserves to be preserved; human society deserves to be renewed. Hence the pivotal point of our total presentation will be man himself, whole and entire, body and soul, heart and conscience, mind and will" (GS 3).

From all this we may conclude that evangelization is not in competition with the creative autonomy of human evolution. Evangelization is not a substitute for evolution and progress; it is rather the salvation of the latter. Thus evangelization necessarily presupposes all the dynamic realities which form the intrinsic warp and woof of human evolution. Its task is to proclaim the good news about the eschatological "salvation" of human history, a salvation which is already operative now in history but which will reach its culmination only outside history.

For discussion of this paper, see Appendix, p. 163.

Mission work is nothing else but the diffusion of this message, carried out by the Church in her role as trustee and interpreter of the gospel. Thus the role of the Church is not to promote human evolution but to save it. She is not the trustee of some formula for human evolution that can enter into competition with the other techniques which the human mind discovers slowly and painfully in the course of history. The Church must take account of the state in which this evolution finds itself, in order to inject into it the added force of salvation that is already at work preparing human history for its culmination in the kingdom of heaven.

Now human evolution develops on many planes and dimensions: political, social, economic, cultural, and even religious. Mission work, as such, cannot confuse its evangelizing task with some imported model of a political, social, economic, cultural, or religious nature, even if this model has already been evangelized. Mission work should contribute *evangelization itself* not *some evangelized reality.*

Every attempt at evangelization presupposes a new process, in line with the situations to be found among the people and structures to which we bring the good news. Taking matters as defined above we can draw two fundamental conclusions.

RELIGIOUS PLURIFORMISM OF THE GOSPEL

Mission work does not have the right to violate conscience, be it that of the individual or the community, by forcefully imposing evangelization on it. It cannot present evangelization as if it were a "technique" for human evolution and betterment that offered better scientific guarantees than the techniques which might be utilized by the individuals or peoples to be evangelized.

For this reason, evangelization is gravely compromised when mission work comes in a form that is linked up too closely with imported political, social, or cultural models (mainly of a colonial nature). It then fails to appear as the salvation of the realities lived by the native population; it seems rather to be a substitute for these realities, offering presumably superior realities and imposing them with a greater or lesser degree of violence.

Besides showing the necessary respect for the consciences of individuals and communities who are to be evangelized, we must realize something else. We must realize that the gospel does not, of itself, comprise a "religion" of its own. The gospel proclaims the salvation of the religion it encounters, but it does not propose a new type of "religion."

Saint Paul fought all his life to preserve the religious pluriformism of the gospel from the monopolist tendencies of Judeo-Christians. Within the bosom of the nascent Church, Jewish Christians sought to take full control of the gospel and to equate it with the ensemble of their traditions and religious practices. Thus, to be a Christian, you would first have to be a Jew; and the gospel would seal the universal and exclusive validity of Jewish religious practice.

Saint Paul fought this monopolist effort on the part of Jews. When he came to the meeting in Jerusalem (Acts 15), he defended the religious pluriformism of the gospel against the narrower views of Saint James' followers (Gal. 12:2); these Jewish Christians, living in Jerusalem, dreamed of extending Sion's religious dominion over the whole world.

In the area evangelized by Saint Paul, there existed only two categories of religious man: Jew and Greek. The gospel could not be equated with either, nor could it suppress either. Instead it was supposed to bolster both, taking them over and sublimating them without destroying the valid and distinctive differences they already possessed.

Saint Paul never gave up his status as a Jew. Throughout the eastern area of the Mediterranean, he continued to preach in synagogues, telling his co-religionists that Jesus was the Christ proclaimed by the prophets and psalmists of the Old Testament. But when he confronted the other type of religious man, the Greek, he proclaimed Christ directly to him without demanding that he practice the venerable, age-old traditions of Israel.

Thanks to this "kerygmatic" process, which was plurireligious, diverse communities took shape. In them the gospel was lived out in different, pluralistic forms, without losing its purity at all. The Christianity of the first three centuries offers wonderful testimony to this religious diversity within its overall unity. This diversity is manifested principally in the great richness and variety of the Eastern and Western liturgies.

When the Church subsequently succumbed to the "temporalizing" contagion of the decadent Roman Empire, there reappeared the "religious imperialism" against which Paul had fought so hard. The old Roman dictum, *Cuius regio eius religio*, acquired validity once again. Roman imperialism, revitalized by the expansionist tendencies of Christianity, attempted to make the world into "one single region"; and it saw this "monoreligious" Christianity as the major tool for its expansion and consolidation.

Thus, quite contrary to its essence, Christianity turned itself into *a* religion: not "one more religion" but the "one and only" religion. The admirable work of Saint Paul to embody the gospel in different religious forms gave way to a fanatic, destructive proselytism. In the scattered debris of the old Roman Empire, Christianity entered the lists against other religions. These religions, in some way or other, accepted the same God of Abraham, Isaac, and Jacob; so they were well disposed toward listening to the "religiously universal" message of the gospel.

GIVE FREELY. . .

Now if evangelization is not a substitute for the betterment of man, but rather his gratuitous salvation, then it follows logically that mission work can be worthwhile and valid only in a context of *absolute gratuitousness*: "You received without charge, give without charge" (Matt. 10:8). It is the consciences of individuals and peoples that are supposed to receive the gospel—as a purely gratuitous gift offered by God on his own initiative.

Consequently, when the work of evangelization is "aided" by the support of aid programs, political or social influence, cultural contributions, or even religious monopolies, then we have a real violation of people's consciences; for the latter cannot benefit from any checks placed on their total liberty.

Thus the reality of an established church works against the essential aim of mission work. For such churches win their political, social, economic, and cultural supports at the expense of the "gratuitousness" of the gospel message, which they are supposed to offer freely to consciences.

Political confessionalism, in itself, implies a pathological situation in the Church. The Church is afforded certain guarantees for the exercise of her mission, but only on the condition that it unite in solidarity with the fundamental directives of the ruling political machine. When one bestows social, political, or cultural authority on a religious function (e.g., the episcopate), that amounts to pawning the gratuitous nature of the evangelical *kerygma* for the sake of indubitable advantages of a temporal nature that will automatically accrue.

Such collusion (a religious function combined with temporal authority) validates the attitude of protest that the faithful often adopt toward the *temporal* dimension which has been illegitimately tied up with a properly religious function. When Emperor Charles V found himself going to war against the pope, he consulted the best theologians of his day. They authorized him to engage in war against the "head of the Papal States," even though he revered the person of "the Bishop of Rome and the spiritual head of Catholicism."

Today it frequently happens that the illegitimate tieup between temporal authority and a religious function is economic in nature. That is why it is always lawful for the faithful to "protest" the social and economic structure of the Vatican State, which is bound up with the great capitalist trusts of America and Europe. This does not stop these same people from revering the religious dimension of the same person who is being attacked on account of the socioeconomic picture.

When churches find themselves in a missionary status—and this should be their permanent situation, as opposed to being established churches—they can accept the lessons of history and avoid the faults which have been so detrimental to the universal proclamation of the gospel.

Freedom of conscience must be respected as much as possible. And, to this end, we must make sure that the religious function is kept completely clear of tieups with social, cultural, economic, or religious realities.

MISSION WORK AND FORMS OF IMPERIALISM

In a word, mission work can be wholly worthwhile only in a climate of absolute respect for the consciences of individuals and communities we seek to evangelize. So we must avoid the great temptation of "imperialism" that plagues the missionary, for it gives him a subtle but profound superiority complex, on the temporal level, toward those he is supposed to evangelize. It ramifies into various forms:

Historico-racial imperialism   The missionary presents the gospel as the exclusive patrimony of a superior people, impregnated with excellent traditions. He transmits this patrimony to the native population with an air of condescension, as if they were his inferiors.

Socioeconomic imperialism   The missionary presents the gospel as a component of certain capitalist "development projects." He stresses the economic contribution of the countries that are exploiting the evangelized country both socially and economically.

Political imperialism   The presence of certain missionaries from the mother country insures that the latter will be able to engage in political propaganda. When France suspended or expelled the religious orders, for example, missionaries in some of the French colonies were enjoying astonishing privileges.

Cultural imperialism   Mission work helps greatly to export the culture of the home mission country, without paying much attention to the indigenous culture. For example, some French bishops spent thirty years in China without learning a word of Chinese (*cf.* Père Lebbe).

Religious imperialism   Some missionaries have not even tried to evangelize other religions. They have brusquely substituted a Western religion for them: specifically, the Roman religion.

All these forms of imperialism are a direct attack on freedom of conscience, on the consciences of those to whom the gospel is directed. They seriously compromise the sacramental validity and effectiveness of the church's *kerygmatic* thrust, as it has operated throughout the world in every historical epoch.

APPENDIX

I: Two General Discussions

1. Non-Christian Religions

INTRODUCTION BY J. LÉCUYER We have tried to group this morning's topics under two general headings: (1) the problem of non-Christian religions with respect to salvation; (2) the novel aspect of Christianity and the need for missionary activity. The main questions could be outlined as follows:

1. NON-CHRISTIAN RELIGIONS AND SALVATION

1: Clarification of the notions of "nature" and "supernatural"
   Meaning of the terms
   Biblical equivalents (spirit and flesh . . .)
   Can one speak about the "supernatural" with reference to non-Christian religions?

2: Can the term "religion" be reserved exclusively to the external and human aspects of the religious phenomenon?
   Is it possible to reduce these aspects to "idolatry"?
   Must one say that these questions are posed in Christianity as well (ambiguity)?

3: What do we mean by *economy of salvation*?
   Are there more than one?
   If there is only one, to what extent does it go beyond the Church?
   How are we to understand the Church as sign, sacrament, community, instrument of the kingdom?
   What about other religions in the economy of salvation?
   Does the Jewish religion have a place apart?

4: The concepts of *revelation* and *salvation*.
   Are these terms univocal when used with reference to Christianity and other religions?

2. NOVEL ASPECT OF CHRISTIANITY AND NEED FOR MISSIONARY ACTIVITY

1: Is the essential novelty of Christianity fraternal charity?

2: Its tieup with faith in the incarnate, crucified, risen Christ, the foundation of our hope.

3: To what extent is it necessary to know that God revealed himself as "Love," and to proclaim this to men?

4: Is it enough to preach "brotherly love"?

5: Concretely what is the motive for the missionary vocation and its labors? love of God? God's glory? God's will, according to Christ's command in Matthew 28?

Some of you have asked that we go back to Lyonnet's paper. That is why the second series of questions was drawn up. As far as the first set of questions is concerned, it seemed that we should clarify some of the terms that cropped up frequently in our discussions. Among them are the concepts of "nature" and "supernatural." Perhaps De Lubac would tell us what he thinks about them?

H. DE LUBAC   In this area I have no personal view of my own. I simply reiterate what our Christian faith tells us. The term "supernature" is a recent one that is neither biblical nor traditional. Revelation and Christian tradition do not offer us the notion of some human nature that is not called to a higher destiny; no abstract nature exists, to which we would add on something like a supernature. But faith informs us, if you will, about God's plan; he created man and destined him to participate in the life of the Trinity. This does not mean that there is no difference between nature and the supernatural. On the contrary, there is a radical distinction between the two. By God's grace, nature is summoned to divinization. There is as much difference between nature and the supernatural as there is between creature and creator, man and God. And the Fathers themselves reiterate: "If a person says that man is divine by nature or essence, then he is uttering blasphemy." However, man is made for the supernatural; God creates him so that he may share in God's own life. Thus there is an intimate union between nature and the supernatural because man is summoned to union with God, because God created in order to communicate and share himself. Thus, by God's own plan, there is a radical distinction between nature and the supernatural and, at the same time, the no less radical destination of man to union with God, to the supernatural.

As far as the biblical equivalent is concerned, the terms "spirit and flesh" were offered in the outline. From a concrete viewpoint, these particular biblical terms would correspond more to the opposition between "nature" and "grace." Man, *qua* flesh, is sinful man who must undergo a conversion. There must be a *metanoia* and for such a *metanoia* man needs the transforming power of grace. If we want to transpose the opposition between "nature" and the "supernatural" to the biblical plane, then the more suitable terms would be "image" and "likeness," as they were interpreted by the Greek Fathers. Image is the order of creation, hence, the order of nature. Within creation man is already the image of God. But this term calls out for a complement, a transfiguration. It calls out for "likeness," which suggests the gratuitous transformation involved in man's divinization. Speaking in general terms and leaving aside the case of those who can really live through grace, one cannot speak of the supernatural, in the strict sense, in non-Christian religions considered objectively. One can certainly talk about evangelical preparation, ordination to the supernatural, and elements ordered toward, or in the process of becoming, supernatural; but one certainly cannot talk about the supernatural *simpliciter*.

J. LÉCUYER   Daniélou said that non-Christian religions, insofar as they are creations of man's genius, do not include the supernatural. That would not prevent the grace of God from being able to operate in these religions, if I have properly understood De Lubac's explanation.

A. SEUMOIS   Would not the fact that prophecy exists in non-Christian religions, as an active preparation for the New Testament covenant, also imply a ministerial activity of a supernatural character? Likewise in what we call the "pre-sacraments," there is a disposition toward the supernatural in an appeal for the redemptive intervention of Christ; there is a disposition toward the Christian sacraments, which goes beyond the framework of the natural components of these religions as culture-linked systems.

J. DANIELOU   To be saved, there must be an act of faith. Hence we must have the action of grace in non-Christian religions. But it would be very ambiguous, in connection with the non-Christian religions, to speak of "revelation" in the objective sense of "biblical revelation": i.e., in the sense of a divine authority who speaks, which is the direct work of God.

J. M. SETIEN   Religion, even a non-Christian one, has something objectively supernatural. After all, if the religious acts of non-Christians have something of the supernatural, how could the non-Christian religion itself not have something supernatural, since the religious acts are the manifestation of an act of faith?

A. VANNESTE   We simply cannot separate the subjective and objective elements. Faith is made manifest in one's adhesion to a determined *credo*. One cannot wholly deny a supernatural character to non-Christian religions.

D. GRASSO   I don't see any real difficulty. In non-Christian religions there are truths which bear supernatural values, at least implicitly. Saint Thomas said that there were also prophets in non-Christian religions. God revealed certain truths in the non-Christian religions, and so the grace of God can operate to make it possible for some people to make the act of faith.

H. DE LUBAC   My aim just now was to explicitate the notion of supernatural in terms of ultimate destination. But we must maintain the distinction between subjective and objective. The fact that man may be moved by God's grace does not signify that he receives a supernatural revelation to transmit. It is quite possible that the founders of non-Christian religions were animated by grace, but that does not mean that their systems were objectively supernatural. Saint Thomas does talk about prophets, but not about religions as such; and these prophets are certainly a prefiguration of the Christian religion. The paradox is that through these nonsupernatural systems, which are sometimes shot through with error, a man can make a supernatural act with the help of God's grace. But if a man makes supernatural acts under the impulse of God's grace, it does not follow that he has received supernatural enlightenment to establish an objectively supernatural religious system.

J. M. GONZALEZ-RUIZ   We are all mixed up. We seem to be equating supernatural religion and revealed religion. In many non-Christian religions there are supernatural truths and supernatural acts, even though these religions are not revealed. God has always manifested himself in a supernatural way. Communal and individual acceptance of the manifestation of God's gratuitous gift is supernatural, and thus one can say that the religious system is supernatural. But only Judaism and Christianity are revealed religions; only they are the realm of the *apocalypsis*.

H. DE LUBAC   Obviously everything true and good comes from God. One may challenge the terminology, but it is after all traditional. What we must maintain is the radical distinction between the natural manifestation of God in nature, through the creation order, and the supernatural manifestation of God in the Old and New Testament, which culminates with Christ. The former is ordered to the latter, but we must not confuse the two. And we must of course understand that both are gratuitous, that they represent God's challenging summons to man.

A. VANNESTE   The radical distinction seems untenable to me. There are not two revelations by God, just two pathways of revelation. Creation itself is already a certain presence of Christ, for everything has been created in Christ.

J. DANIÉLOU   There are two ways of approaching the problem. We can say that the thing that saves is faith in Christ, in the New Testament sense. So we may then ask how those who do not have Christ's revelation can benefit from the salvation given in Jesus Christ. In this way we preserve and safeguard the absolute priority of revelation and explicit faith in Christ, the normal pathway of salvation. Now we can also say that faith in Christ exists everywhere in a diffuse, implicit way. Thus we no longer give any privilege to faith in Christ, or any priority to salvific revelation in Jesus Christ. But this is the wrong way to pose the problem, for then we can no longer justify the missionary activity of the Church. We run into the confusion involved in theories about implicit or anonymous Christianity, which turns our perspectives backwards. I am not unaware that Saint Paul talks about the "patience of God" in his letter to the Romans, when he considers the ages before Christ as the time of God's compassion. On the other hand, Paul passes quite severe judgment on the pagan religions which refuse to hear Christ's summons.

J. MASSON   If we view religion as an "system," we cannot escape the dilemma. But religion is, first and foremost, an existential group, a community of living people. So how can we deny that these communities receive the grace of God? How can we avoid saying that in certain groups, in India for example, there is supernatural intervention by God?

E. SEUMOIS   We do not talk often enough about the paleo-Christian economy, resulting from the protoevangelical covenant (or, at the very least, the protoevangelical promise). In it we have the promise of a future redeemer, hence the concrete possibilities of salvation in Christ for all men even before the fulfillment of redemption in history. This economy is very distinct from the Old Testament economy, valid exclusively for the chosen people of the Old Testament. And both are ordered to the New Testament economy, the only juridically legitimate one after Christ and valid for all peoples.

G. DELCUVE   Aren't we talking a bit too much on the intellectual level here, on the level of knowledge about God? A life lived out of love is a life lived in human and religious groups.

A. VANNESTE   We must suppress the radical distinction between natural revelation and supernatural revelation, but at the same time we must give full value to the tension between non-Christian religions and the Christian religion. Every man bears within himself a supernatural vocation, but he must become that to which he is called. The expression "anonymous Christians," used with reference to non-Christians, is exact; but it is sometimes abused, insofar as its use implies that they can be content with being "anonymous Christians." These anonymous Christians must move out of their anonymity; they must become truly that which they are only in embryonic form. Christianity is the full explicitation of that which lives in every man.

H. DE LUBAC   Are we saying that natural man is an implicit Christian? We simply cannot mix everything up. Not all men are anonymous Christians, but all men are called to become anonymous or explicit Christians. That's quite a different story.

A. CAMPS   We have to re-read Colossians: everything has been created in Christ. In biblical tradition, the other religions are not outside Christ. In a certain sense they are supernatural.

S. LYONNET   There are people who have lived with grace and who have expressed it in their rites; that is explicit. Can we really exclude, a priori, the possibility of a supernatural element in certain religious groups of men?

J. MASSON   Believing in this possibility is very important for missionary work, even if we cannot say exactly what its elements are in the concrete. For the missionary it is an indication that a summons to grace exists in his field of labor.

G. DELCUVE   It is really what we call "appeals" or "inner expectations." And if there is such preparation and expectation, then evangelization is precisely the response to it.

A. M. HENRY   Undoubtedly there is a certain amount of ambiguity in non-Christian religions. Like everything else human, including the religious factor, they tap good, less good, and evil wellsprings. Where is grace, where is the activity of the Holy Spirit, in this overlapping? We would be fools to say: Grace is here. We would be just as foolish to say it is not here at all. Saint Paul does tell us that faith alone justifies. But does faith begin with our explicit formulation of it? And does this explicit formulation always correspond with the heart which, in reciting a given credo of faith or a given catechism response, professes or does not profess Jesus Christ? We can readily affirm that faith justifies the sinner, or that contrition takes away sin. That is certain. But no one can say that this particular man is contrite (who can be sure?) and hence justified. Still less can we say that he is justified (hence contrite). All the time we have merely fragile, transitory signs. God alone sees into the heart. But we do have some wondrous signs. Think of Toukaram, Gandhi, and Tagore, just to mention India. They gave such felicitous expression to certain Christian truths. And in this connection one cannot help but think of Al Hallaj. Moslem he was, but was he not one of the great mystics of the world? Massignon said that the Sufis who adhered to him adhered to Christ secretly and invisibly, insofar as he was a mysterious echo of Jesus' teaching—though perhaps an echo that was strange to the Judeo-Christian heritage. All these things truly do exist. And the history of the Church tells us clearly that there is often an osmosis between Christianity and the other religions, with the result that the gospel has influenced other religions themselves even outside the frontiers of the Church. Things are more mixed up than one might realize from a quick, superficial look at world religions.

J. DANIÉLOU   It is true that the spirit of Christianity is everywhere. But that is not our problem. What is important is the transition from the radiation of Christ's message to the act of faith. There we run up against a gulf. We can say that God takes care of this, but we cannot base the Church's activity and pastoral work on that.

J. LÉCUYER   Time limitations compel us to move on to the second part of the agenda. The fundamental question is the relationship between charity and faith in Christ's resurrection, which is our hope of being resurrected with him. To what extent can this charity exist in a man before the word of God has been brought to him? Perhaps Lyonnet could start us off by going back to his paper of yesterday?

S. LYONNET   What is primary for Saint Paul is the act of faith, through which man accepts God's activity. Let us assume a person does in fact have this charity. Then, on the one hand, he may not know that this charity comes to him from God; in this event, we must teach him that it does, because it is beneath a man to act for unknown motives. On the other hand, he may refuse to receive it from another; in this event, he is cutting himself off from the only source that can give it to him. He then ceases to love in a truly disinterested way. If he refuses to accept its divine origin, then his charity is not authentic; that would be his sin.

G. DELCUVE   Is it wise to make such a sharp distinction between faith, hope, and charity—as we usually do? Is not our acceptance of God one and the same act?

S. LYONNET   Yes, indeed, this act of charity is an extremely concrete act.

J. M. SETIEN   The distinction between implicit or explicit faith, as a condition for having charity, does not satisfy me. Let us take any person who has the charity to give his life for others, say a Marxist. Can he or can he not act under the action of God's grace without having faith, whether it be explicit or implicit?

S. LYONNET   This grace must be accepted, for man is a free being. Faith would be the acceptance of God's gift, first implicitly and then, when he knew its divine origin, explicitly.

I. DE LA POTTERIE   I fear that in speaking about fraternal charity we remain solely on the moral plane, thus reducing theological charity to do-gooder work. Authentic Christian love looks toward the *koinonia*, toward authentic communion with other men and God.

J. M. GONZALEZ-RUIZ   Then how would you interpret the parable of the Good Samaritan? I think we have over-intellectualized faith. It is an act of acceptance, and there are many degrees in it. On the lowest level, man does not perceive what he is doing. We can talk about the *initium fidei* and a listening attitude, but that is already faith.

K. MÜLLER   I should like to ask De la Potterie if there exists a moral act that would not be a supernatural act at the same time.

I. DE LA POTTERIE   What is specifically Christian is love for one's enemies. In that case, yes, there is really a supernatural act. But is that so commonplace outside Christianity?

J. FRISQUE   In concrete human experience we find experiential elements which permit us to say that this unbounded charity, this love even for one's enemies, gives us an indication of supernatural life even when it does not go by that name. It tells us that this life is there among men who are on the way to Christ, who are seeking out God, the God that will speak his name in Jesus Christ. When we speak of charity as "doing good to others," we may well be running into that attitude of acceptance which someone just said was the sign of faith.

I. DE LA POTTERIE   But it is obviously impossible to make an empirical judgment on the quality of a human act.

J. FRISQUE   Well I'm certainly not trying to talk on the quantitative plane. Insofar as human beings, even outside Christianity, are led to work out an integral human experience that is analogous to the gospel, we have an indication of a "direction toward." It is an attitude linked to faith.

2. Mission Work and Development

INTRODUCTION BY T. VAN ASTEN   Missionaries have always worked for man's betterment. Their charity found expression in work for human and cultural development that was integrated into the daily activities of the parish or the diocese. But today development has taken on national and international dimensions, and it has become the work of specialists. Missionaries feel lost and drowned in this effort by technical experts, where the gospel is in danger of being forgotten. Whether they are involved in development work or in evangelization, they feel guilty.

Missionaries would like to hear answers to such questions as the following:

1: In what way is evangelization the soul of all development work? In other words, what are the relationships between technological development and evangelization, insofar as the latter refers to preaching the Word and administering the sacraments?

2: In what way is development work a missionary activity? In what way is it an evangelical task? In other words, what is the role of the Church, as a sacrament and instrument of salvation, vis-à-vis development? Is it to animate consciences so that people become fully aware? Is development, as such, the work of civil society and governments first and foremost? What is the role of ecclesial institutions in development?

3: Missionaries have little to say about certain theories relating to the theology of development, which are clothed in European and Western outlooks. These theories suggest that development must or should begin, of necessity, with secularization. Should we pose the problem in terms of secularization? Our question here is: Can we project onto other continents the hypothesis that development is to come in and through secularization?

RELATIONS BETWEEN EVANGELIZATION AND TECHNOLOGICAL DEVELOPMENT

J. DANIÉLOU   The problem posed here is the relationship between evangelization and development. Now it seems clear to me that there is always a specific place for evangelization. Mission work is not simply aid to development. Moreover, we must distinguish between the first steps of evangelization and the implementation of a pastoral effort. The role of the priest and that of the layman is quite different. The latter specifically bear Christian witness in the secular domain. The role of the former is to give spiritual animation. Today there is a tendency to reduce the role of the priest to that of the layman. In the primitive Church, by contrast, it was the laity that fashioned the place and role of the priest; the latter has his own proper place in the construction of the Church.

J. M. GONZALEZ-RUIZ   Evangelization can never be identified with development. Evangelization can never curb true development. Evangelization offers to development a sense of historical transcendence. It offers important values. For example, it gives deeper meaning to man's autonomy, it maintains the unity of human nature against all sorts of idols, it protects man against the fanaticism of a terrestrial heaven, it guards man against the grave danger of centralization, etc.

I. DE LA POTTERIE   Evangelization, like development, should be carried out on a much broader scale today. It should give universal, worldwide value to the evangelical message, just as the mystique of development has taken on universal dimensions. In this connection we must develop the cosmic themes of the Bible, since we are faced with a development project organized on a world scale.

A. BOUCHARD   Dividing up our missionary tasks between priests and laymen, as Daniélou suggested, is fine. But doesn't one of the reasons for the present-day unease of priests reside in the fact that their role has been reduced to being ministers of the sacraments? Psychologically, the professional role of the priest is important. So too is the role of the missionary in development.

A. M. HENRY   We would all agree, in line with *Populorum progressio* (n. 21), that evangelization fulfills the whole of man, both individually and collectively, and that it alone fulfills him. Now faced with the ever growing resistance it is meeting from certain religions and cultures, the road is clear for mission work. It should present to the world men who are more "human" than others. Or, to put it another way, it should offer the human ideal that peoples are groping toward in the dark. It should do this in such a way that these peoples are led to ask Christians: Who are you? What is your faith? For example, human beings are seeking unity, but they realize they cannot achieve it on their own with their own inner resources. The gospel points out the road to this universal charity. The latter ultimately ties in with the integral development of man, according to *Populorum progressio*. Universal love for others, and anything else of this sort, is more or less an idol to the extent that it is closed in upon itself: i.e., to the extent that it is not truly universal. But it ceases to be an idol and reunites with the thrust of Christ's charity to the extent that it stays constantly open, ready for new steps forward, alert to new demands, etc. But the gospel does not just show men the road to total love. It is a force for every believer. By means of the proclamation of the gospel and its sacraments, Christ communicates his grace. Without the latter, men could not get far with love.

J. FRISQUE   We cannot ever reduce development to its technological and economic aspects. We must always get back to the notion espoused in *Populorum progressio*: the integral development of man. And, in fact, the people engaged in development work manifest cultural, spiritual, and religious dimensions that go far beyond these economic and technological aspects.

G. DELCUVE   Development aid would be a summons, because it reveals man's limits. In certain missionary circumstances, only development would be possible. And this would be a real evangelization, a true revelation of Christ's charity.

J. M. SETIEN   I come back to my distinction between apostolate and evangelization. For me, Christian social action is an apostolate; but it is not yet evangelization, the proclamation of the Word in the strict sense.

S. LYONNET   Section 12 of *Ad gentes* is devoted to "the witness of Christian charity." What it says in one paragraph can greatly clarify the problem we are discussing here. Note what it regards as "true witness to Christ" ordered to people's "salvation": "Closely united with men in their life and work, Christ's disciples hope to render to others true witness of Christ and to work for their salvation, even where they are unable to proclaim Christ fully. For they are not seeking a mere material progress and prosperity for men, but are promoting their dignity and brotherly union, teaching those religious and moral truths which Christ illumined with His light." These truths, in other words, were already known but only imperfectly. Their work is both human "development" and authentic "evangelization" at the same time.

A. CAMPS   Some of our distinctions are indeed Western ones. Everything that actualized the kingdom of God in this world—the quest for justice, the work for unity and peace, etc.—is evangelical work.

J. MASSON   The growth of peoples should be taken in its global sense. In like manner, the intention of the one who evangelizes should consider his work in its totality: the growth of the whole man on every level. This is the goal of all missionary work. We do well to underline the text of *Ad gentes* (n. 12), just cited by Lyonnet. For there the Church claims nothing for herself, except the duty of serving human beings in charity and faithful service. It thus becomes senseless to make chronological distinctions.

J. LÉCUYER   Indeed it is the aim of mission work that is important. It is the *intention* that differentiates the heralds of Christ from all other philanthropists.

J. FRISQUE   I think the only essential element is witness that speaks of Christ; this is more than a simple intention.

G. DELCUVE   The goal of missionary work is to lead men to Christ, by revealing his presence through the missionary. It involves the very life of the one who is bearing witness. Now is this witness, first and foremost, a tool for conversion? No. The fact that I, through my commitment, hope to lead men explicitly to Christ does not prevent me from respecting human autonomy and the freedom of the one I am helping.

A. SEUMOIS   Certain indications are to be found in *Ad gentes* that may help us to settle the problem of the relationship between evangelization and development. They underline the properly spiritual function of the people consecrated to missionary activity. They do not talk about the older institutions tied up with an "indirect apostolate," that is, an apostolate that has a directly secular aim (e.g., schools, hospitals, etc.). They talk about clerical demeanor. When they do talk about such activities (schools, hospitals, social projects, etc.), they do so strictly with reference to the laity, especially the laity of a given country. And it is in the framework of governmental institutions, not of institutions with a specific Catholic stamp. The same outlook is to be found in *Populorum progressio*. It is up to the laity to operate in the development sector, with civil institutions and enterprises. There is an enlightening commentary on these views in a talk which Cardinal Agagianian gave to the first meeting of the Union of Superiors General.* The missionary exercises an in-depth role in development through the repercussions of his evangelizing work. But technical work in development is especially the domain of the laity, and it should preferably be carried out within civil projects. Our older institution responded to certain crying needs; and they were meant to supplement other efforts, even though they often held the field alone. Now they should be increasingly integrated into government projects, even if this involves concentrating on modest pilot projects. Such projects may be less grand, but they may also exert greater influence as examples of socio-Christian principles.

A. FIOLET   Just what is evangelization? What is the administration of grace? Is it something intellectual, or a change in our concrete life-style? That is what we want to give to others. If we do not choose to change our Western habits, our social and economic structures, etc., dominated as they are by sin, then we will not be able to preach Christ. For to preach Christ is to summon people to conversion, to a change in their life-style in accordance with the gospel. It does not mean we summon them to convert to our Western structures.

THE ROLE OF THE CHURCH AS A SALVATION INSTITUTION IN DEVELOPMENT

C. H. BUTTIMER   We have spoken a lot about priests and lay people, but thousands of brothers and nuns are in development work. It is even the essential part of their missionary work: e.g., educational formation, intellectual training, medical work, etc. They would ask the same question as priests, even more insistently because it involves their distinctive work. Is their work truly missionary? I should simply like to remind the theologians that these people are engaged in missionary work, and that they have problems too.

T. VAN ASTEN   I really think that everything we are saying here about the relationship between evangelization and development applies to all the laborers in the mission field.

J. LÉCUYER   I should like to comment on what Fiolet said earlier: "There is no witness without God's word. But is it possible to be a sacrament of

*Cardinal Agagianian, "La promotion ecclésiale de la religieuse missionaire," *Documents Omnis Terra*, November 1967, pp. 31-21; *Le Christ au Monde*, January 1968.

salvation furnished by Christ without abandoning certain Western structures?"
Do you think that all our Western institutions are sinful in themselves? Should
we assume that we must first make a revolution in the West before bearing
witness elsewhere? Personally, I don't think so.

J. M. GONZALEZ-RUIZ   What we must first challenge is our own lack of
faith, which causes us to doubt the victory of the kingdom. In particular, we
lack the faith to challenge our own institutions and to start a true ecclesial
revolution. We lack faith, for example, when we think it is impossible to
establish a church in a Moslem country because the latter is impenetrable.

J. M. SETIEN   I personally distrust the insistence placed on charitable
witness when it is reduced to the individual level. Development is a social task. It
is the Church, as such, that must bear witness in this work. But our witness of
charity will be null and void if we operate within the framework of certain
Western institutions.

D. S. AMALORPAVADASS   Here I speak of an area I know, India. Even
though India needs foreign aid and is grateful for it, it has less appreciation for
the services rendered by the institutions of the Church—which often seem too
clericalized and paternalistic—than for those performed in collaboration with
other communities, religions, and civil institutions or agencies. Sometimes
Indians do not understand the type of testimony offered by the Church's
traditional institutions. Indeed it sometimes happen that they bear just the
opposite witness, or it is so interpreted. In such cases the Church does not show
up as a sacrament of salvation, since it becomes a sign that is not understood.
Insofar as development is concerned, the Church should collaborate more and
more with government, working with government institutions and agencies. This
does not mean that the Church does not have her own role to play. But she must
use her imagination. We must create another organization that will allow the
Church to inspire development work in a global way, for that is her
responsibility and she is always meant to be an educator. Secondly, the direction
and management of ecclesiastical institutions for development should be left to
lay people. What is more, we must begin to train lay people who will enter
secular institutions and structures, as leaven in the dough.

A. CAMPS   I think that Amalorpavadass's remarks hold true everywhere.
The role of the Church should be to foster the creation and implementation of a
true development community.

A. M. HENRY   Underdevelopment is one of the sins of modern times.
Must the Church save the world from this sin? How is she to do it? Up to now,
we have created a few islands of prosperity, owned by the Church, in an ocean
of poverty. That resolves nothing in terms of the development of nations. We
must help them to develop themselves, we must put ourselves in the service of
specialized organisms instituted by underdeveloped countries themselves.

C. G. AREVALO   1. We must stress the role of the Church as a
community. Development should be conceived as the establishment of a
harmonious human community, that is, a community living in peace, justice and,
ultimately, charity. Christian communities should be visible signs of Christ's
grace. The role of the local church is to present a model vision of a community
living in charity, totally at one with Christ, and fully integrated into the life of
the nation.

2. When some theologians speak of the role of the Church in development, they stress that the Church first has a role to play in the West. She must promote and organize the forces protesting those Western structures which prevent ecclesial institutions from being clearcut signs of charity in development work, which make them seem to be tied up with a colonial or neocolonial spirit. It seems to me that there is much truth in this position.

J. FRISQUE   As far as Christian institutions are concerned, we must look at each institution and the situation in a given country in order to judge the situation. It may turn out that they are useful, or that they have been, and that they have been part of the Church's real mission. The question is whether they are instruments of tutelage *today*. If they are, then we must give them up. As far as the respective role of priest and layman in missionary work is concerned, it is difficult to go into detail here. But one certainly cannot resolve the present crisis by dividing up their tasks in terms of their functions. The crisis is not dealt with that easily.

H. DE LUBAC   To return to an idea voiced a moment ago, I don't think we must wait for Western society to be perfect before we begin to act. It does not seem to me that turning the Church into a vast protest organization will resolve the missionary problem. However, I would not want to discourage certain particular vocations.

THE PROBLEM OF SECULARIZATION IN DEVELOPMENT WORK

T. TSHIBANGU   Although one may say that a given group of people is deeply religious, this does not mean that we cannot establish their destiny and way of living once and for all. It is possible that the secularization movement may hit Africa one day. But there is reason to hope that the African character will resist this movement, because this character is more sensitive to "lived values" than to *a prioris*. More intuitive than systematic, the African can make a synthesis of Christian commitment through secular institutions without losing his sense of God. That is what I feel, at least.

A. BOUCHARD   It seems to me that one cannot get away from secularization, properly understood, as a component of the Christian message. For example, we will not be able to avoid the declericalization of the Church, and of the priesthood itself. We will not be able to content ourselves with transferring clerical institutions to the laity.

D. S. AMALORPAVADASS   No country is immune to secularization, but there is also another current at work. The major religions themselves, pressured by the political structure of nations, have committed themselves to development work. We must take the Western conception of development, but we must also adapt it to particular circumstances.

J. M. GONZALEZ-RUIZ   We might like to think that the problem of secularization would not hit mission lands. Unwittingly we might want to recoup there what we have lost in the West, insofar as the Church's influence on society is concerned. But as Bouchard pointed out, secularization is a biblical theme that must be kept distinct from secularism.

I. DE LA POTTERIE   Indeed, in our Western milieu, we often confuse secularization and secularism. Secularization is included in the biblical message, but we must be careful not to present secularism as a missionary duty.

II: Closing Public Session

The chairman of the meeting, Charles Henry Buttimer, opened the session by asking C. G. Arevalo to present the conclusions of the symposium (see next section of this Appendix). *The papers of Camps, Gonzalez-Ruiz, and Tshibangu (10, 11, and 12) were followed by a public discussion open to all those present. Participants who were not members of the symposium proper are designated "observers" in the text below.*

−Editor

A. SACCHI *(observer)*   To reduce the unease of missionaries with regard to the present theological debate, we must indicate the firm points involved. Could you spell out the theological consensus? Where are we starting from? Where should we end up?

A. CAMPS   That is why I insisted on the need for pastoral institutes to re-educate missionaries and to help them to understand and follow present-day developments in theology.

G. DELCUVE   I agree. But it would be very useful to tie in the work of such institutes with Western institutes, especially when we are dealing with liturgical research and the right way to live Christianity today.

S. LYONNET   The "pastoral institutes" to which Camps refers are already in existence. The one recently set up at Abidjan seems to meet the request of Delcuve. Besides involving African professors and European professors living in Africa, it also invites European professors to give courses. But its chief benefit may well be the common life shared throughout the year by its African and European "students": priests, religious, and laity. They live together, reflecting together on the principal problems of pastoral work.

P. A. POTTER (*observer,* World Council of Churches)   At the request of your chairman, I would sum up the Protestant experience this way. 1. There has been an evolution in the notion of adaptation itself (now called "indigenization"). We have the same problems. We have set up study centers that engage in deeper studies. Problems crop up when it comes to the point of experimenting with the ideas raised in such discussions. This is especially true when it comes to re-educating our "preconciliar" leaders! 2. We have a foundation for theological education, through which we have already organized symposia to deal with basic questions. Here our problems involve the scholastic way of understanding theology at the present time. We tend to transmit traditional items of knowledge rather than to reflect jointly on what God has given to the world, on what man gives, and on what God does in the countries where these people live. Today we feel that the latter theological approach is very necessary for a better comprehension of mission work today.

P. MERTENS *(observer)*   We all are agreed on dialogue. That is of primary importance. But the problem is to find native theologians in the arena. Our reflection is still too dominated by Western theologians, who tell the natives what to think. That is not yet dialogue.

F. CLIMACUS *(observer)* I would offer two biblical texts as the motive force behind mission work, in line with the conclusions read by Arevalo: 1. "If you make my word your home you will indeed by my disciples, you will learn the truth and the truth will make you free" (John 8:31-32); in proposing the truth, the missionary brings liberty to men. 2. "May they all be one. Father, may they be one in us, as you are in me and I am in you, so that the world may believe it was you who sent me" (John 17:21).

T. A. STANLEY *(observer)* In the past we exported Christianity as a certain datum. Now we export it hesitatingly. My problem is this: Could our uncertainty itself escape exportation?

A. CAMPS The changes and groping efforts of the West are also present in non-Western countries. The solution is not to export our uncertainty but to enter into dialogue. In this way we can join together to create a new reality: A Christianity that feels at home everywhere, be it in India or Japan.

G. S. SCHNEPP *(observer)* There is always the same dilemma to be faced. Faith is a gratuitous gift. We cannot say that it is found with certainty in non-Christian religions. Thus they are not pathways of salvation. For this reason I do not understand the *Theological Conclusions*, which say that individuals receive salvation through these religions.

S. LYONNET The Christian religion is essentially a life of charity, of disinterested love for others; fallen man is radically incapable of leading this life. He can only love in this fashion if Christ loves in him, whether he knows it or not. So if he loves his neighbor, he does the will of God even if he does not know it explicitly. One can conclude that he has not rejected the gift which God offers to all men; he is on the road to salvation.

D. S. AMALORPAVADASS The reality involves a tension between what one receives and what one has already. Today we have a certain number of universal problems. We will find their solution by attacking them together in dialogue. To be wholly ourselves, we should like to form and keep contact with Westerners, even to avoid the borrowings already made.

X. ROWNTREE *(observer)* Indeed we would like to enter into dialogue. But we do not find theologians coming among us in South Africa. My impression is that the underlying change is in the political rather than the ecclesial order.

J. URQUIA *(observer)* The conclusions just presented do not reply to the questions of missionaries. That holds true for Camp's conclusions as well, for they are historical rather than theological.

J. M. GONZALEZ-RUIZ I agree. The conclusions are not the result of discussion. There have been several outlooks expressed, but we were afraid to scandalize missionaries. So we end up with a watered-down document. I personally think that differences of opinion can enrich our missionaries. For example, some have said that non-Christian religions do not constitute a supernatural milieu, that only individuals do. I do not agree. Thus the question is not closed. We should continue to discuss and debate this point. In the New Testament, the tension between the "now" and the "yet to come" is essential. But some churches stress the "now." I think that the "yet to come" is even more important for missionaries. An advent theology is a powerful stimulus to activity.

J. FRISQUE   The whole discussion will be published. The purpose of the conclusions was to spell out some of the questions posed, not to reply to all of them. They affirm what can be affirmed, without being based on a particular theological position. They are a bedrock response which leaves open unresolved questions and thus will allow for profound changes in the practical order. They are a point of departure. The questions that crop up on the scene are not small matters. We must tell missionaries: the people around you are en route with respect to the manifestation of Jesus Christ.

A. CAMPS   One of the sources of unease is that we envisage religions a bit too analytically. We must look at them globally in order to escape the limitation of "adaptation" theology.

A. VAN DER WEIJDEN (observer)   Shouldn't we pose the question of nonbelievers? It is a key issue, one that should put us on guard against the danger of an outdated theology which is too centered on non-Christian religions.

G. DELCUVE   I must say that our approach to religions was meant to be global. I must also say that unbelief is a threat everywhere. There is no room to pose religious questions because many of our contemporaries say they have no need of religion. Refoulé says that we must create room for questioning even before we create room for religion. Here development may be able to help us. At some point it enables people to discover man's limits, and hence to pose basic questions.

A. M. HENRY   I should like to offer an elementary and basic reply. It is obvious, but it is well said. For me the certainty of certainties is the necessity of mission work. Missionaries are called upon to help men love one another. If they don't do it, no one will; and something essential will be missing in the world. The world will deteriorate. That must be said. But this brotherly love requires that men have faith. If they reject this force, which comes from God rather than from themselves, they will be incapable of loving each other as much as the unity of the human family requires. For the latter requires that we love strangers, peoples of other cultures and religions, and our enemies—even unto death—so that this unity can be achieved. To simplify the matter, let me say that once upon a time we preached faith, thinking that hope would follow from it; now charity involves moving from the opposite direction. We must first love men, thus raising the hopes of those who have no hope. In this way non-Christians will be led to ask questions to which we will offer an answer: Who are you? What is your faith, which allows you to love us so much? Faith, then, will not be tacked on; it will well up from within. This will be the primary benefit of the new approach. Secondly, moral theology will find its true stature and meaning in the primacy of charity. Finally, if charity demands respect and attentive listening to others, and sometimes the ability to make demands on him, then the primacy we give it will meet all the questions posed to us by development.

T. A. STANLEY (observer)   I fear that we are moving in the wrong direction when we look for a theology that varies with different cultures. All the studies of the coming future tell us that we are moving toward a world culture.

A. CAMPS   There will be a certain unity, thanks to technology and the social communications media. But I do not think we will arrive at a single culture. Moreover, we must not forget that the Holy Spirit is always at work. In Japan, for example, we see Christianity growing in influence, affecting life-styles and new religions even when the number of conversions to it is not growing proportionately.

A. VANNESTE   African theologians feel that the various cultures will survive, even though there is a thrust toward unification.

J. WETZSEIN *(observer)*   Today we distinguish between Christ and the Church. How should missionaries present the Church?

A. BOUCHARD   At the invitation of the moderator, I would say that Camps has answered that question. We must not borrow Western structures as such. In the past, missionaries did not have the authority to change the structures of the Western Church. Today they must sow the seed, allowing it to develop in accordance with each respective culture. That is what Saint Paul did in the Greek world. Then we must confirm the positive results, as Paul did for his work at the Council of Jerusalem.

A. CAMPS   We must stress the notion of "living together." It is more than community.

W. HOLLENWEGER (*observer*, World Council of Churches)   The question we are asking at the World Council is the missionary structure of the congregation. Our conclusions are those of Camps. But we have not yet surmounted the categories of the Middle Ages. The reality is the Spirit pushing us toward "living together," despite the vocabulary employed. The problem comes when we give names to this Spirit, names that are alien to him. We shall try to discover the reality through polyspiritual celebrations. Unity is celebrated in pluriform theologies and liturgies. Experimentation will provide us with the answer.

D. GRASSO   One cannot love Christ without loving the Church, his representative on earth. And the Church will always have human structures. So the Christ-or-Church dilemma does not exist. I have another point to make. I do not think that one can say that non-Christian religions are pathways of salvation. They are a preparation for the Gospel. Christ is the only pathway of salvation.

DISCUSSION OF ARTICLES 11 AND 12

I. DE LA POTTERIE   I agree with Tshibangu that it is possible to revitalize theology by starting, as it were, at the other end, as hermeneutics demands. In other words, we should start with today's problematic issues, and modern hermeneutics gives us an example to follow. It seeks to make a synthesis between the word and its meaning today. Hence we should indeed study the concrete situations of the present day. Moreover, Christianity must incarnate itself in these specific and particular situations. We can usefully back up our ontological philosophy with an existential philosophy, indicating the insertion of faith into concrete human cultures and living situations. I would add that Christianity must incarnate itself into concrete structures. I do not see how we might envision a deinstitutionalized Christianity. We cannot invoke the incarnation economy to reject all institutions.

J. FRISQUE   I am very much in accord with the ideas expressed by Gonzalez-Ruiz. But I am disturbed by the outlook in which they were expressed.

There is tension between the liberal and conservative wings of the missionary effort. The solution, however, will come through common exploration. For all have the same basic intention even if they find themselves in different historical situations. I do not think that the best way to be tolerant is to pass harsh judgment on our predecessors.

J. M. SETIEN   The real problem is witnessing to charity by concrete acts, not just by ideas. Missionaries must devote themselves to the task of criticizing and prophesying in the face of collective institutions, if evangelization is to be stripped of certain censurable forms. They must enlighten Christians and help them to find their vocation in solving the burning issues of peace and development. But how do we find a bridge between secular tasks and witness to Christ? How do we link development work to the witness of charity?

J. M. GONZALEZ-RUIZ   I did not at all mean to adopt the mentality described by Frisque. I agree about the need for common research. Excuse me, if my bad French gave that impression.

MLLE. STIEVENS *(observer)*   Revelation concerns not only God but also man. It is a progressing phenomenon, carried out in a fashion similar to development. Are development and revelation dependent on each other? Is there not a close relationship between the development of revelation and human development? I would also have two questions in connection with the conclusions: 1. What are the universal structures that constitute the image of God in man? 2. What stages must be respected in fostering these structures?

A. FIOLET   At the invitation of the moderator, I would say that we must spell out the implications of the Incarnation. It involves the full completion of what man is and what creation is. God fashions the world and its history. Revelation and creation are complementary works by God. The Church's missionary task is precisely the full unfolding of the grand plan God had in mind when he created man. As we read in Chapter 1 of John's Gospel, creation finds its fulfillment in its "complement." And this world is the realm in which God effects this "complement." Thus grace is not an addition to human nature; it is the plenitude and full employment of this nature. Grace is already here, but we must recover it. Mission work means guiding man toward that which he is and can be in Jesus Christ.

D. GRASSO   Culture must reach a certain maturity before the fullness of revelation can be transmitted to it. We must show this culture what it lacks. For example, the notion of "fatherhood," essential to revelation and the Trinity, may be underdeveloped in a given culture.

J. M. GONZALEZ-RUIZ   If I have understood correctly, the problem of myth and language has been posed. Faith needs a language, and normally it is expressed in anthropological terms. But that does not mean that it consecrates those terms. The content of language is quite distinct from language itself.

A. M. HENRY   I should like to offer an embryonic answer to the questions posed by Mlle. Stievens. Our theology is obviously tied up with our anthropology: this type of man gives you this type of God, and vice-versa. Tell me who your God is and I'll tell you what kind of man you are. Or, putting it the other way, tell me what kind of man you are, and I'll tell you who your God is. Now if your God is a God of law codes or a Moloch, you will always be more or less fatalistic and fearful. You will not be a man in favor of development but rather a man with a fixed conception of the world. If your God is a "big daddy" without any consistency, then you will not feel a need to progress and develop constantly. One of the great obstacles to development is actually paganism. For it sees the world as being inhabited by all sorts of dark, invisible forces. They must be kept in balance rather than disturbed. It is, in short, a fixed world. If something moves at some point, the imbalance must be counterweighed by sacrifices of atonement. In the underdeveloped world, this pagan mentality is often the major obstacle to new ideas, action, and development. Christian faith, by contrast, is based on hope and engenders an outlook geared to progress, evolution, and dynamic effort. It usually engenders the type of man who will steer the course of development.

I. DE LA POTTERIE   It is true that one can best understand the progress of revelation with reference to human progress. Teilhard attempted this new synthesis. But I should like to return to the question of myth, that was just raised. Any given myth must furnish its own "meaning." It must discover the symbolic value of natural realities, which call for a "going beyond." Consider the symbolic value of the "father-son" theme. Essentially it involves a relationship of love and mutual giving. Anthropology will study this on the human plane. Theology will go further to apply it to the relations in the Trinity and their meaning for us. If this particular symbolic theme is degraded in a given culture, we must first restore its full human import. That would be the role of authentic development. Then revelation will add to it a dimension and a dynamism that will redound to the total fulfillment of this human community.

III. Theological Conclusions

It must be pointed out that these conclusions represent a compromise formulation, particularly with regard to the relationship between non-Christian religions and salvation. One participant, J. M. Gonzalez-Ruiz, felt obliged to publicly dissociate himself from this text.

—Editor

1. Why Missions?

Missionaries have always been convinced of the absolute necessity of mission work among non-Christians. Today, however, this conviction is being put to the test. In many countries with an ever-growing population, conversions are diminishing or becoming altogether impossible. At the same time another line of thought is evolving. It recognizes the positive role that can be played by non-Christian religions in attaining the salvation achieved, once for all, by Jesus Christ.

This gives rise to several questions. Are we to convert non-Christians at any cost, and bring them into the Church? Would it not be better to help them make progress in their own religion? Isn't there a danger that conversion to

Christianity will uproot them? In any case, what is to be the authentic stimulant of missionary activity today?

1. NON-CHRISTIAN RELIGIONS AND SALVATION IN JESUS CHRIST

Here we do well to recall some fundamental truths:

1: The Spirit is at work in the heart of every individual and nation. But to the extent that non-Christian religions are creations of man's religious genius in search of his destiny, they cannot be pathways of salvation. For the one and only pathway of salvation comes from the initiative of the Father: it is Christ, known by faith and accepted in charity.

2: However, non-Christian religions contain authentic values. Thus they constitute a real preparation for the gospel, even when they are suffused with errors and deviations. Purified and elevated by grace, these values can be a means of arriving at the act of faith and charity that is necessary for salvation. It is not out of the question that in these religions, in their rites and beliefs, we may find supernatural elements—wherever they may come from.

3: Far from rendering the proclamation of the gospel useless, the existence of non-Christian religions adds a new argument in favor of its importance. If we affirm that these religions can prepare the way for the gospel, we are saying that in them there exists an ordination to Christ which can only be fulfilled by the proclamation of the gospel. If supernatural elements are found in them, then they must be brought back to their source and their plenitude: the Incarnate Word living in the Church.

2. WHY MISSIONS?

Missions are fully justified within the perspective just presented:

1: If grace is communicated to men by God for their salvation, thus ordering them to Christ, then it is precisely mission work that allows them to reach full knowledge of his mystery within their own living conditions.

2: It is mission work that reveals to men their true nature, the means of truly achieving their hopes for unity and peace (which are the basic preoccupations of the present-day world), and the ultimate meaning and destiny of their lives.

3: If Christ mandated the Church to proclaim the Good News to the whole world, and to plant the novelty of the gospel everywhere, he did so that everything might gradually be subjected to his lordship. By inviting all nations to opt for Christ and become his disciples, the missionary works for God's glory. The Church thereby unveils its catholicity and fashions the eschatological flowering of God's kingdom.

3. MISSIONARY APPROACHES

In the realm of concrete attitudes and behavior patterns, several points deserve attention:

1: Missionaries never start from zero. Through dialogue, they must discover the authentic values present in non-Christian religions, in order to purify and elevate them by inserting Christ's gospel in them. In this way, Christ will be manifested to non-Christians, not as a stranger but as the one they have been looking for. *Quod ignorantes quaeritis, hoc ego annuntio vobis* (Acts 17:23).

2: If a real dialogue is to be established and carried on successfully, certain conditions are absolutely necessary as prerequisites: Missionaries, be they priests or laymen, must truly immerse themselves in non-Christian cultures, in order to comprehend them from within and to encounter people as they are, on the very level of their own religious experience. The missionary economy must reproduce the mystery of Christ himself, which happens to be an economy of Incarnation, Death, and Resurrection. The conversion of individuals should be viewed in the perspective of converting nations and achieving universal salvation.

2. Mission Work and Development

True missionaries have always worked on behalf of man's betterment. So long as this aid remained on the human level of the parish or diocese, no special problem was posed. *Today*, however, development and its organization have become complicated. It has taken on national, continental, and even worldwide dimensions. Thus it has become the affair of specialists, and simple missionaries are in danger of no longer understanding their own role in it. Mission theology and development theology should help them to be faithful to their missionary vocation, their work of evangelization, and their contribution to development in this new context. For they often feel that Christ's mission is submerged in a great technological and humanitarian effort instead of being its inspiration and impetus.

But missionaries are perplexed by the contradictory opinions of theologians. If some theologians stress the irreducible and primordial character of proclaiming the Word and administering the sacraments, then missionaries engaged in development work by force of circumstances feel ill at ease. If other theologians stress the capital role of development, then missionaries engaged in the traditional apostolate begin to have doubts. The chief difficulties can be related to three questions, to which the theologians gathered here are trying to provide a response.

RELATIONSHIP BETWEEN EVANGELIZATION AND DEVELOPMENT

1: We take development in the sense of *Populorum progressio*. Thus it entails integral development, the development of the whole man and of all men. It is the carrying out of the gospel's new commandment: "Love one another as Christ loved you." In this respect, work on behalf of integral development is an authentic pathway of evangelization. The stakes involved go beyond the temporal. Taken in the concrete, this task engages the whole man and demands a radical option from his spiritual liberty.

2: To the extent that this task engages man, development becomes a reality involving more than just things; it is a witness that speaks of Christ's lordship over the world. This witness should be recognized as evangelization in the strict sense, as an expressly religious act. This spoken witness, which is one of the ways of evangelization, also demands that the authentic word of salvation be proclaimed—revealing the mystery of our divine vocation and responding to the "problems and aspirations of today's human beings" (report of the doctrinal commission of the Synod, D C No. 1505, Nov. 19, 1967, col. 1985).

3: Thus there is a necessary tieup between these two pathways of evangelization. The second pathway of evangelization, Word and sacraments, reveals the deeper and ultimate meaning of development, it confers on it a dynamism that is no longer purely human. To the extent that Christians are visible instruments of Christ's mediation, they render an irreplaceable service to development. For adherence to the Word communicates new import to the responsible nature and unity of the human adventure.

4: Where the proclamation of the Word is impossible, work on behalf of development preserves a truly missionary sense when it is animated by this spirit. It contributes to the fulfillment of God's kingdom in all its dimensions. But from the start the missionary must have this intention, and his witness must speak this intention. After all, Christ began to teach and to act.

ROLE OF THE CHURCH, AS SALVATION INSTITUTION, IN DEVELOPMENT

1: The whole contribution of the Church to development must be performed in a spirit of service, not of tutelage: Christ did not "come to be served but to serve" (Matt. 20:28).

2: The fittingness of creating or maintaining Christian institutions, or of preferably involving oneself with nonecclesial structures, must be judged in the light of this principle.

3: In any case, the role of the Church in this domain is one of educating. And her goal is to inspire these communities with the charity that has its ultimate source in Christ.

HYPOTHESIS OF SECULARIZATION AND OTHER CONTINENTS

1: We get the impression that two trends are evident in both Africa and Asia. On the one hand, the phenomenon of secularization is beginning to show up, with all its ambiguity. On the other hand, non-Christian religions are making more and more of an effort to integrate temporal tasks into their own religious vision.

2: But there is still reason to hope that the genius of these continents will preserve them from certain extremes that the West has encountered.

3: In this connection we must always keep in mind the distinction between secularization and secularism, a distinction that is easily forgotten in practice.

4: Rightly understood, secularization recognizes the "just autonomy" (GS 36) of terrestrial realities, without threatening the ultimate orientation of all human activity.